SOUTHWESTERN INDIAN
BASKETS

The publication of this book was made possible by generous support from the Brown Foundation and the National Endowment for the Arts.

SOUTHWESTERN INDIAN
BASKETS

Their History and Their Makers

Andrew Hunter Whiteford

with a Catalogue of the School of American Research Collection

SCHOOL OF AMERICAN RESEARCH PRESS : SANTA FE, NEW MEXICO

SCHOOL OF AMERICAN RESEARCH PRESS
Post Office Box 2188
Santa Fe, New Mexico 87504

DIRECTOR OF PUBLICATIONS: Jane Kepp
EDITOR: Tom Ireland
DESIGNER: Deborah Flynn Post
TYPOGRAPHER: Business Graphics, Inc.
PRINTER: Dai Nippon Printing Co.

DISTRIBUTED BY UNIVERSITY OF WASHINGTON PRESS

Library of Congress Cataloging in Publication Data

Whiteford, Andrew Hunter.
  Southwestern Indian baskets.

  (Studies in American Indian art)
  Bibliography; p.
  Includes index.
  1. Indians of North America—Southwest, New—
Basket making. I. School of American Research
(Santa Fe, N.M.) II. Title. III. Series.
E78.S7W53   1988   746.41′2′08997079   88-3255
ISBN 0-933452-23-3
ISBN 0-933452-24-1 (pbk.)

Frontispiece. Hopi Indian woman with baskets, about 1920.
(Photo by H.C. Tibbitts, plate no. 1648; courtesy
Roderick Hook.)

Contents

Illustrations

Preface

I never met a basketmaker I didn't like. There seems to be something about the whole experience of exploring the fields and woods to find the right plants, gathering and processing them, and eventually weaving them into a basket that produces a satisfying sense of accomplishment. The work requires enormous patience, great manual dexterity, skill, and knowledge of techniques, designs, and customs. I cannot explain how this complex of talents and experience combines to endow basketmakers with a lively sense of humor, an interest in people, constant curiosity, and a remarkable tolerance of inquiring strangers, but it occurs so commonly that it may be one of the unrecognized universal traits of humanity. Maybe basketmakers everywhere are like this.

Although I have worked with American Indian baskets for many years, it was not until 1980, when I became a research curator at the School of American Research, that I became totally immersed in the rich tradition of southwestern basketry. At the request of Barbara Stanislawski, then director of the School's Indian Arts Research Center, I began a project to recatalogue the basket collection. It continued with the support of her successor, Michael Hering, with the goal of producing a published catalogue, for which the School of American Research was awarded a grant by the National Endowment for the Arts in 1984. The objective, as conceived by the School's president, Douglas W. Schwartz, and formulated and guided by its director of publications, Jane Kepp, was to make the holdings of the School known and available for public appreciation and scholarly research. My study of the collection was to be the basis for a general review of southwestern baskets. I am grateful for the opportunity to attempt this.

The distinction between *baskets* and *basketry* should be recognized. The craft or art of basketry is an ancient and universal technique in which strips of plants are intertwined or interlaced in one way or another to create a mesh or netting that might be either rigid or flexible. Baskets, on the other hand, are containers made by this technique, but they are only one of many kinds of basketry produced by the the Indians of the Southwest. Because of space limitations, this study deals only with basket containers and cannot describe the use of basketry for the construction of fireplace hoods, fences, traps, house doors and shutters, dance masks, sandals, sunshades, tumplines, and even as forms to hold stones for the piers of bridges over the Rio Grande.

Ever since Washington Matthews's pioneer observations in the 1880s, southwestern baskets have been examined and described. Every new study is indebted to those that preceded it, and every new work, such as this one, must repeat some of what has been said before. I have depended mostly upon the writings of J. M. Adavasio, Jerold Collings, Frederic Douglas, John Gogol, Joyce Herold, George Wharton James, Mary Lois Kissell, Otis Tufton Mason, Earl Morris and Robert Burgh, Helen Roberts, Bert Robinson, Clara Lee Tanner, Harry Tschopik, Jr., and Gene Weltfish. I have drawn upon many others, particularly some of the California scholars, but the writers I mention here developed the basic body of observations, comparisons, and interpretations upon which any study of southwestern Indian baskets must be based. In this book I have tried to summarize many of their observations and interpretations, to look at them critically in the light of new information, and to develop a synthesis which will facilitate our understanding of basket typology and of the many factors which have affected the development of basketmaking among the Indians of the Southwest.

Most of the studies of southwestern baskets have been largely descriptive, a necessary approach to define the kinds of baskets made by each of the many tribes. Styles of baskets, their functions, the designs with which they were decorated, and the techniques by which they were constructed have been well delineated, particularly in the classic work of Morris and Burgh (1941) and in the many reports by Adavasio (1974, 1977, and others). These scholars also examined the historical development of basketmaking in the Southwest, with additional contributions by Kidder and Guernsey (1919) and Weltfish (1930, 1932). The dynamics of cultural diffusion and the diverse forces that change basketry are extremely difficult to define, but some of them have been discussed in the studies by Ellis and Walpole (1959), McGreevy (1985b), and Tschopik (1938, 1940).

The changes that have occurred and the influences that have directed them are extremely difficult to explain. There is no satisfactory explanation yet for the Mescalero Apaches' use of stacked-rod-and-bundle coiling, nor for the similarities between the Western Apaches' distinctive twined burden baskets with U-shaped reinforcing rods and those of the early Hidatsas and Arikaras. The way in which the Navajos transferred the pattern for their wedding baskets to the San Juan Paiutes is a mystery to me, and I cannot pinpoint the Pueblo source from which the Navajos acquired their two-rod-and-bundle style of coiling baskets — nor why this was not passed on to the Southern Paiutes along with the wedding-basket design. I do not know the sources for the Hopis' distinctive baskets, nor why none are made on First Mesa, nor how the coiling and plaited wicker techniques became identified with Second and Third mesas, respectively. And where did the Rio Grande Pueblos learn how to make their plaited wicker willow baskets?

Conundrums such as these led me into the ethnological and historical literature with less than satisfactory results. I perused the files and collections of many museums, and I talked with many people, including archaeologists and the basketmakers themselves. Most of what I gleaned from these sources is included in the book, but the problems remain of much greater interest than my elementary explanations.

I am aware of a number of the omissions in this study. Some types of baskets are not illustrated because they are not represented in the collection of the School of American Research, which is the focus of the report. Some tribal groups were eliminated because of lack of space, budgetary limitations, and their absence from the collection. Under other circumstances some attempt would have been made to discuss the fine baskets of the Chemehuevis, the meager production of the River and Delta Yumans, and the Southern Utes.

I am convinced that the next developments in the study of southwestern baskets will come from two sources. The first will emerge when archaeologists become knowledgeable about basketry and recognize that it is worth preserving and studying. The second will come from detailed field studies of native American basketmakers, studies with the depth and sensitivity of Bunzel's work with Pueblo pottery and Reichard's with Navajo weaving. The tools for description and comparison are available. The challenge now is to apply them in the study of basketmaking as a living, changing art.

Acknowledgments

Many people contributed to this study, and I can express my appreciation and my pleasure in knowing them only by recognizing them here. They gave their time and shared their experience and knowledge because of their deep and lively interest in baskets and basketmakers. If I have failed to include anyone here it is only because my memory and my notes are deficient — not my gratitude.

The staff members of the School of American Research were a pleasure to work with, and I am especially grateful for the support of Douglas W. Schwartz and Jane Kepp. I also appreciate very deeply the support and co-operation provided by my assistant, Lucy Fowler; by my dedicated volunteers, Peter Babcock, Phyllis Strickland, and Manya Wentworth; and by Barbara Stanislawski, Michael Hering, Ann Merritt, and Lynn Brittner of the School's Indian Arts Research Center.

My work was constantly stimulated and challenged by such friends and students of basketry as Garrick and Roberta Bailey, Bruce Bernstein, Florence H. Ellis, Catherine Fowler, Kate Peck Kent, Barbara Mauldin, Susan Brown McGreevy, Tu Moonwalker, and Bettina Raphael. Some of them, and our daughter Linda, read parts of my manuscript, all of them looked at baskets with me, and most of them disagreed and argued with some of my interpretations. Their interest and friendship sustained me and made the project a rich experience. Among the many traders and collectors to whom I acknowledge a lasting debt are Dennis Kirkland of Casa Grande; Al Townsend of Inscription

House; John Foutz of Kirkland; the late Virginia Smith of Oljeto; William Beaver of Sacred Mountain; Joyce and Melvin Montgomery of Peridot, San Carlos; Sylvia Leakey and Bernice and Herbert Beenhouwer of Santa Fe; Mr. and Mrs. M. H. Blakemore of Santa Fe; Melissa and Ray Drolet of Shonto; and Don Lee and the Reverend Arthur Guenther of Whiteriver.

Many of my museum colleagues took the time and trouble to admit me into their collections and to discuss them with me. Among those who were very helpful were Raymond Thompson and Clara Lee Tanner of the Arizona State Museum; Armand Labbé of the Bowers Museum; Joe Ben Wheat and Frederick Lange of the University of Colorado Museum; Joyce Herold and Barbara Stone of the Denver Museum of Natural History; Phyllis Rabineau, Phillip Lewis, and Ronald Weber of the Field Museum of Natural History; Ann Marshall and Diana Pardue of the Heard Museum; Druscilla Freeman and Jane Troszak of the Logan Museum of Anthropology; J. J. Brody and Marian Rodee of the Maxwell Museum of Anthropology; Nancy Ostreich Lurie and Thomas Kehoe of the Milwaukee Public Museum; Nancy Fox and Barbara Mauldin of the Laboratory of Anthropology, Museum of New Mexico; Robert Breunig and Laura Graves Allen of the Museum of Northern Arizona; Kenneth Hedges of the San Diego Museum of Man; Linda Isenhart, James Snead, and William L. Merrill of the National Museum of Natural History, Smithsonian Institution; Patrick Houlihan and Daniela Moneta of the Southwest Museum; Malinda Blustain and Kathy Skelly of the Peabody Museum of Archaeology/Ethnology, Harvard University; and Isabel MacIntosh of the Philbrook Museum of Art. There were other collections and curators also, but these were the ones with which I spent the most time and from whom I required the most assistance.

In the photographic archives of the Museum of New Mexico, Richard Rudisill and Arthur Olivas gave friendly support and guidance, and Thelma Heatwole of Phoenix sent me her fine Pima photographs. I also wish to note the skillful editing of the manuscript by Thomas Ireland and the talents of Deborah Flynn Post in designing this book. Most of the photographs of baskets in the School of American Research collection were taken by Vince Foster. Molly Toll, of the Castetter Herbarium at the University of New Mexico, kindly provided most of the botanical identifications. For providing insight into modern basketmakers such as John McQueen, I am indebted to Charlotte and Robert Kornstein of Bellas Artes Gallery, Santa Fe.

I am deeply grateful to the many native Americans who accepted my intrusions and were willing to discuss and to demonstrate their skills and techniques in making baskets. I do not wish to intrude further on their privacy, and I cannot recognize them all here, but I wish to express special appreciation to Norma Atone and her family of Chuichu; Linda and Mike Guzmán of Cibecue; Evelyn Henry and her family of San Carlos; Lydia Pesata's family and Ardella Veneno of Dulce; Joyce Ann Saufkie of Shungopavi; the various members of the Lehi family of Hidden Springs; and Elbys Hugar, Freddie Peso, and others of Mescalero. Participation in the 1983 Southwestern Basketweavers Symposium, organized by the Museum of New Mexico, introduced me to many basketmakers and taught me a great deal about baskets.

Finally, I thank my wife, Marnie, who not only fed me and humored me while I struggled with the word processor, but also provided extra ears and eyes during field studies, translated what I could not hear or interpret, and deciphered the notes she laboriously wrote while I mumbled descriptions or chatted happily with basketmakers. She contributed to this book in many more important ways that need not be described to be appreciated.

Figure 1. Women of San Juan Pueblo winnowing wheat, about 1935. After the grain was threshed by combine or the trampling of animals, the women poured it from baskets so the wind would blow the chaff away. This practice is still followed occasionally. (Courtesy Museum of New Mexico, neg. 55192; photo by T. Harmon Parkhurst.)

1

The Ancestry of Southwestern Baskets

Few of the ancient native American arts have survived into the twentieth century, but where they have endured, some modern Indians have developed them into new forms of artistic expression. Indian arts produced for the past century in the southwestern United States have received international recognition for their fine craftsmanship and unique aesthetic qualities. Many modern designs and forms derive from ancient tribal traditions; others are new and original. The weavings, pottery, silverwork, and basketry made by southwestern Indians have often been exhibited, purchased, and analyzed. Baskets, although not always as popular with the general public as the other arts, have been esteemed for many years and collected zealously by artists and connoisseurs. Old baskets are prized not only for their age, but also for their technical excellence and beauty.

Baskets made at various times by Indians of the Southwest tell a great deal about the Indians' life patterns and provide some clues to their ancestry. They made baskets out of many different materials, in many shapes, and for many uses (fig. 1). They devised enormous baskets for storing nuts and grain; large burden baskets to sling on their backs for carrying heavy loads; flat baskets for serving food; a variety of bowl shapes to hold corn, pollen, or beads; deep basket bowls to cook food; and bottle-shaped baskets to hold small seeds or, with a coating of pine pitch, to carry water. Baskets were also used as drums, resonators for rasps, cradles for babies, and important instruments

Figure 2. Basket dance at San Ildefonso Pueblo in 1920. The women carry baskets which they give away to friends at the end of the dance. None of the baskets in the picture was made at San Ildefonso. (Courtesy Museum of New Mexico, neg. 106876; photo by Sheldon Parsons.)

for many ceremonies (fig. 2). They were made with a variety of techniques and decorated with designs and colors that transformed many of them into decorative works of art.

Baskets have always been hand crafted, without the use of any mechanical contrivance. Since early times, a knife or other cutting implement and a simple awl were all that was needed to make most kinds of baskets, but the most important tools have always been the weavers' hands, used along with their teeth and fingernails. The essential ingredients in basketry continue to be the ingenuity and manual skills of the weavers. Making baskets is a time-consuming and arduous task, and the survival of the craft through thousands of years is surely an indication of the usefulness of baskets and the satisfactions they provide for both their makers and users.

Today in the Southwest, some tribes are making large quantities of baskets; other tribes are making almost none. In recent years modern manufactured goods have largely supplanted baskets in daily use, but some people have continued to make them for ritual and ceremonial purposes and to sell. Basketmaking has declined in some tribes but flourished in others for varied and complex reasons. Knowledge and training are required to make good baskets. Besides a thorough knowledge of technique, weavers must have a broad understanding of native materials, where they can be procured, and how to prepare them. They must also know the aesthetic traditions of their group, the ceremonies in which the baskets might be used, and in recent times, the markets where they can be sold. Usually, the women make the baskets. They must be artists, technicians, ecologists, botanists, and merchants, as well as assiduous workers. The knowledge and inspiration for making good baskets almost always come from previous generations of basketmakers. Many forces can unite to break the fragile link by which any craft tradition survives, and for some southwestern tribes, the link in the basketmaking tradition has already been broken.

CULTURAL ORIGINS

As difficult as it is to trace the historical development of modern baskets, important archaeological clues reveal the origins of certain kinds of baskets and help establish the influences of certain groups on others. Although organic materials disintegrate rapidly, baskets and basket fragments have been preserved through many centuries in dry caves where they were protected from moisture. Some of these caves contained baskets that were made more than seven thousand years ago.

The ancient people of the Southwest made baskets long before they acquired pottery or planted corn. For thousands of years, their only containers were fiber bags and baskets, among their most prized possessions. Basketmakers devoted great care to the construction and often to the decoration of baskets, although their baskets were always functional and served many purposes. They produced many different forms, and by the beginning of the Christian era they had invented almost every technique that has been used in the Southwest for making baskets. Many ancient techniques and uses were passed on to the Indians of recent times, and some have survived to the present.

About 8500 B.C., peoples of the Archaic culture inhabited the region extending from Oregon through the Great Basin to the Southwest. They reached the Southwest about 7000 B.C. and developed into three distinct divisions: the San Dieguito-Pinto in the southwestern section, the Cochise in the south, and the Oshara in the north (Irwin-Williams 1979:33). During the approximately seven thousand years that the peoples of the Archaic culture occupied the Southwest, they developed from nomadic hunters and gatherers into sedentary villagers who raised corn and beans — a farming pattern continued by later prehistoric cultures.

About the beginning of the Christian era (A.D. 1), the Cochise Archaic developed into the Mogollon culture, whose people made some of the first pottery in the Southwest. Besides being excellent farmers and weavers, they made twined utility baskets and coiled baskets, some with fiber-bundle foundations, but more with two-rod-and-bundle coils. Although the Mogollon cannot be traced directly to any of the historic peoples, it influenced all of them and lasted until A.D. 1200, when it culminated in the Mimbres culture, famous for its beautiful pottery. In the final phases of the Mogollon, its people had close contact with the descendants of the northern Oshara Archaic, who developed into the Anasazi.

Through the centuries, the Anasazi also changed from hunters and gatherers into farmers, exchanging goods and ideas so freely with the Mogollon people that the two cultures gradually merged. The first Anasazi to develop from the Oshara Archaic were called the Basketmakers. They learned pottery-making, acquired corn and beans, developed a pattern of village life, and by the beginning of the eighth century A.D., evolved into the first of the Pueblo peoples, who continue to flourish in the Southwest today (fig. 3).

As their name implies, the Basketmakers created magnificent baskets of many kinds — bowls, jars, pitched bottles, and burden baskets decorated with red and black geometric designs. Their early coiling was done with a single rod, but later baskets were coiled with two rods and a bundle, and less frequently, with fiber bundles. They used a great variety of stitching techniques and perhaps invented the long-enduring yucca-splint plaited ring basket.

Basketry continued to flourish among their descendants. The Anasazi, or prehistoric Pueblos (A.D. 700 to 1300), partially replaced baskets with pots, but they continued two-rod-and-bundle coiling and some one-rod coiling, and they adopted three-rod bunched coiling at a later time. Some of their baskets were beautifully decorated in red and black, and the old yucca ring baskets were also colored.

The third major culture to develop from the Cochise Archaic was also influenced by the neighboring Mogollon and evolved into a distinct tradition known as the Hohokam, perhaps as early as 100 B.C. Strongly influenced by the culture of what is now Mexico, and perhaps settled from there, this culture produced sophisticated agricultural systems in the desert region of southern Arizona, large villages, distinctive pottery, textiles, and other fine crafts, including basketry. Their baskets were twined, plaited, and coiled with various kinds of foundations: one-rod-and-bundle and two-rod-and-welt, but more frequently, two-rod-and-bundle, three-rod bunched, and fiber-bundle. The Hohokam tradition lasted for almost seventeen centuries, but for unknown reasons it had disappeared by the time the first Spanish explorers reached the area. In its place, they found the people who were probably the lineal descendants of the Hohokam, the contemporary Pimas and Papagos.

In the extreme western part of the Southwest, in and near the valley of the lower Colorado River, another cultural tradition emerged. The Hakataya, as it is known, may have developed from the San Dieguito-Pinto tradition of

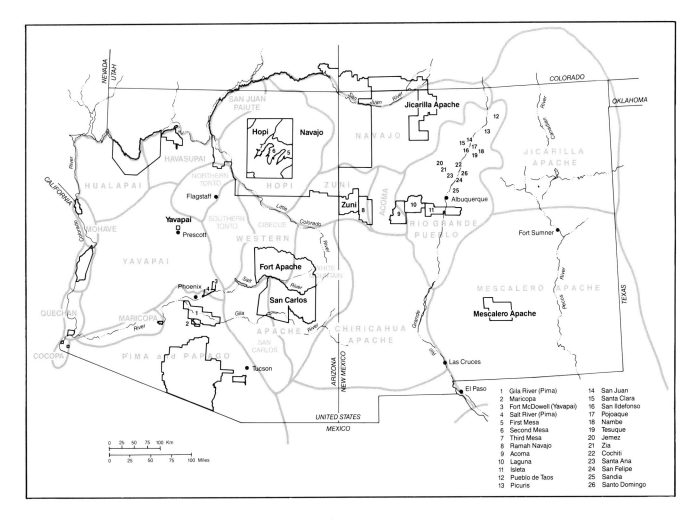

the ancient Archaic. The Hakataya people generally lived in small bands, hunting, gathering wild foods in their vast, arid land, and practicing a little agriculture. Although strongly influenced by both the Hohokam peoples and the Anasazi, they developed a distinct culture pattern which eventually evolved into the common ancestor of the later Yuman-speaking tribes (the Yavapais, Hualapais, Havasupais, Quechans, Maricopas, Cocopas, and Mohaves). Very little is known about early Hakataya basketry, but the historic Pai peoples continue to coil their baskets with three bunched rods.

All the tribes mentioned so far are linked by direct ancestral lines to the very early occupants of the Southwest. This is not true of the one large remaining group of Indians, the Southern Athapascans. Consisting of the Navajos and the various divisions of the Apaches, none of these people descend from the ancient Archaic, nor are they related to any other southwestern peoples.

Figure 3. Locations of tribal areas and reservations in the southwestern United States. The large areas outlined in gray are approximately the territories occupied or used by the tribes in the early part of the nineteenth century. The angular areas outlined in black are the reservations now occupied. (Map by Katrina Lasko.)

Their ancestors migrated into the Southwest from the far north (probably the vicinity of the Mackenzie-Yukon Valley) sometime between A.D. 1200 and 1500. The Navajos first settled near the Rio Grande Pueblos and learned many things from them, probably including the making of baskets. Occupying the semiarid region of northern New Mexico and Arizona, the Navajos eventually became shepherds, weavers, and silversmiths, living in scattered settlements with small gardens. The Apaches spread out into the mountains, where in recent times most of them have developed forest resources and raised cattle. The eastern Apaches — the Jicarillas and Mescaleros — were also influenced by the Pueblos, but the basketry of groups that moved west into Arizona (San Carlos, Cibecue, and others) was affected more strongly by the designs and techniques of the Yuman-Pai tribes of that area. All the Southern Athapaskan peoples were excellent basketmakers, and most of them have continued to practice the craft.

PREHISTORIC BASKET TECHNIQUES

The earliest known basketmaking people in the Southwest were the ancient hunters and gatherers of the Archaic culture. They trapped, snared, and speared every kind of small animal and bird and also hunted big game such as deer, elk, and mountain sheep. However, the wild plants they gathered formed the basis of their diet. Moving about in a pattern governed by the ripening of seeds, fruits, nuts, and roots, they gathered the produce in baskets made for that purpose. From what is known about the use of baskets by historic hunting and gathering peoples such as the Paiutes, it seems certain that these ancient people also used baskets for transporting loads on their backs, cooking, parching seeds and nuts with hot coals, and winnowing them to separate the kernels from the hulls.

The people of the Archaic period made all of their earliest baskets by twining — the oldest technique used in the New World and still used today by many Indian basketmakers (fig. 4). Twining employs three separate elements or strands: one group of strands forms the vertical parallel warps, across

Figure 4. Havasupai basket with oblique pattern produced by twill, or diagonal, twining. Each weft twist encloses two warps; the courses at the top and in the middle that enclose four warps are done in three-strand twining. SAR B.389, 9" diameter. (Photo by Vincent Foster.)

and around which the two weft strands are twined and twisted (fig. 5). One weft is passed in front of the first warp and the other behind it. The two wefts then cross each other, changing positions so the front weft now passes behind the next warp and the other weft comes in front of it. Then the wefts cross each other again to enclose the next warp. Three-strand twining is used for reinforcement or a change in texture. It is heavier than two-strand twining, enclosing two warps on the outside of the basket and a single warp on the inside (fig. 5d).

Even in very early times, Indian women made many different kinds of twined baskets. Hard, rigid baskets were made with stiff, heavy warps. The same technique, but with soft, supple warp strands and soft wefts, was used to produce textile-like carrying bags, mats, and capes. Twining was also varied by spacing the warps and/or the wefts. Sometimes the parallel warps were placed close together while the twined wefts were separated (fig. 5b), or both the warps and the wefts were separated to make open-work baskets for sifters and sieves. The twined wefts could also be compacted tightly against each other to make a basket with a hard, impervious wall (fig. 5c).

The early Archaic basketmakers used many of the same materials that are used today. Shoots (osiers) of willow, squawberry sumac, mulberry, and other bushes were used whole, especially for warps, and split into narrow, flexible splints to be twined together for wefts. For soft baskets and bags the fibers of Indian hemp (*Apocynum*), various kinds of yucca leaves, and the bark of the greasewood bush (*Sarcobatus vermiculatus*) were twisted into cords and used for both warp and weft elements.

For almost four thousand years (6000 B.C. to 2000 B.C.), the people of the different divisions of the Archaic culture spread over the Southwest, living by hunting and gathering, and making many twined baskets. Slowly, their lives changed. New people, probably filtering into the area from the Great Basin, brought with them a basketmaking technique known as coiling. Baskets made in this way gradually increased in popularity, and by 2000 B.C. the people of the later Archaic (Cochise and Oshara) were making eighty-five percent of their baskets by coiling and only fifteen percent by twining.

The only thing twining and coiling have in common is that they both produce baskets. While twining is basically an interweaving, textile-like process, coiling involves wrapping and sewing. In coiling, the basketmaker bunches together some twigs or grass stems with her left hand and wraps them into a slender bundle with a long strand of grass or yucca fiber. She then twists one end of the bundle into a spiral disk and begins to wind the loose bundle around it. As she coils it around, she sews the new bundle to the starting spiral by wrapping the sewing strand around it and threading it through a hole made in the edge of the center disk. She continues to enlarge the spiral, using the wrapping-sewing strand to fasten the new section of coil to the previous coil until a circular coiled mat is produced. This is the start of her basket (fig. 6).

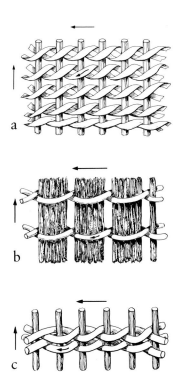

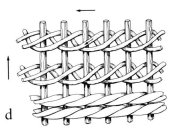

Figure 5. Diagrams of twining techniques. *a*, Plain twining with stiff, spaced warps. *b*, Plain twining with close warps and spaced wefts. *c*, Plain twining with spaced warps and close wefts. *d*, Three-strand twining. (Drawings by Arminta Neal.)

Figure 6. Baskets coiled with a bundle of fibers usually start with a tight spiral. In coils with rod foundations, the rods are thinned so they can be bent easily. (Photo by Deborah Flynn.)

Figure 7. Diagrams of coiling techniques. *a,* One-rod coiling with interlocking stitches. *b,* Three-rod bunched coiling with noninterlocking stitches. *c,* Three-rod stacked coiling. *d,* Two-rod and bundle coiling. (Drawings by Arminta Neal.)

Basketmakers may have preferred coiling to twining in the past, as they do now, because it is simpler in some respects, and because shorter, rougher, more uneven materials can be used, as well as a wider range of materials.

During the Archaic, basketmakers proved the axiom that "baskets can be made out of almost anything." They also invented almost every coiling technique used subsequently by any native peoples of the Southwest. Almost any vegetal material can be wrapped into a coil, but coiled baskets fall into two general categories: coils of fiber bundles and coils of wooden rods or sticks. The two can also be combined. Various styles of coiling appeared at different times in different regions, some lasting a short time and disappearing, others seeming to last forever. One-rod coiling (fig. 7a), one of the earliest and most enduring methods, was used before 5000 B.C. by the people of the Oshara Archaic in what is now the Four Corners area, and it continued to be used throughout the Anasazi period. It produced stiff, hard baskets, mostly bowl shaped. Three-rod bunched coiling (fig. 7b) appeared about the same time in the Southwest. Three sticks or rods, usually of the same diameter, are wrapped together in a triangular formation, producing substantial baskets with corrugated sides. This technique is now used by the Western Apaches, the Pai tribes, and others.

The basketmakers of the Cochise Archaic invented a quite different kind of rod coiling and passed it on to their Mogollon descendants. This method is called stacked-rod coiling because the two or three rods in the coils are stacked one on top of the other (fig. 7c) instead of being bunched together, producing baskets with thin and rather flexible walls. This technique was used by the Mescalero Apaches, the Southern Paiutes, and, recently, the Navajos. Another long-lasting type of coiling made by both the Cochise and Oshara people combined two rods with slender bundles of yucca or other fibers (fig. 7d).

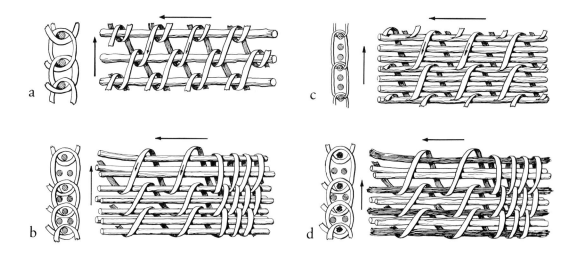

This two-rod-and-bundle technique, as it is known, was used by the Mogollon people. It was also the favorite of the Anasazi Basketmakers and continued to be used by the early historic Pueblos and the Navajos.

The Mogollon and Hohokam people devised, or possibly acquired from Mexico, a distinctly different type of basket coiling, perhaps as early as 2000 B.C. No rods were used in these coils; they were constructed entirely of a bundle of vegetal fibers: yucca, beargrass, rush stems, and other materials. Some coils were thin and hard, others relatively thick and soft. The technique remained dominant in much of the western section of the Southwest, where it is used by the Papagos, Pimas, and the modern Hopis.

The prehistoric peoples of the Southwest used a number of other coil foundations at one time or another, including bundles with rod cores, one rod and bundle, two rods with a flat slat or welt, and half rods, but these foundations never became popular, and they had disappeared by historic times. Decorations and the use of various types of sewing also produced different kinds of baskets. Complex sewing is no longer used by any of the modern peoples of the Southwest, but in earlier times, open-work baskets were made by separating the coils with fancy knots or wrapping in the stitching. In recent times, only three kinds of stitching have been common: interlocked, noninterlocked, and bifurcated or split. Interlocking stitches have almost always been used in one-rod baskets, and they are rare in the Southwest. With these stitches, the sewing splint may or may not penetrate the preceding coil, but it always passes through the stitch below it. This process creates a spiral pattern, as the stitches lie diagonally above each other (fig. 7a). In the more common noninterlocking stitching, the sewing splint passes through the lower coil between the preceding stitches. Because they lie almost directly above each other, they form a straight line on the basket (fig. 7b).

Bifurcated or split stitching was often produced accidentally when the basketmaker's awl penetrated the previous stitch, usually dividing it in two. This usually occurred on the interior (nonwork) surface of the basket, but occasionally a careless worker would split some stitches on the exterior. Accidental and uneven stitches detracted from the appearance of the surface, but on rare occasions, the basketmaker deliberately and carefully split each stitch to create a distinctive texture. This process was rare in prehistoric baskets, but it was developed in modern times, especially by the Papagos (fig. 8).

About 2000 B.C., the people of the Archaic cultures received new ideas and influences that gradually changed their entire way of life. Primitive varieties of maize and squash diffused into the Southwest from Mexico, and the hunters slowly began to become farmers. Gardening was sporadic at first, but beginning around 100 B.C., the crops became important enough that the people began to settle in simple villages and take care of their fields.

Figure 8. Detail of Papago basket in which stitches were deliberately split to create a pattern. (Photo by Vincent Foster.)

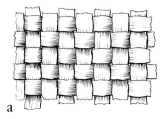

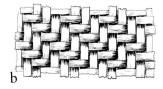

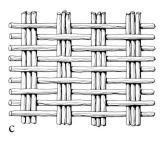

Figure 9. Diagrams of plaiting techniques. *a,* Plain splint plaiting. *b,* Twill, or diagonal, plaiting. *c,* Plaited wicker. (Drawings by Arminta Neal.)

Along with domestic crops, and probably also from Mexico, came plaiting — a simple basketmaking technique in which the warp and weft elements are usually alike and are alternately passed over and under each other. There are various patterns. In plain plaiting, a checkered pattern is produced (fig. 9a). The interwoven splints may be compacted to produce a solid surface, or separated to make sifters or sieves. Yucca ring baskets in this technique are the most enduring kind of basket in the Southwest, and they are still made and used by most of the modern Pueblo peoples. Plaited yucca ring baskets have continued unchanged from their first appearance, in about 2000 B.C., to the present. In many of them, twilled effects in herringbone (fig. 10) and diamond patterns were produced by changing the intervals at which the weaving elements crossed each other.

Plaiting was used by most of the prehistoric peoples and the modern inhabitants of the Southwest to intertwine rough branches and twigs into traps, weirs, corrals, and the walls of houses, some of which were plastered later. Strong, rigid baskets for food storage and carrying loads were constructed with whole-rod warps of willow, sumac, or other woods, and wefts were made from the slightly thinner and more flexible stems of rabbitbrush (*Chrysothamnus* sp.) or the terminal branches of willows (fig. 9c). This technique is called wicker basketry, but it should be noted that wicker is a product, not a process: wicker can also be made by twining (fig. 5a). Large wicker circular trays, "peach baskets," and donkey panniers were once made by many Pueblo groups, and Hopis in the villages of Third Mesa make colorful plaited wicker baskets today.

Figure 10. A typical Rio Grande Pueblo ring basket twill plaited of yucca splints. SAR 1984-4-36, 15" diameter. (Photo by Vincent Foster.)

BASKETMAKING IN THE MODERN ERA

As early as 1894, Washington Matthews (1894:202), an army surgeon and one of the first students of Navajo religion, predicted that basketmaking would soon become extinct in the Southwest. George Wharton James (1903), a knowledgeable collector, expressed the same fear just a few years later. Basketry did decline severely in many tribes and disappeared completely from some. By 1950 the Western Apaches had almost completely stopped making the fine coiled baskets for which they had been renowned only fifty years before (fig. 11), although they continued to make twined burden baskets, chiefly for ceremonial use. In the 1980s, tentative steps were taken to revive the production of coiled baskets and twined burden baskets, and pitched bottles took on new shapes and designs in response to a growing market for them. Among the Eastern Apaches, the Mescaleros gave up making their distinctive coiled baskets entirely by 1980, but the Jicarillas continued to produce their colorful baskets for the market.

The Pimas and the Papagos of Arizona made elegant coiled baskets, perhaps for hundreds of years. By the middle of the twentieth century, Pima women had turned their attention to more profitable work, and basketmaking nearly disappeared. A few weavers continued to make traditional baskets into the 1980s, and some young women began to produce fine horsehair miniatures. The Papagos, however, more limited in agricultural resources and job opportunities than the Pimas, became the most productive basketmakers in the Southwest. They substituted easily available yucca for traditional materials, invented

Figure 11. Western Apache coiled bowl. The corrugated surface produced by the three bunched rods shows clearly. The bowl is sewn with willow, black devil's claw, and red yucca root and decorated with typical human and animal figures. SAR B.304, 17" diameter, 10" high. (Photo by Vincent Foster.)

new and quicker coiling techniques, and produced baskets in great quantities, providing a substantial source of income for their families.

Basketmaking has also been maintained and developed into the modern era among the Hopis, the Havasupais, and the San Juan Paiutes, all of northern Arizona. The Hopis of Second Mesa still make many colorfully decorated coiled baskets similar to those made there for generations, and the women of Third Mesa make traditional stiff, plaited wicker baskets and plaited yucca-splint ring baskets of an ancient style. Many Hopi baskets are used in ceremonies, but most of them are made for sale. Very little basketry is produced at the other pueblos. Some yucca ring baskets were made at Zuni in the early 1980s, and the women at Jemez Pueblo on the Rio Grande still make them today. Open-work plaited wicker baskets, perhaps of Spanish ancestry, are made at several Rio Grande pueblos, but the ancient tradition of coiling has disappeared.

Basketmaking among the Havasupais of the Grand Canyon has waxed and waned, but it has never died out completely, and decorated coiled baskets continue to be made. For many years the San Juan Paiutes made and used their old-style coiled and twined utility baskets in limited quantities, but the craft was really sustained by their production of coiled wedding baskets for the Navajos. In the 1970s, new designs were introduced, production

Figure 12. Contemporary San Juan Paiute baskets recently arrived at Sacred Mountain Store, ready to be catalogued by the trader, William Beaver. (Photo by A. H. Whiteford, 1983.)

increased, and a "new wave" of Paiute baskets was created (fig. 12; McGreevy 1985b). The Hualapais fashioned their own renaissance by organizing basket-making classes and actively marketing their distinctive twined basket bowls.

The Navajos made excellent coiled baskets and water bottles in the early historic period, but by about 1890 the women had found the weaving of textiles so much more pleasant and profitable than basketmaking that they began to buy and trade for baskets made by the San Juan Paiutes and other tribes. During the early years of the twentieth century, many traders and dealers thought Navajo basketry had become extinct. In fact, some women always made baskets, and in 1969, classes were organized to teach the craft to young women. It caught on rapidly and has blossomed in the 1980s, in-corporating new designs, shapes, and techniques (Mauldin 1984:35–38).

Although the Indian peoples of the Southwest have been subjected to many hardships during their histories, ranging from near-catastrophic changes in climate to domestic tensions and foreign invasions, they continue to sur-vive and, some of them, to flourish. Like people everywhere, their life patterns have changed with time, and they are constantly faced with the demands and uncertainties of the future. Nevertheless, they have preserved their traditional cultures to a remarkable degree. Their growing appreciation for the unique qualities of their languages and ancient beliefs promises that these institu-tions, as well as traditional crafts, will be preserved for future generations.

Figure 13. Southern Paiute (Kaibab) women wearing twined hats and carrying twined burden baskets. They also carry basket trays for gathering and winnowing seeds. (Courtesy National Anthropological Archives, Smithsonian Institution, neg. 1607; photo by John K. Hillers, 1873.)

2

The Southern Paiutes

The traditional way of life of the Southern Paiutes provides a model for understanding the uses and changing roles of baskets among other historic and prehistoric peoples of the Southwest. Consisting of many bands, they occupy an area extending from north-central Arizona westward into California, maintaining close relations with the Navajos and the Upland Pai tribes. Only the small San Juan band, who live on the northwest corner of the Navajo reservation (see fig. 3), and to a lesser extent, their neighbors of the Kaibab band, are relevant to a discussion of southwestern baskets.

The ancestral homeland of the San Juan Paiutes is arid steppe-desert country surrounded by mountains — hot in summer and cold in winter. Extremely varied, it produces many kinds of food resources if one knows where to find them and how to use them. This the Paiutes did with great skill. They were not "pawns of a harsh environment, but rather . . . culturally adapted people capable of exploiting a variety of conditions in numerous ways" (Euler 1966:14).

The accounts of the Franciscan friars Silvestre Vélez de Escalante and Francisco Atanasio Domínguez, who met the Paiutes in 1776, preserve information about their aboriginal adaptations and use of baskets. The most detailed descriptions of the people and their land, as well as some excellent photographs, were produced by Major John Wesley Powell in research conducted between 1867 and 1880 (Powell 1874, 1875). Powell collected many baskets and other implements from the Paiutes, and the items are still stored in the Smithsonian Institution and other places. Excellent analyses of the manuscripts and collections by Don and Catherine Fowler and their colleagues from the University of Nevada have made it possible to compare Powell's information with that gathered from other tribes at later times (Fowler and Fowler, eds. 1971; Fowler, Euler, and Fowler 1969; Fowler and Matley 1979). Because of their work, the baskets of the eastern Paiute bands can be distinguished from those of the western Paiutes of California (Owens Valley, etc.) and Nevada (Moapa, Las Vegas, etc.). Comparison of Southern Paiute baskets made a century ago with more recent baskets reveals the changes that have occurred in form and technique during this time and tells a great deal about the changes that occurred in the lives of the Paiutes — a wealth of detail that is not available for many other tribes of the Southwest.

As early as 1852, the outside world was changing the lives of the Southern Paiutes. Mormon missionaries and colonists had taken over their few verdant valleys for growing crops and pastured their cattle in the grassy meadows that had been the Southern Paiutes' major source of wild foods (Euler 1966). Major Powell saw that it was becoming impossible for them to maintain their traditional way of life and proposed the establishment of a reservation where the Paiutes could be protected. No reservation was formed, and by 1910 the ethnologist Edward Sapir found that the tribe's traditional crafts and activities were no longer being practiced. Isabel Kelly found very little activity in 1932 and 1933, but at her request, some older women made examples of baskets they remembered having seen (Kelly 1964). Their reconstructions were remarkably similar to baskets collected by Major Powell half a century before, but such baskets had not been used in recent years. When Stewart conducted a detailed survey of the Southern Paiutes in the late 1930s (O. Stewart 1942), he reported that the old crafts were practically extinct.

FOOD AND BASKETS

The Southern Paiutes, like the ancient Archaic peoples, depended upon their baskets for survival. In addition to hunting large and small game, they raised some corn, beans, squash, and pumpkins; but roots, seeds, and nuts were their most important foods. The Paiutes gathered a variety of foods that is almost inconceivable to people who buy their food, or even to those who raise it. Isabel Kelly (1964) and Omer Stewart (1942) give comprehensive lists, but even a brief summary will indicate the complexity of the Paiute diet: acorns, piñon nuts, cactus fruits and stems, yucca fruits, lily bulbs, mescal crowns, ants, locusts, caterpillars and other insects, sunflower seeds, and berries of all kinds. The seeds of grasses and other small plants were among the most important foods. Each plant grew in particular places and had to be gathered at a particular time, so Paiute life was scheduled according to a biological calendar. The great depth of knowledge necessary to utilize these natural resources was passed from one generation to the next.

Pine nuts, harvested in the piñon forests above six thousand feet, were one of the most important foods. However, the crop was undependable. Some years the nuts grew in immense quantities; other years there were none. In good seasons the Paiutes ate many of the sweet nuts immediately, processed some for tomorrow, and stored others for the unpredictable future. As the nuts were knocked off the trees or picked from the ground, they were gathered in basket bowls or trays and then dumped into large conical carrying baskets to be hoisted on someone's back and carried to camp with a broad tumpline braced across the forehead (fig. 13; Fowler and Matley 1979:fig. 18).

The carriers, or burden baskets, used for this purpose were generally large — 18 inches high and 16 inches across at the rim. Some were made by twining, others by coiling. Two-rod stacked was the most common type of coiling used for carriers among the Southern Paiutes. The scraped rods and finely split segments used as sewing splints were generally willow or sumac. The walls of these large coiled baskets were fairly thin and rather flexible, but the baskets made by twining were equally strong and even lighter. The stout warps lent rigidity, and the slender wefts kept the carriers light but sturdy. In some baskets the wefts were woven closely to hold small seeds and nuts; in others they were spaced apart to make open-work baskets for carrying firewood or mescal roots. Most of these baskets were made with twill twining.

Even in these strong conical carriers, two areas were especially subject to wear and tear: the pointed bases and the rims. The bases were strengthened in two ways. First, the Paiutes used warp rods that were long enough to be crossed at the center of the basket and bent up to serve in the sides. Where they crossed each other, the rods were bound together to form a hard, pointed base composed of several layers of wood. Second, the finished bases were covered with a cap of stout rawhide to protect them when they were set on the ground for loading. The rims, which could be broken easily when the loaded baskets were being lifted or when the baskets were lying empty around the camp, were made in double thickness. The upper ends of some of the warp rods were bent along the rim and wrapped into a stout bundle, then attached to the final rows of weft twining with sewing splints. In addition, a stout rod of willow or juniper (1/4 inch in diameter) was sewn on top of the bundle of warp ends. With such reinforced bases and rims, the carriers of the Southern Paiutes were very strong and durable.

The straps used for carrying these large baskets were made of skin or braided vegetal fibers such as Indian hemp. They were tied through the wefts and around several warp rods, or attached inside to short wooden pegs to distribute the weight over a larger area and avoid breakage.

Very few Southern Paiute baskets were decorated in the early days, but some carriers had dark bands enclosing light-colored zigzag lines just below

Figure 14. Detail of a San Juan Paiute basket showing the diagonal fag ends of a sewing splint caught under the following stitches. Various tribes used this technique, but it is rare on fine baskets. SAR 1986-7-15. (Photo by Deborah Flynn.)

Figure 15. Anna Lehi Whiskers, of the San Juan Paiute band, winnowing piñon nuts. Hidden Springs, Arizona, 1984. (Photo by A. H. Whiteford.)

the rims. Dyed splints were sometimes used, and the designs made with them were the same both outside and inside the baskets. In other baskets, twining with splints on which the bark had been allowed to remain on one side resulted in a decoration that showed on the outside and was reversed on the inside. The brown bark contrasted with the lighter, peeled splints and was twisted to the inside or outside of the basket to make the light and dark parts of the design. Occasionally, the Southern Paiutes intensified the decorations by painting over them.

Bowls and tray-shaped baskets, generally coiled, were also used in the gathering and carrying of berries, nuts, and other foods. Many bowls were shallow with flat bottoms; others were nearly hemispherical. Some deep cylindrical bowls were used to cook mush by dropping heated stones into them until the mixture of meal and water was cooked. These early coiled baskets were sewn with willow or sumac splints passing through the upper rod in the coil below and usually splitting the preceding stitches. The rims were finished with simple lashing, sometimes diagonal. The fag ends of the sewing splints were clearly visible because they were laid diagonally along the coil and partially covered by succeeding stitches (fig. 14). Later Paiute basketmakers continued to use this coiling procedure.

Some of the the large, circular shallow trays, between 14 and 20 inches in diameter, were coiled. Others were twined, and both served various purposes. Piñon cones were spread on them and beaten lightly to dislodge the nuts, which were then parched by mixing them on a tray with live coals. So the basket would not burn, the mixture was kept in motion until the shells of

the nuts popped open. The trays were protected with a coating of cactus pulp or a thin coating of clay. When the nuts were partially roasted and the shells cracked, they were rolled gently between a grooved rock and a handstone (mano) until the shells and kernels separated. The mixture was then winnowed by tossing it in a tray so the lighter shell fragments were scattered by the wind; or else the winnower might blow them away (fig. 15). The nuts were usually roasted once more and stored or used immediately.

This process for preparing seeds and nuts was common throughout the Southwest, and the baskets used were similar in many tribes. Some people, including the Southern Paiutes, made trianguloid trays for winnowing (see fig. 13). They were made with stiff rod frames enclosing a mesh of closely set warp rods held together with spaced rows of twined splints. Open-work twined trays were used for parching and sifting.

When the seeds or nuts were parched and winnowed, some were eaten raw. Many were ground into meal, which was used to prepare dough for pancakes or biscuits cooked on flat rock griddles, or mixed with water for soups, stews, or mush. The Southern Paiutes picked berries and dug roots like everyone else, but they also gathered the seeds of at least forty-four species of grass. They were able to harvest millions of miniscule seeds from grasses, pigweed, lamb's quarters, and other plants with basket seed fans or beaters (fig. 16). Such implements were used by many California tribes and a number of southwesterners. They were generally fan shaped or made like an oval open-work basket on a handle — somewhat like a tennis racquet — but the simple ones were little more than willow rods spread at the ends and bound together at the butts. No beaters have been found in southwestern prehistoric sites dating from before the Numan-speaking (Shoshonean) peoples arrived about 500 to 700 years ago, but they were used by the Southern Paiutes in the middle of the nineteenth century, and it is possible that they came originally from southeastern California.

As the name indicates, the seed beaters were used to knock or flail the ripe seeds from standing grass stems. Women hit the seed heads with a lateral stroke to bend the stems over the rim of a basket bowl or tray, which caught the seeds as they fell (fig. 17). The Southern Paiutes generally used racquet- or spoon-shaped beaters, made from an oval willow hoop with rods lashed across its length. The rods extended past the hoop and were bound together to form the handle. Sumac splints were twined back and forth across the oval at intervals of an inch or so to keep the warp rods in place and slightly separated from each other. Some beaters were made without a hoop: the outer warp rods were simply bent and lashed together to form a rim. In some beaters, the cross pieces were roughly plaited back and forth. Although they were made hastily, they were probably as effective as those made with care.

To increase efficiency and durability, a flat wooden blade was sometimes attached to the end of the beater. This fender protected the rim and

Figure 17. Mabel Lehi, San Juan Paiute, demonstrates how seeds are beaten from a bush into a small open-twined carrying basket. These implements are still used occasionally. Hidden Springs, Arizona, 1984. (Photo by S. B. McGreevy.)

Figure 16. Modern seed beaters of the San Juan Paiutes. *Top,* SAR 1986-7-96, 22" long. *Bottom,* SAR 1986-7-98, 16" long. (Photo by Vincent Foster.)

provided a hard, sharp edge. The Paiutes once carved fenders out of oak or other hard wood, but recent blades have been made of galvanized tin or a piece of iron.

To hold fine grass seeds and berries and keep them safe from rodents, the early Paiutes made globular basketry jars with short, flaring necks. They also used such jars as "treasure baskets" to hold small personal items (C. Fowler, personal communication, 1985). Some of these baskets were twined and decorated with brown bands enclosing zizags or with crisscrossed lines forming diamonds.

Most of the jar- and bottle-shaped baskets of the Paiutes were coiled with two stacked rods. Even the large ones rarely had carrying straps, and the use of a single loop handle suggests they may have been made for pouring rather than carrying. The Southern Paiutes also covered some bottles and jar-shaped baskets with piñon pitch specifically for storing and transporting water.

These water containers were usually ovoid with subconical or rounded bases and pitched both inside and out (fig. 18). The pitch consisted of the natural resin that oozes from piñon trees. It was melted to a thick syrup and brushed on the baskets after they had been rubbed with a mush of pounded cactus leaves or powdered juniper leaves to fill the spaces between the stitches. The pitch was poured into the baskets, and heated stones were rolled around inside to keep it from hardening before it could flow into all the openings. When it hardened it turned a transluscent amber color and became impervious. These water jugs lasted so well and could be repaired so easily that the Paiutes and other Indians preferred them to metal containers and continued making them into the 1930s. Now they are being made again to sell to collectors and tourists.

In the old days, women wore twined basket hats of sumac splints to protect their foreheads from the weight of baskets carried with tumplines (see fig. 13). Some hats were hemispherical; others had a point on the top formed by wrapping the starting ends of the warps together. The thick rims consisted of a bundle of splints lashed together with the bent ends of the warps. Simple designs were created with barked splints, as in carriers, and occasionally with splints of black devil's claw (*Martynia proboscidea parviflora*).

The San Juan Paiutes rarely decorated their baskets. In the 1920s and 1930s, they told researchers that they had used no decorations before beginning to emulate their neighbors to the west, the Kaibab Paiutes, who had

Figure 18. Old Paiute water jar. The outer coating of pine pitch has almost disappeared, and the two stacked rods in the coils show clearly between the spaced stitches. The carrying loops are of braided horsehair. SAR 1984-4-23, 14" high. (Photo by Vincent Foster.)

Figure 19. A wedding basket of the kind made for the Navajos by the Southern Paiutes, collected in the 1920s. They are usually made with three-rod bunched coils in this traditional design. SAR B.369, 17" diameter. (Photo by Vincent Foster.)

been taught in school to copy designs from Navajo textiles (Kelly 1964:80). Nevertheless, it is clear that some of the baskets collected by Powell from the San Juan and Kaibab bands between 1867 and 1881 were decorated.

Almost all of these decorated coiled baskets were made with three-rod bunched foundations rather than the more common stacked rods (Fowler and Matley 1979:figs. 2, 107). Because stacked-rod coiling was so common among the Southern Paiutes, and also because it was used extensively by their Numic-speaking relatives to the north, stacked-rod baskets probably represented their traditional coiling technique, and three-rod baskets were probably late innovations or intrusions from elsewhere. Three-rod bunched baskets were traditional among the neighboring Havasupais and Hualapais, with whom the San Juan Paiutes had close and sometimes friendly relations (Euler 1966:75). Such decorated baskets were probably acquired by the early Paiutes from the Pai people.

No discussion of Southern Paiute decorated baskets would be complete without considering colored "Navajo wedding baskets" (fig. 19), which will be discussed more fully in the Navajo chapter. The Southern Paiutes produced great numbers of these baskets, and much has been written about them (Newman 1974; McGreevy 1985a). The San Juan Paiutes and some of the Southern Utes have been making these baskets for the Navajos since 1890, and probably earlier (Matthews 1894). Their distinctive design seems to have no precedent in early Paiute basketry, and the three-rod bunched foundation with which they are coiled was not traditional among either the Paiutes or the Navajos. The early Navajos used principally two-rod-and-bundle coiling, but they also coiled some three-rod bunched baskets and still do today, especially on the western part of the reservation. Both the Navajos and the Paiutes may have learned three-rod coiling from the Pai tribes or the Apaches, but it is not known which tribe acquired it first.

The rim finish was one traditional Navajo feature adopted by the Southern Paiutes in the making of wedding baskets. In old Navajo baskets, the rims were finished with diagonal plaiting, producing a herringbone design. A well-known legend describes how a supernatural being first taught the Navajos this pattern (see chapter 3), but many modern Paiutes insist that they have always used it — a contention unsupported by the design of old Paiute coiled baskets.

Almost without exception, both old and new Paiute baskets were coiled from right to left in the usual southwestern fashion. The description of coiling direction as "clockwise" or "counterclockwise" is confusing because the coiling inside the baskets appears to be the opposite of that on the outside. To eliminate this confusion, it is critical to identify the "work surface" — the face of the basket on which the basketmaker worked. This surface can usually be identified by its greater smoothness and regularity. Also, it is less likely to have accidental split stitches, and the fag ends of the sewing splints can usually be detected (Adavasio 1977). Shallow bowls and trays were usually held diagonally on the worker's lap while she used her awl on the far side of the basket. She perforated the inside surface and held the unbound materials in her left hand while sewing the coil from right to left (fig. 20).

Figure 20. Marie Lehi, San Juan Paiute, coiling a shallow bowl. She sews on the interior surface, building the coils from right to left. Hidden Springs, Arizona, 1984. (Photo by A. H. Whiteford.)

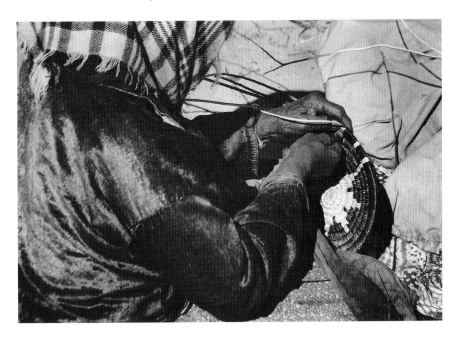

Figure 21. In coiling a deep bowl or jar, Anita Antone, a Papago from Bigfields, Arizona, works on the outside of the edge closest to her. The coils move from right to left as in shallow baskets, but on the interior of the basket they appear to turn in the opposite direction. (Photo by Deborah Flynn, 1983.)

When sewing a deep bowl or olla-shaped basket, a woman usually worked on the side closest to her, using her awl on the outer surface and still building the coil from right to left (fig. 21). This is why the coils seem to be turning counterclockwise inside shallow bowls, while they turn in the opposite direction inside deep baskets. Actually, both were coiled in the same direction. The importance of identifying the work surface in determining the direction of coiling has been pointed out many times (for example, Weltfish 1930), but it is often forgotten.

MODERN BASKETS OF THE SAN JUAN PAIUTES

The San Juan Paiutes of Hidden Springs, Arizona, and Navajo Mountain, Utah, have lived in contact with the Navajos since at least 1864, when some Navajo families took refuge with them to escape imprisonment at Bosque Redondo. Although changing conditions made it impossible for the Paiutes to follow their traditional way of life, they preserved the fundamental concepts of their culture while adopting a veneer of Navajo lifestyle. Like Navajos, they raise corn and keep flocks of sheep and goats. Paiute women wear the velveteen blouses and flowing skirts of the Navajos, and some have learned to weave "Navajo" rugs and make "Navajo" baskets. A few Paiutes and Navajos have intermarried, and some Paiutes speak Navajo in addition to their own Numic language, but they are not accepted as equals by the Navajos, and for many years have been a remote and virtually forgotten people.

Many of the San Juan Paiutes at Hidden Springs and Navajo Mountain still make wedding baskets to sell to Navajos, traders, and craft dealers. Because they are always in demand, these baskets provide a steady source of income. In recent years, older women have made the only other baskets — a few simple coiled pieces for gathering berries or piñon nuts. Ghosts of the past, these baskets were made only for home use because there was no outside market for them:

> Hence, even though production of utilitarian basketry has not been necessary for many years, San Juan Paiute weavers continue to make "old-timer baskets" in order to preserve individual and collective memories of the "old ways." Other types of current craft production, including cradleboards [which are used], basketry hats, hunting implements and certain games also belong to this category of historical preservation. (McGreevy 1985b:26–27)

San Juan basketmaking moved into a new dimension in the 1970s when women from Hidden Springs began dealing with the trader at Sacred Mountain Store on the highway to Tuba City. William Beaver and his Navajo wife, Dollie Begay, knowledgeable and dedicated enthusiasts in all aspects of traditional Indian arts, encouraged the Paiute women to learn everything possible about "old-time" baskets from their mothers and grandmothers. They purchased the baskets the Paiutes made and soon owned a large collection, including reproductions of old conical burden baskets made with plaited willow splints and some crude, heavy pieces coiled and sewn with yucca. Some hats and pitched water bottles were made with two-rod stacked coils. Two and three stacked rods were used to make shallow parching trays and flat-bottomed bowls similar to the nineteenth-century baskets collected by Major Powell. What happened to San Juan basketmaking after this auspicious beginning has been thoroughly described by McGreevy (1985b) and will only be reviewed here.

The Beavers were optimistic that the old skills could be revived. They also thought that Paiute basketmakers might be able to create some new basket styles, other than the usual wedding baskets, that could be sold to the outside world. If so, the Paiutes might establish a reputation as fine basketmakers, enabling them to develop a stable source of income for their families — something they needed very badly. Although the San Juan Paiutes possessed land of their own at one time, it had been incorporated into the Navajo reservation in 1933, and the expanding Navajos were slowly pushing the Paiutes away from their water supplies. Available resources could not even support their small population of about two hundred people. In 1985 they were petitioning the government for official recognition as a tribe and for access to land and essential services (Bunte 1985).

With William Beaver's encouragement and guidance, Paiute women began to explore new designs and colors. The daughters and granddaughters of Marie Lehi, the eighty-seven-year-old matriarch of the tribe, were especially involved. Beaver brought them books and pictures of the basket decorations of other tribes, and a "new wave" of Paiute baskets emerged. In spite of concern that neither the traders nor the Navajos would buy these nontraditional baskets, production increased, and Beaver purchased most of the new work. As he said, "The response was great. . . . Soon some beautiful baskets started showing up. . . . Many times they'd say, 'I got it out of one of those books. . . .' They were also bringing in some baskets that they said were their own designs . . . and that was great, because here was new creativity" (McGreevy 1985b:29).

Made with new techniques and a range of designs that is still expanding, the new baskets were full of color and vitality. Three types of designs can be distinguished: improvisations on the wedding-basket pattern, new interpretations of traditional designs from other tribes, and designs that seem to originate with the Paiute weavers. Variations on the wedding-basket pattern range from simply changing the circle of points to forming them into something resembling Navajo *yei* figures (fig. 22; McGreevy and Whiteford 1985: figs. 40–55). Designs adapted from other tribes, in which the source is often identified, include a number of traditional Navajo Spider Woman crosses (fig. 23), Washo-like flame figures, groups of angular meanders similar to Havasupai designs, whirlwinds, and geometric "cog wheels" (McGreevy and Whiteford 1985:figs. 56–81). The most interesting baskets are those with "original designs," including gaily colored butterflies (pl. 1), figures of horses and other animals, and flowerlike petal designs (McGreevy and Whiteford 1985:figs. 82–102).

To achieve the brilliant colors of the modern baskets, the Paiutes dye the sumac and willow splints with commercial solutions; but some of the women are working with a variety of plants to produce their own vegetal

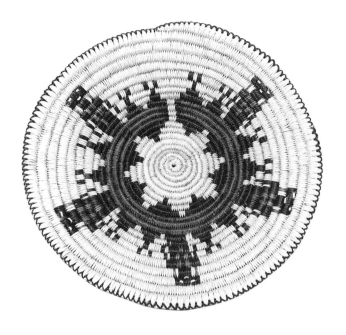

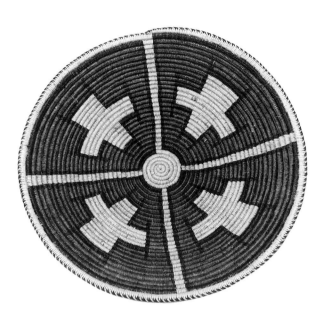

dyes. Several kinds of coil foundations are used: traditional two-rod and three-rod stacked; three-rod bunched, the usual method in wedding baskets; and five-rod bunched, a new idea with the Paiutes, but widely used by Navajos in the area. All of these kinds of coiling have been used by other people at other times, but a final rod foundation may be something new: four-rod bunched. This technique produces a smooth surface on one side, where the rods are stacked above each other, and a sharply corrugated surface on the other side.

The vigor with which the San Juan Paiutes are developing their newly discovered creativity in basketry and their campaign for federal recognition may portend a better future for them and their children. As a result of Beaver's enterprise, in 1985 they and their baskets were honored with a large exhibition at the Wheelwright Museum of the American Indian in Santa Fe. This exhibition brought the Paiutes a great deal of favorable attention in local and national publications, and the School of American Research purchased the entire collection. At the same time, the Paiutes formed a new basket cooperative — the San Juan Southern Paiute Yingup Weavers Association — and with help from the National Endowment for the Arts, they published an attractive color brochure offering their baskets for sale through the mail. The fortunes of the San Juan Paiutes give real indications of improving. It would be a special kind of poetic justice if the ancient basketmaking skills that once enabled them to survive in their struggle with nature were to serve them once again, this time to cope with pressures from the alien societies that now surround them.

Figure 22 (left). San Juan Paiute variation on the Navajo wedding basket design. These green *yei* figures were favorite motifs of Grace Lehi of Hidden Springs, Arizona. SAR 1986-7-44, four-rod bunched, 13" diameter. (Photo by Vincent Foster.)

Figure 23 (right). The Navajo Spider Woman cross, a design popular with modern San Juan Paiutes. Creating a negative design on a dark red-brown background was a Paiute innovation. Made by Rose Ann Whiskers of Hidden Springs, Arizona. SAR 1984-21-1, three-rod bunched construction, 19" diameter. (Photo by Vincent Foster.)

3

The Navajos

The Navajos have always been different from the Paiutes, although they are neighbors and live in similar high, dry lands of wild beauty, sparse resources, and difficult climate. Unlike the Paiutes, the Navajos have always been adventurous, aggressive, and mobile. They are also proud, extraordinarily inquisitive, adaptive, creative, and imbued with a strong sense of tribal identity. And they are relative newcomers to the Southwest.

The Navajos descended neither from the ancient Archaic peoples nor from the prehistoric Mogollon or Anasazi, but from the Athapascan-speaking tribes who migrated into the Southwest sometime between A.D. 1200 and 1500. The Athapascans, a hunting people from the far north, moved down from the Mackenzie-Yukon Valley, following the eastern foothills of the Rockies (Gunnerson 1979; Eggan 1979) and/or an intermontane route through the valleys of the Great Basin (Opler 1983a). When they reached the Southwest, they began raiding the Pueblo villages, and in the process of taking booty and captives, they gradually acquired so many other aspects of Pueblo culture that their original pattern of life changed forever.

One change was an evolution into distinct groups, each with its own cultural pattern. Some Athapaskans became the Apaches. Others — the Navajos — settled in what is now northern New Mexico and created a lifestyle that combined their traditional ways with ideas and techniques acquired from the Pueblo people. They planted fields of corn and other crops, and they settled into semipermanent family camps. Their ceremonial life became more elaborate, and their crafts flourished.

The most intimate contact between Navajos and Pueblos came after the Pueblo Revolt of 1680, when the Spanish reconquest forced many Pueblo people to flee their villages and take refuge among the Navajos. At this time many of the Navajos were living around Gobernador Canyon in the upper Chama Valley, an area which they regarded as their homeland and called Dinetah. Here they took in the Pueblo refugees, who, as prospects faded for an early return to their Rio Grande villages, settled down to live with their former enemies. During this period, from 1700 to about 1770, the Navajos acquired many of the skills and practices which have now become traditional with them. Some were Spanish traits that were first acquired by the Pueblos: the domestication of cattle, sheep, and goats, the use of wool in weaving, and several new crops such as peaches and melons. The Navajo population increased, and taking along their growing flocks of sheep, goats, and horses, they expanded into the vacant territory to the west.

The Navajos maintained their independence from the Spaniards, but during the subsequent period of Mexican rule they were continually at war with white settlers and other Indians. When the Mexicans lost the Southwest to the United States in 1846, the Navajos' fierce independence, constant raiding, and opposition to encroaching settlers finally brought the concentrated force of the United States Army against them. After several years of resistance and flight, the Navajos were starved out and the survivors rounded up. In 1864 more than nine thousand Navajo men, women, and children made the "Long Walk" to imprisonment at Fort Sumner in central New Mexico. There, at a place called Bosque Redondo, they were kept under dismal conditions for four years, until the government concluded that the Navajo tribe was finally broken.

In 1868 the prisoners were released to make their way back to the fragment of their homeland assigned them as a reservation. With a few government-issued tools and two sheep apiece, the Navajos began reestablishing their herds, planting crops, and growing in numbers again. From the depths of poverty and humiliation they became so successful that the government was forced to expand the reservation several times to accommodate their settlements and their growing herds of livestock.

The Navajos demonstrated their technical proficiency and aesthetic sensitivity through the adopted crafts of weaving and silverwork. Pottery was never important to them as an art form, probably because it was incompatible with their seminomadic way of life. Baskets probably gained importance in early times for uses similar to those of Southern Paiute baskets. Yet in spite of the Navajos' relatively late arrival in the Southwest, the history of their basketry is hazy.

Little is known about the Navajos' prehistory, probably because their early camps left few remains for archaeological recovery (Brugge 1983:489–523). A few burials and caches have been found in dry rock shelters, and an important one in northwestern New Mexico (Vivian 1957) included six Navajo conical pots dating earlier than 1775, along with a large pitched basketry jar and a burden basket. The jar was made in one-rod coiling and sewn with noninterlocking stitches. Because sewing on one-rod coiling in the Southwest was always done with interlocking stitches as far back as the Basketmaker II period (Morris and Burgh 1941:11), the basket in the cache seems to be more typical of the cultures of the Great Basin. The burden basket of plaited wicker with corner reinforcements of two U-shaped rods — a type also common to the Pueblos — was still used by the Navajos at the beginning of the twentieth century (Franciscan Fathers 1910). Except for these two pieces, almost nothing is known about Navajo basketry before the nineteenth century.

The lack of information does not necessarily mean that early Navajo baskets were either scarce or of inferior quality. On the contrary, some Spanish accounts from the mid-eighteenth century reported that Navajo baskets were important trade items: "They wove some textiles, and [dressed] some buckskin and [wove] baskets from small shrubs that they called 'lemitas' [sumac] with which they barter for other articles with the other Indians of this Kingdom, and also with the Spaniards" (Codallos y Rabal 1744, cited in Hill 1940:400–401). Navajo baskets were regarded so highly that Spanish officers serving on the northern frontier are said to have carried them home as gifts for their families. Unfortunately, these baskets have all disappeared, though some may be preserved in Mexico or Spain (Garrick Bailey, quoted in Sandlin 1983).

TRADITIONAL HISTORIC BASKETS

Undoubtedly, the Navajo people were making and using baskets for many purposes before they were imprisoned at Bosque Redondo. After their release, their poverty made baskets especially important because the natural materials for their construction were free. They used them, as they had before, for gathering seeds and roots, cooking, carrying burdens, parching and winnowing, and for other domestic and ritual functions.

Pitched water bottles and jars continued to be important to the Navajos in their arid land (fig. 24), and they were still making some coiled bottles, pitched inside and out, in the Ramah area as late as 1940 (Kluckhohn, Hill, and Kluckhohn 1971). Like the Paiutes, the Navajos rolled heated stones inside the jars and bottles to spread the piñon pitch, and they applied the boiling liquid to the outside with a brush. Often they rubbed red clay into the surface before applying the translucent amber pitch. The coiling was generally done with two stacked rods and sumac stitching, as in Paiute bottles (Kluckhohn, Hill, and Kluckhohn 1971:107). Bottles were usually spheroid or ovoid, with

Figure 24. Navajo girls of the early 1900s carrying water jars. Many of the Navajos' baskets were obtained in trade from the Southern Paiutes, but they also made a variety of forms themselves. (Courtesy National Anthropological Archives, Smithsonian Institution, neg. 55,621; photo by George Wharton James.)

high, wide necks that were straight or slightly flared, and jars were wide bodied with short necks, sloping shoulders, and flat bottoms. Some pitched baskets were small, but others could hold three to five gallons of water or seeds. The early jars had double handles of elbow-shaped twigs; later baskets had two loops of braided horsehair.

The Navajos used burden baskets, like the one found in the early cache, probably as late as the 1920s (Kluckhohn, Hill, and Kluckhohn 1971:61; Gilpin 1968:153). They were semiconical and made with rough, plaited wicker withes of sumac on a frame of U-shaped oak rods. The rims were finished by wrapping the warps around a rod ring or by being "pushed into the basket" (Franciscan Fathers 1910) and wrapped with a splint or skin thong. In most respects they were like the burden baskets of the Pueblo Indians.

Basketmaking declined among the Navajos during the 1880s to such an extent that many people (for example, Matthews 1894) believed it would soon become extinct. Even in 1910, the Franciscan Fathers (1910:292) wrote, "The number of Navajo basket weavers is very limited. . . . It is apparent that for reasons of their own, the Navajo are perfectly agreeable to the competition of their neighbors among whom basketry flourishes sufficiently to allow the Navajo weavers to retire." Baskets were rapidly being displaced by trade goods such as metal buckets, canteens, plates, cups, and pots. As textile weaving grew in economic importance, Navajo women spent most of their time weaving rugs for the market and had little left for the arduous tasks involved in making baskets. Finally, there was the onerous complex of ritual taboos which Navajo women were forced to observe while making baskets. They were forbidden to have intercourse, no one was allowed to touch them, and their sumac materials had to be placed so nobody would step over them. The women were kept in isolation to observe dietary restrictions, they could not work while menstruating, and they had to undergo ceremonial cleansing before and after the making of a basket (Tschopik 1938). Basket water bottles were an exception: although they were used in many rituals, they were not considered sacred, and there seem to have been no restrictions placed upon making or using them.

CEREMONIAL BASKETS. While basketmaking declined in the early years of the twentieth century, the Navajo population increased, and the complex of ceremonials continued to be a central focus in Navajo life. Frequent rituals were required, "first, to restore and maintain health; second, to obtain increase of wealth, the well-being of home, flocks, and fields, the security of himself and his relatives; and perhaps third, to acquire certain ceremonial property, such as white shell or turquoise bead tokens to wear as protection from lightning and snakes" (Wyman 1983a:537). In ceremonies, baskets were needed to hold sacred pollen, corn meal, prayer feathers, medicines, stirring rods, firedrills, reed cigarettes, flints, claws, colored earth, and other things, usually belonging to the medicine man, or singer, as part of his ceremonial bundle.

Baskets were also turned over and beaten as drums, or used as resonators with a rasp. Some rituals required baskets with particular designs, such as wedding baskets; but for others, various kinds of baskets were acceptable. The number and frequency of ceremonies demanded many baskets.

Characteristic of the adaptability they have shown throughout their history, the Navajos commissioned baskets from tribes in which the women were not subject to basketmaking taboos. Without breaking the sacred pattern, they relieved themselves of annoying restrictions, freed time for rug weaving, and continued their ritual life. This solution was also economically efficient. The price of wool dropped disastrously during the financial panic of 1893 in the eastern part of the United States, and the Navajos were in economic trouble by the following year (Kent 1985:17). Through the influence of traders, Navajo women began to produce rugs for the growing market in Indian handicrafts. Rug weaving became a major economic activity, absorbing all the time the women might have spent making baskets, but providing the cash to buy them instead. Within a short time, so many of the baskets used by the Navajos were made by the San Juan Paiutes and Utes that predictions of the extinction of basketry among the Navajos seemed to have come true.

Fortunately, this did not prove to be the case. Some Navajo women continued to make baskets throughout the twentieth century, but their production filled only a fraction of the demand. In Ramah, a small area in the southeastern part of the reservation, Navajos made twenty-two baskets in 1936–37 and bought twenty Paiute-made baskets. During this time, 120 full ceremonials were held, creating a demand for baskets that far exceeded the supply of imported and locally produced baskets combined (Tschopik 1940:455). On the western edge of the reservation, where Navajos told the ethnologist Omer Stewart (1938:95) that all their baskets were made by "foreign" Indians, he wondered "how the few Utes and Southern Paiute Indians known to be making these baskets can keep the numerous Navajo supplied." The size of the population and the number of ceremonies clearly indicates that the Navajos must have needed a large number of baskets, as they do today.

The apparent discrepancy between the number of baskets needed for ceremonials and the number being produced can be explained at least in part by changes in Navajo culture. Traditionally, every ritual required a new basket, or at least one that was in perfect condition, having never touched fire or held bloody meat. The baskets were so sacred that when they became worn or damaged, they were cached in trees or bushes where the sheep would not walk on them. Even scraps of baskets could not be burned or thrown away, and fine baskets were buried with the dead until the 1930s (Kluckhohn, Hill, and Kluckhohn 1971). Since the early part of the twentieth century, most of these traditional beliefs and practices have disappeared or been modified. Perhaps when non-Navajos began making ceremonial baskets, the conditions governing their use changed. New baskets were no longer required for every ceremony, and different kinds of baskets became acceptable. Ceremonial baskets could now be sold, given away, or reused in other rituals, filling the gap between the large number required for ceremonials and the much smaller number of new baskets being produced.

The exchange and purchase of ritual baskets is still important today. Most modern Navajos buy them at the trading post or purchase them directly from the weavers. Depending on the wealth of the family, the importance of the ceremony, and the prestige of the medicine man or woman who will conduct it, some people buy the cheapest baskets available, while others buy the finest they can afford. Some or all of the baskets used in the ritual become part of the medicine man's fee, which may also include livestock, jewelry, and cash. Popular medicine men accumulate many baskets, which they usually turn in to the trading post for exchange of goods or cash. But they are expected to be generous, and give many of them to friends and relatives, who may, in turn, sell them, save them for future rituals, present them as gifts, or keep them as mementos of important ceremonies (Rain Parrish, personal communication).

WEDDING BASKETS. Marriages are one of the few occasions for which a special kind of basket is required. The famous "Navajo wedding basket" is characterized by an encircling band of deep red, bordered on its inner and outer edges with black triangles (fig. 25). The design is believed to be symbolic:

> The center is the beginning of life, moving outward. Then the rain comes. These are black clouds. The red lines are the red and pink in the sky and clouds. The outer white part is the increase of the People. This can be any size till the basket is finished. The pathway is to let the People emerge: a way out. (Newman 1974:84, quoting a Navajo medicine woman)

The "pathway" is a required break in the encircling band (or in any design) that creates an opening from the center to the outer edge of the basket. Sometimes referred to as the "doorway," it is an essential feature in every Navajo ceremonial basket and orients the basket to the east, as required in most rituals. For this reason, weavers always end the coiling where the pathway intersects the rim, enabling the medicine man to orient the basket properly by touch even when the light is dim or the design is covered with corn meal (Chapman and Ellis 1951; Bennett 1974).

Wedding baskets may be used in various ceremonies but are required only for marriage rites, not a sacred ceremony as such because a medicine man is not involved, no sand paintings are prepared, and other sacred activities are absent.

A small container of water, and a wedding basket containing ceremonial gruel or mush are set out by the bride's father. As part of the

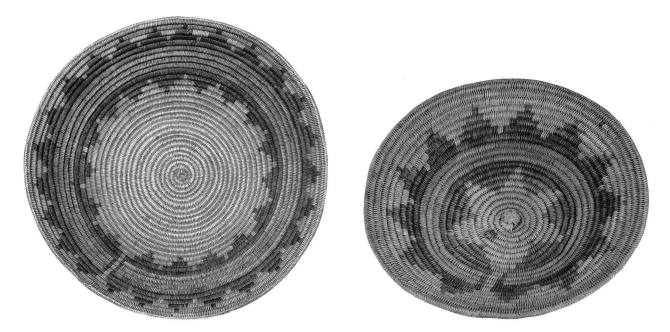

Figure 25. Two Navajo wedding baskets. Both are three-rod construction and were probably made by Southern Paiute women. *Left,* SAR B.368, 18" diameter, collected before 1920. *Right,* SAR 1981-25-5, 15" diameter. (Photos by Lynn Lown.)

ceremony, he draws lines with pollen across the gruel basket — first from east to west with white pollen and then south to north with yellow pollen — and circles the basket. After dipping water from the water bottle over each other's hands, the bride and groom eat gruel from the east, south, west, north, and center of the wedding basket, with remaining portions eaten by the guests. (Witherspoon 1983:528)

The guest who eats the last portion of the mush is allowed to keep the basket.

Wedding baskets have been produced by the Southern Paiutes and Utes for the Navajos since before 1890, but the exact date is uncertain. Thousands of these baskets have been used by the Navajos, and they have provided a steady source of income for their makers. They are generally between 12 and 14 inches in diameter, and they are invariably made of squawberry sumac (*Rhus trilobata*) with narrow sewing splints and coil foundations of three bunched rods. The rims are always finished with a herringbone pattern of diagonal plaiting, and they are coiled from right to left. When the baskets are turned over to be used as drums, the coils appear to be turning in the required sunwise direction.

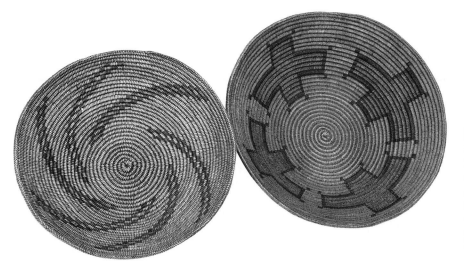

Figure 26. Traditional Navajo designs on two-rod-and-bundle bowls. *Left,* SAR B.238, whirlwind spiral in red with black outlines, 12" diameter. *Right,* SAR B.232, four red Spider Woman crosses outlined with black, 14" diameter. (Photo by Vincent Foster.)

Figure 27. Traditional Navajo designs on two-rod-and-bundle bowls. *Left,* a red band outlined with black and edged with angular hooks is fairly common. SAR B.250, 12" diameter, 4" high. *Right,* this simple zigzag band may be ancestral to the classic wedding basket design, which is rare on old two-rod-and-bundle baskets. SAR B.251, 13" diameter. (Photo by Vincent Foster.)

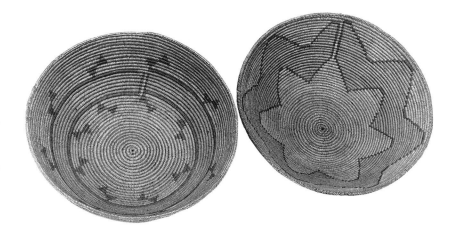

TRADITIONAL DESIGNS AND CONSTRUCTION

The wedding basket design is rare in the large number of nineteenth-century Navajo bowl-shaped baskets preserved in museum collections such as the Smithsonian Institution, the Field Museum of Natural History, and the Peabody Museum. Most of these old baskets are decorated with traditional motifs such as the square crosses called rain crosses or Spider Woman crosses (fig. 26), spirals or whirling vanes (fig. 26), and encircling bands of red bordered with angular hooks or crosses (fig. 27). Some of the edges of the bands are terraced, notched, or indented to form petaled stars at the center of the basket, vaguely reminiscent of a wedding-basket pattern (fig. 27). Some large

baskets that may date from the 1870s have unusually complex arrangements of terraced figures (fig. 28). Most of these designs and motifs also occur on early Navajo blankets, and it is possible that they were derived from baskets that preceded them (Kent 1985:17).

The only colors in the traditional baskets were black and a deep, russet red. Weavers made black in several ways, resulting in a range of colors from dark gray to jet. Powdered surface coal or slightly roasted ochre (hydrated iron oxide) was boiled with sumac leaves and piñon pitch, and the sewing splints were steeped in this solution until they absorbed the color. To dye splints red, the pot was filled with a mixture of juniper roots and the crushed bark of mountain mahogany root (*Cercocarpus* sp.) with a touch of alder bark (*Alnus* sp.) and the ashes of burnt juniper or cedar needles.

The most distinctive feature of old baskets with traditional designs is their construction: coil foundations of two sumac rods topped with a hank or twist of yucca fibers. The walls of these baskets are smoother and thinner than those made with three bunched rods. They are also slightly flexible and less suitable as drums. Because the fiber bundle becomes compressed on the top of the final coil, the rims of these baskets are usually flat instead of rounded, as when finished over a rod. As in wedding baskets, the rims are always woven in a herringbone pattern created by carrying the final splint, or an added splint, back and forth in a figure-eight pattern (fig. 29). Clearly another element of the coiling complex that the Navajos acquired from the Anasazi, this technique was common as early as Basketmaker II times (200 B.C. to A.D. 400) and continued in use through Pueblo III (A.D. 100 to 1400) (Kidder

Figure 28. These fine baskets are exceptionally large, and the complex designs of red, interlocking terrace figures outlined in black are unusual. Both are coiled with two rods and a bundle. *Left*, SAR B.266, 18" diameter, said to have been found in a cave west of Cochiti Pueblo, New Mexico. *Right*, SAR B.267, 20" diameter, purchased from the White Mound Trading Post in Houck, Arizona. (Photo by Vincent Foster.)

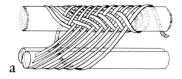

Figure 29. The rim finish called herringbone or false-braid, which was common to the early Navajos, Jicarilla Apaches, Havasupais, and Pimas. *a,* Expanded view of the weaving process. *b,* Oblique view of finished rim. (Drawings by Arminta Neal.)

and Guernsey 1919:30; Morris and Burgh 1941:23). Because it was used on old Navajo baskets but not on the old baskets of the Southern Paiutes, it appears to have been adopted by the Paiutes when they began making wedding baskets for the Navajos, though some contemporary San Juan Paiute weavers believe that it "originated with them" (McGreevy 1985b:31).

The Navajo story of the origin of this attractive rim finish is an important piece of southwestern basket tradition:

> In the ancient days the Navajo woman invented this pretty border. She was seated under a juniper tree finishing her work in the old, plain way, when the god Hastseyath threw a small spray of juniper into her basket. Happy thought! She imitated the fold of the leaves on the border and the invention was complete. (Matthews 1894:19, condensed by Mason 1904:516)

Most Navajo ceremonial baskets have an open hole at the center, formed at the start by bending a thinned portion of a rod into a circle and sewing the first coils to it (Newman 1974:77–79). To keep pollen and corn meal from leaking through the hole, it was plugged with a wooden peg or scrap of cloth, usually removed by traders and collectors.

Besides the Navajos, some Rio Grande Pueblo people also coiled their baskets with two-rod-and-bundle foundations. The construction first appeared in the Archaic DeSha complex around 6000–5500 B.C. and continued to be used by various Anasazi groups from about A.D. 400 until A.D. 1600, and perhaps later. Undoubtedly, it was transmitted to the Navajos from the Pueblos:

> Today . . . the Navajo represent the only Southwestern group to manufacture two-rod and bundle coiled basketry (Weltfish 1930). There seems to be little room for doubt that the Navajo took over this trait from the earlier inhabitants of the Pueblo plateau after they arrived in approximately their present position. The trait seems not to have been reported outside the Southwest, and the probability that the Navajo invented this basketry type in an area in which it had been manufactured since early times seems unlikely. (Tschopik 1939:127)

By the end of the nineteenth century, the Navajos were making very few two-rod-and-bundle coiled baskets with traditional designs, and their ceremonial needs were filled largely by the increasing supply of wedding baskets from the Utes and Southern Paiutes. Some Navajo women continued to make wedding baskets, generally with three-rod bunched foundations, a coiling technique that may have been acquired from the Pueblos at the same time the Navajos learned to make two-rod-and-bundle baskets. The eastern Pueblo people were using both techniques as late as Pueblo IV times (A.D. 1400 to 1800) (Morris and Burgh 1941). However, like the San Juan Paiutes, the western Navajos lived near the Pai tribes and the Western Apaches — a traditional stronghold of three-rod bunched coiling. This proximity suggests that three-rod bunched coiling in both Navajo and Paiute wedding baskets had a western origin and that the Navajos learned it from the Paiutes, rather than the other way around.

In any case, it is curious that so few old two-rod-and-bundle Navajo baskets were decorated with the wedding-basket pattern. As a speciality, early wedding baskets may have always been made with three-rod bunched foundations, but there are too few documented early specimens to be sure.

It is not clear why Navajos abandoned the ancient and nearly ubiquitous technique of two-rod-and-bundle coiling. To a limited extent, it persisted in some parts of the eastern reservation. As late as the 1930s, a few Ramah women were using it (Tschopik 1940:445–46), and even in the 1980s, occasional baskets with two-rod-and-bundle foundations were made in the Blanco Canyon area.

Today (1986), the process of coiling baskets is practically the same among all the basketmakers of the Southwest. Fine splints of sumac, or less frequently, cottonwood or willow, are used for stitching. The long, thin stems are cut during the winter when the sap is down and tied in bundles to be stored until it is time to use them. Good material is not always easily available. Women sometimes go long distances to find it or trade with people who live near the source. Newman (1974:71) mentions, "Weavers from Navajo Mountain must travel as far as Farmington, New Mexico, or Blanding, Utah, where they buy it from the Ute people or cut it themselves."

To prepare sewing splints, the sumac stems are soaked until they are flexible, then split lengthwise into three equal strips. The splits are started with a knife, then one section is held between the weaver's teeth while she pulls the other two apart (fig. 30). Good basketmakers control the pressure

Figure 30. Marie Gregg, Cibecue Apache, splitting mulberry splints with her teeth. (Photo by A. H. Whiteford, 1986.)

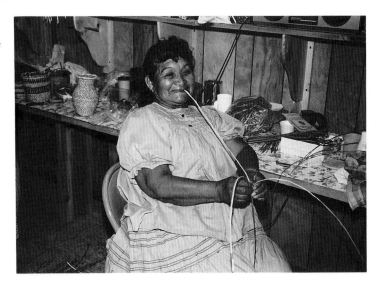

so that all the segments are equal in thickness. The pith and the bark are scraped from the strips, and they are split again to produce thin wooden strands or splints, smoothed and evened by scraping them with a knife or pulling them through a hole in a piece of tin. When a new sewing splint is required, a splice is made. One end of the new splint, called the moving end, is passed through the sewing hole made with the awl, and the splint is pulled through. The final end is left protruding from the coil to anchor the splint. This is called the fag end. Because the wood stiffens when it dries, the rods and sewing splints must be soaked in water and kept covered with damp sand or a moist cloth while the basket is in progress.

The only tools necessary to make baskets are an awl (a sharp piece of metal set into a wooden handle, like an ice pick), a knife, and perhaps a piece of tin for a scraper. Awls were once made from splinters of bone, cactus spines, hard wood, and possibly antler. The weaver holds the awl and the end of the sewing splint in her right hand, while her left hand holds the foundation materials in place. She makes a hole between the fiber bundle and the sumac rods or through the upper rod, inserts the sharpened end of the splint, pulls it through from the other side, brings it up over the new coil, and pushes it into a new hole just a fraction of an inch further along. As she pulls the splint through, she tightens it around the coil. This is the basic coiling procedure. The weaver pauses only to add a new length of splint or rod or a colored splint for decoration, or when she must put the basket aside to attend to other domestic duties.

CREATIVE PEOPLE AND INNOVATIVE DESIGNS

By the middle of the twentieth century, the few remaining Navajo basketmakers were scattered widely across the enormous reservation, and their numbers were still dwindling. At Shonto, on the western reservation, six women were making a total of a dozen or so baskets each year (Adams 1963: 83), and the Navajo Mountain area had no more than five basketmakers in 1971 (Shepardson and Hammond 1970:106). The sad state of the craft was about to change, however: programs were already being organized to revive the basket arts among the Navajos. At the Rough Rock Demonstration Center, operated by the Navajo tribe in Arizona, a woman who lived near Inscription House was brought in to teach basketmaking in 1966. Two years later, one of her first pupils was hired to do the same thing at the Navajo Community College. Classes also started at Navajo Mountain in the early 1970s. By 1973 more than one hundred Navajo women were making baskets in the northwestern section of the reservation, and basketmaking was being offered in the high schools.

Navajo basketmaking continued to expand during the 1980s, particularly in the northwestern part of the reservation. Weavers produced baskets

ranging in size from miniature (3 inches in diameter) to enormous (60 inches) and experimented with designs and colors never used before. They coiled with three-rod bunched foundations, five rods, and even with seven rods. Thick, five-rod coils may have been copied from the Jicarilla Apaches, but there is some evidence that the style was taught at Navajo Community College. Navajo women may have adopted it because they could make baskets faster with five-rod coils than with thinner coils. Two or three rods were also stacked above each other, especially by Shonto weavers, who also made water bottles coiled with bundles of fibers, wood splints, or sumac shavings. The stacked-rod technique is a revival of an old type of coiling once used for water bottles by the eastern Navajos (Kluckhohn, Hill, and Kluckhohn 1971:107), and it was also a traditional process among their Paiute neighbors. The great diversity of coiling techniques reflects the freedom and enterprise of the weavers and indicates the breadth of knowledge and experience the women were able to acquire at workshops, exhibitions, fairs, and classes.

Although basketmakers rarely put identifying marks on their products, the work of certain weavers has been recognized and appreciated by collectors and dealers. Women whose craftsmanship is outstanding or who create

Figure 31. An example of the eclectic approach of some modern Navajo weavers: Sally Black with a large basket decorated with an Apache central design and broad Pima-style squashblossom border. (Photo by Deborah Flynn, 1984.)

original or beautiful designs are known and remembered. Some very creative work has been done by Sally Black of Medicine Hat, Utah (fig. 31), and by her mother, Mary Holiday Black, who is noted for very large wedding baskets that have been purchased for wall decorations. One of Mary's baskets in the Wheelwright Museum of the American Indian measures 5 feet in diameter and is very tightly and evenly stitched.

When Sally Black was sixteen years old, she created or adapted a design incorporating colored *yei* figures similar to those woven into rugs by her mother (Roessel 1983:600, fig. 8). Her grandfather warned her not to use such figures in her baskets, but she was not deterred. The Heard Museum has her first *yei* basket, made in 1978; a later example was purchased in 1981 by the School of American Research (pl. 2). Unlike earlier Navajo basketmakers, Sally is a full-time professional. She uses the traditional sumac and willow for her baskets and gets her mellow colors from commercial dyes. Her mother continues to be a creative basketmaker, and her younger sister and her sister-in-law make olla-shaped baskets in many sizes, some with brightly colored designs. The commitment of these women to basketry and craft production is part of Navajo tradition, but their individual creations are their own. Their future baskets will reflect the broadening horizons of the younger generation.

Innovative designs do not always guarantee commercial success. New designs and shapes are purchased by dealers and traders only if they believe the baskets will appeal to the general public. Collectors must learn to appreciate new or distinctive designs, and weavers must be encouraged to create them.

Never before have Navajo basketmakers produced the variety of designs now found on the northwestern part of the reservation near Oljeto, Kayenta, Shonto, and Navajo Mountain. The collection of the late Virginia Smith at the old Oljeto Trading Post exemplifies this variety. Started in 1955, it includes many small baskets about 8 or 9 inches in diameter, and a number of fine miniatures, some of which are square. The majority of the baskets are plaques or shallow bowls between 10 and 15 inches in diameter, though some are as large as 18 inches, and there are a few deep bowls. Many of the designs are adaptations of old patterns: the cogwheel, the encircling band bordered with angled figures, and the simple four-petaled pattern. Some are variations on the wedding basket, but others have no known precedent. Single and double bird figures, which may be eagles, are a specialty of Zonnie Bowsley, who designs them with natural wood colors and green and red dyes. Shonto weavers also make excellent baskets with bird figures (fig. 32), and a basket made at Inscription House is decorated with black and red butterflies. A number of designs with *yei* figures by Maude Little and Melissa Ray of Shonto and Mae Black of Oljeto may have been inspired by Sally Black's creations, although some may predate hers. Virginia Smith remembered that the first *yei* baskets appeared at Oljeto about 1976.

The similarities in these designs indicate a great deal of interaction among the weavers of the area, but they do not copy each other's designs exactly. The deep cylindrical baskets with Hopi kachina figures that are made near Monument Valley seem to have some of the few patterns taken from non-Navajo sources. These baskets are coiled with two-rod stacked foundations. Around Shonto and Oljeto, the weavers use both two-rod and three-rod stacked, and three-rod and five-rod bunched coiling.

In most contemporary coiled basket bowls, the sumac-splint stitching is regular and tight, but sometimes it is rather rough and split on the nonwork surface. In three-rod bunched coiling, the stitches usually split the upper rod in the coil below, and both fag and moving ends are clipped short. The stitches also generally split the upper rod in the coil below in two-rod stacked coiling, and pass under it in three-rod stacked coiling. It is also common in stacked-rod baskets for the moving ends of the stitches to be laid diagonally under two or three of the following stitches, while the fag ends are clipped short. Many of the rims are finished with a false braid or herringbone pattern, others with vertical or diagonal lashing.

Pitched jars, most of which have sloping sides and little or no neck, are among the most common modern baskets on the western reservation (fig. 33). They are popular with basketmakers because they are easy to make. Some traders discourage their production because they do not sell well: one remarked that he buys them only to encourage the weavers, hoping they will do something else. These baskets have little relationship to traditional Navajo water bottles besides the use of piñon pitch and stacked-rod construction, but they do resemble early and contemporary baskets of the Southern Paiutes. The stitching is spaced, so the underlying coil foundation (three-rod stacked or a bundle of wood splints) shows clearly. The long fag ends of the stitching are

Figure 32. Life forms such as these eagles are occasionally found on modern Navajo baskets. The four crosses or "coyote tracks" here have red centers. Purchased at Shonto Trading Post, Arizona; weaver unknown. SAR 1984-13-1, five-rod construction, 18" diameter. (Photo by Vincent Foster.)

Figure 33. Modern Navajo pitched water jars. Left, coiled with bundles of willow splints, lightly pitched. Made by Mei Bedone, Shonto, Arizona. SAR 1984-21-5, 8" high. *Center,* coiled with three stacked rods, thick clear pitch, braided horsehair loops. Made by Yenora Platero, Bloomfield, New Mexico. (Courtesy Case Trading Post.) *Right,* coiled with three stacked rods, lightly pitched, red design, braided horsehair loops. Made near Shonto, Arizona. SAR 1984-8-1, 7" high. (Photo by Vincent Foster.)

laid along the coil and held under two or three following stitches, and the moving ends are handled in the same way. These baskets are also characterized by lashed rims, flat bottoms, and two thin loops of braided horsehair. They are coated inside and out with a thin layer of pitch.

Some women in the eastern part of the reservation have recently started making fine jars coiled with three stacked rods, much superior to the modern pitched jars of the west. These baskets are tightly sewn with broad sumac splints and covered inside and out with a clear amber coating of piñon pitch. The handles are made of thick braids of soft hair.

Whatever inspired so many Navajo weavers to create baskets with new techniques and original designs, these changes have successfully transformed the craft among the western Navajos. The old taboos have long been abandoned, and a valuable source of income has been developed for many families. Not everyone has joined the basket revolution, however. Some weavers disdain it completely and continue to make traditional wedding baskets (Mauldin 1984:37). The new-style baskets are destined for the outside market, but traditional baskets continue to be used in rituals, and even some of the younger basketmakers sometimes make a wedding basket for a special occasion.

The Navajos always seem to have been able to move their culture in several directions at the same time. While they were once content to consign the production of most of their wedding baskets to the Paiutes, they resumed basketmaking when it became economically attractive, once again applying their traditional creativity to the ancient craft.

4

The Apaches

The Apaches are related to the Navajos through their language and common origins: both speak Athapaskan, and they were both part of the migration from northwestern Canada that arrived in the Southwest between A.D. 1200 and 1500. Some of the Apache groups moved into the mountainous region of what is now southeastern Arizona, where their descendants still live. These Apaches had their first sight of white men when Francisco Vásquez de Coronado passed through the area on his first expedition from Mexico in 1540. Further east, on the plains between the Canadian and Red rivers, Coronado met another group of Apaches, the ancestors of the Llanero band of the Jicarillas. Pedro de Castañeda, one of Coronado's company, called these nomads Querechos or Tejas, noting that they traded buffalo meat and skins with the Pueblos of Taos, Picuris, and Pecos and raided them for corn and women.

Archaeological explorations along the Plains-Mountain border suggest that these Querecho hunters were the first Apaches to reach the Southwest (Gunnerson 1969). Morris Opler (1983a:382), an ethnologist who has studied the historic Apaches, disagrees because the excavated materials do not resemble the material culture of any known Apaches. It is certain, however, that some Apaches arrived and dispersed in the Southwest before the beginning of the seventeenth century (Brugge 1983:490).

Even after the Athapaskans settled in the Southwest, they never organized themselves into a single tribal unit, mostly living apart in small, independent bands, but uniting in times of crisis. Those who originally were called Apaches de Nabajo eventually developed fine woven textiles and silverwork, but the other Athaspakan peoples did no weaving, achieving their greatest artistry in beadwork, buckskin, and especially, basketry. While the Navajos maintained contact with each other in their large but contiguous territory, the Apaches split into six distinct tribes. They preserved a common language, the same basic systems of belief and ritual, and to some extent, similar styles of crafts and costumes.

Fifty years after Coronado's first expedition from Mexico, Juan de Oñate brought the first settlers into the Rio Grande Valley. From the beginning, the Apaches defended their rugged mountains against all invasions. For two and a half centuries they fought the Spaniards and the Mexicans, constantly raiding their settlements for horses, food, and captives, then disappearing into their wilderness camps. During this time they were never seriously threatened, and except for their acquisition of firearms, horses, and metal tools, the long conflict had very little effect on traditional Apache life patterns.

With horses, the Apaches developed raiding into an economic enterprise, allowing them to enrich their material possessions and expand their usual diets with corn and other crops produced by their neighbors, both Indian and Hispanic. They were a constant threat to the Spanish settlements until about 1786, when they were bought off with provisions and equipment. When the Mexicans came to power and ended the bribery, the enraged Apaches nearly drove them out of the Southwest.

Conditions changed drastically for the Western Apaches when the United States took over their territory in 1853. The Chiricahua Apaches were singled out as obstacles to westward expansion, and bitter warfare followed, continuing for more than forty years. The discovery of gold in California in 1848 destroyed the Apaches' isolation as thousands of miners passed through their land. Forts were established to protect the newcomers, and all the Apaches were drawn into the long and tragic encounter with the United States Army, eventually resulting in their total subjugation and near extinction.

The miserable survivors of this bitter and uneven struggle were moved to reservations in 1871 to control and "civilize" them. More than five thousand Apaches from various bands were crowded together, some of whom escaped into the mountains. Small groups such as Geronimo's Chiricahuas continued to resist for thirteen years. When the last of the Apaches were finally subdued, all the Chiricahuas and some people from other bands (including some who had served in the army as scouts) were packed into railroad box cars and shipped to prison in Florida. The remaining Apaches were placed on reservations, generally in their traditional regions.

Of the six major divisions among the Apaches (see fig. 3), the Lipan-Apaches and the Kiowa-Apaches are not important to this study because they did not live in the Southwest or make any baskets that we know of. The Jicarilla Apaches, who still live in north-central New Mexico, developed a distinctive type of basketry which they still make today. The Mescaleros of the southeastern New Mexico mountains made coiled baskets different from those of any other southwestern group. Their closest relatives were the Chiricahuas of the Arizona-New Mexico border, whose basketry we know very little about. The Western Apaches, sometimes known as Coyoteros, live in the forested mountains of east-central Arizona and include five major bands: White Mountain, San Carlos, Cibecue, Southern Tonto, and Northern Tonto. The local groups of these bands have been given many different names — Pinal, Arivaipa, Oak Creek, Coyotero, Mazatzal, Carrizo, Mimbreños, and others — none of which were ever used by the Apaches, who knew each other only by their word for "person," *indee,* or *di-nde.*

The baskets of the Apache groups differed from each other in the ways they were made, their shapes, and their decorative designs; and none of them were like the baskets made by their cogenitors, the Navajos. If all the Southern Athapaskans made the same kind of baskets, it could be assumed that they shared an ancient tradition carried from their northern homeland, but none of their baskets resemble those produced by the Northern Athapaskans. Nothing is known about any baskets that might have been made in the northern region five hundred to a thousand years ago, and historically, bark and skin containers were more important there than woven baskets. Some one-rod coiled baskets were made in the north during the historic period, but they were very different from anything made by the Southern Athapaskans. Consequently, there is no evidence to support any conjecture that the Navajos and Apaches carried a basketmaking tradition with them into the Southwest. The diversity of techniques, styles, and designs among Southern Athapaskans is best explained by influences from neighboring tribes in the Southwest.

THE JICARILLAS

The coiled baskets of the Jicarillas are usually large, stout, and strong (fig. 34). Often made in special shapes for particular functions, they are decorated with bold geometric designs and occasionally with animal figures in brilliant, often gaudy aniline colors, which fade rapidly. Some vegetal dyes were also used for softer, subtler, colors on a background that is clear white when the sumac stitching is fresh but that attains a shiny amber color with age. The solidity of traditional Jicarilla baskets results from the thickness of their coils, built on a foundation of three bunched sumac rods, or more characteristically, of five bunched rods — for many years, a distinctive Jicarilla technique.

Figure 34. Jicarilla Apache basketmaker and family. The basket shapes and designs are typical for the early twentieth century. (Courtesy Southwest Museum, Hector Alliot collection, neg. 20800, about 1915.)

The origins of five-rod coiling are difficult to identify because information about the early history of the Jicarillas is sparse. It can be assumed they learned this kind of basketry from the Pueblos, but the evidence supporting this assumption is circumstantial. It seems fairly clear that in the early seventeenth century their ancestors came into contact with the Rio Grande Pueblos, raiding them, but also trading with them and learning from them. The resulting influences transformed their lives. In 1706 the Spanish explorer Ulibarrí found the Jicarillas living in villages across the Sangre de Cristo Mountains from Taos and cultivating crops in irrigated fields (Thomas 1935, cited in Gunnerson 1979:164). They continued to hunt in the Plains, but pressure from the Spaniards on one side and the Comanches on the other forced the several bands to amalgamate, reducing their traditional nomadicism. Even as they changed from roving hunters into settled farmers, external pressures continued. For more than a century, the Spaniards, Mexicans, and finally the United States repeatedly took their land away from them, handing it out to ranchers, miners, and farmers until there was none left for the Jicarillas. They were given a reservation in 1874, but when it was invaded by settlers, the Indians were moved to a reservation with the Mescaleros. Three years later they were moved back to their present location. From then until about 1934, their hardships were largely the result of government mismanagement and commercial greed (Tiller 1983; Cutter 1974; Abel 1915).

BASKET ORIGINS AND STYLES. The origins of Jicarilla basketmaking would be less obscure if something were known about the kinds of baskets made by the people of the northern pueblos during the early part of the nineteenth century. We know only that they did make baskets and that they abandoned basketry almost completely in favor of pottery. The Jicarillas became so skilled and productive in basketmaking that the Pueblos came to depend on them for the baskets they used in their homes and rituals, thus making it unnecessary for them to make their own.

We do know that the northern Rio Grande Tewa villages made stout coiled baskets with both three-rod and five-rod foundations. As the result of considerable research, Ellis and Walpole (1959:17) concluded that "the Jicarillas took their basketry concept from this type" sometime before 1880. Unfortunately, there is little additional information on nineteenth-century Jicarilla baskets except that they were important items in the trade with the Pueblos. It is strange that Otis Tufton Mason (1904) pictures the work of many small and remote tribes in his classic and exhaustive monograph on American Indian basketry, but makes not a single mention of Jicarilla baskets. A similar omission by George Wharton James (1903) is difficult to understand because many Jicarilla baskets from the final decades of the nineteenth century are preserved in collections, and it is apparent that many were being produced in the early twentieth century. As early as 1856, the government agent for the Jicarillas in the Abiquiu area recorded that they were "trying to provide for themselves by selling earthenware and willow baskets" (Tiller 1983:57). Forty years later, "Even the arts and crafts were selling well and bringing in good profits for the craftsmen" (Tiller 1983:30). At the beginning of the twentieth century, some Jicarilla women traveled to expositions such as the St. Louis World's Fair, where Darcia Tafoya was photographed weaving a typical Jicarilla cylindrical basket decorated with large diamonds separated by triangles (Tiller 1983:64). How could Mason and James have overlooked these basketmakers?

Jicarilla women continued to make many baskets during the early part of the twentieth century, but as in most other tribes, their use of them declined. Trade wares from the Pueblos and their own excellent pottery served many functions, and baskets were used chiefly to hold bread and possibly for the storage and winnowing of grain. Demand for Jicarilla baskets by their Pueblo and Navajo neighbors kept the craft alive, and they found another ready market among Hispanic and Anglo farm families of the area, for whom the

Jicarillas produced large five-rod baskets with heavy coils and bright decorations. Deep cylindrical baskets with fitted tops, clearly designed for use as laundry hampers, were common (pl. 3). These strong baskets were made with loop handles or rectangular openings in the sides to facilitate handling. Cylindrical and oval baskets with handles at each end were made in the form of common clothes baskets (pl. 3).

The adventurous and entrepreneurial spirit of the Jicarilla basketmakers of the early twentieth century is reflected to a greater extent in the surprising forms they produced to catch the attention of tourists and other visitors. Some of the most extreme were urn shapes embellished with pedestals and loop handles (fig. 35), modeled on the traditional water bottle, but with excrescences that were clearly foreign. Ring pedestals were also added to large, shallow bowls to form clumsy compotes or fruit baskets. Handles seem to have been a speciality of the Jicarillas. Loop handles were made with a bundle of sumac splints wrapped with other splints and attached to the coils on jars, clothes baskets, and other containers. Rectangular openings also served as simple handles, but the style most characteristic of Jicarilla baskets was formed by turning up a section of the rim coils on opposite sides of the basket and wrapping it with splints to form a loop where it was separated from the coils below (pl. 3). An unusual basket form — never common because its asymmetrical shape was difficult to make — was the fishing creel, with a hinged lid and a rectangular opening for the fish. The Jicarillas also made basket forms such as deep bowls, round or oval.

Traditional Jicarilla baskets from the last decades of the nineteenth and early decades of the twentieth centuries were commonly large, circular trays or slightly deeper bowls. They were decorated with geometric designs and often with blocky animals — deer, elk, horses, or dogs (fig. 36). On some baskets the figures were rendered with tan or brown vegetal colors that blend with the russet of the aged sumac stitching. Most of those in the collection of the School of American Research were made with three-rod coils. Other baskets made at that time were decorated with bright aniline dyes, which often fade into subtle hues (pl. 4). The designs were large, broad, angular, all-over patterns, built on motifs of diamonds, frets or meanders, crosses, plain encircling bands, or zigzag bands (fig. 37). Such designs created a distinctive style of Jicarilla basketry, described and illustrated in detail by Tanner (1982).

The years between 1910 and 1940 were a time of poverty for the Jicarillas. Many died from tuberculosis. Although basketmaking provided some families with a modest income, production declined, and basket forms and decoration were simplified. Conditions began to improve about 1940 as disease came under control and herds of sheep and cattle grew and improved. At the end of the 1950s, the tribe received nearly ten million dollars as a result of land claims against the federal government, and timber, oil, and mineral resources began to produce steady income. The tribal council established the

Figure 35. Late-nineteenth-century pedestaled vase or pitcher derived from the traditional Jicarilla water jar but made for the tourist trade. SAR B.366, 15" high. (Photo by Vincent Foster.)

Jicarilla Arts and Crafts Industry and the Jicarilla Apache Tribal Museum in 1964, enterprises that helped preserve and reestablish Jicarilla basketry.

MODERN BASKETS. During the decades of misery, Jicarilla basketmaking nearly became extinct. A small group of dedicated women — among them Margarita DeDios, Talchan Piaz Largo, Mattie Quintana, Hazel DeDios, Beloria Tiznado, Columbia Vigil, Mattie Vicente, Louise Atole, and Tanzanita Pesata — persevered in the craft, eventually producing a modest renaissance in Jicarilla basketry. Tanzanita Pesata encouraged fine craftsmanship and even in her old age continued to create new forms and designs (Herold 1978:28).

Ten or fifteen women work on baskets almost every day in the tribal museum, built in 1983. They are paid an hourly wage, and their products are marketed through the museum arts and crafts center. Others make baskets at home and sell them to visitors or traders. All the women gather and prepare their own materials and decide what designs to make.

Contemporary work includes shallow bowls about 10 to 14 inches in diameter, a few larger bowls up to 17 inches in diameter, and occasional cylindrical baskets, some with lids. The foundation rods and the sewing splints are of sumac, although willow is also used occasionally, especially in decoration, becoming pinkish-tan when boiled. Commercial textile dyes are generally used to color the sewing splints because they are easy to use and provide great variety. Some women are interested in natural dyes and enjoy experimenting with various seeds, barks, roots, flowers, and other ingredients. One weaver told of her disappointment when she boiled some bright blue berries and got nothing but a dull gray color. Lydia Pesata, Tanzanita Pesata's

Figure 36 (left). Jicarilla Apache basket with animal motifs. Although brilliant aniline colors were used by the Jicarillas as early as 1890, some of the older vegetal dyes continued in use, as in this example. SAR B.169, three-rod construction, 20" diameter. (Photo by Vincent Foster.)

Figure 37 (right). On early Jicarilla baskets such as this one, the designs were simpler and colors fewer than on modern baskets. SAR B.69, three-rod construction with brown vegetal color, 21" diameter. (Photo by Vincent Foster.)

granddaughter-in-law, is acknowledged as one of the most experienced users of vegetal colors. She produces a soft yellow with a flower, possibly golden-rod (*Solidago* sp.); black from boiled piñon gum; soft pink-red from moss (unidentified); maroon-red from chokecherries *(Prunus virginiana)*; deep red from the bark of mountain mahogany root *(Cercocarpus montanus)*; greens from bitterroot *(Tagetes micrantha)* and sage *(Artemisia sp.)*; and orange or red-brown from alder bark *(Alnus tenuifolia)*. Other weavers get various colors by boiling their splints with colored crepe paper. In every case, the splints are boiled for as long as four hours in the dye, then allowed to soak in it for three or four days. No mordant is used. The Jicarillas prefer sumac for baskets because it takes colors more easily than willow. They do not use cottonwood, mulberry, or devil's claw in their baskets.

Jicarilla coiled baskets from the early part of the twentieth century were among the most colorful in the Southwest, and this tradition has been carried on by modern basketmakers (pl. 5). Many colors are used, and pale green and blue have been added to the earlier palette. Most designs seem to be derived from the past. Encircling bands of different colors are common, and some bands are made up of small rectangles indented to create triangles around the rim of the basket and starlike or petal shapes in the center. The indentations are so deep in some of these designs that they produce cogwheels. Complex floral designs and arrangements of triangles and diamonds are fairly common, but life motifs are rare today. Ideas are borrowed from books and visits to museum collections, and original designs emerge occasionally: an American eagle with the stars and stripes on its breast, or a map of the Jicarilla reservation in color. As in the past, some Navajo wedding baskets are still made by some Jicarilla women.

The Jicarillas use a coiling process similar to that of the Navajos, beginning with a small overhand knot or an open circle. Most of the old Jicarilla baskets in the School of American Research collection were started with a circle, the method generally preferred by modern weavers. Because modern baskets are usually smaller than the old five-rod baskets, contemporary weavers are more likely to use three-rod foundations. The splint sewing in modern baskets is generally tight and even, making the coils hard and solid. The coils are worked from right to left and finished with finely tapered ends and well-executed herringbone diagonal plaited rims. The fag ends of the sewing splints are pulled into the coils until they disappear or leave only short butts protruding. The moving ends are usually left hanging on the nonwork surface of the basket until the weaver goes back and trims them short with a knife or fingernail clippers. In many old Jicarilla baskets, the fag ends were bent along the foundation rods and covered by the following four or five stitches. Some modern weavers still use this method, but as one expert basketmaker commented, only "old ladies who were losing their touch, or young weavers who don't know how to do it properly." In a few cases the new splint is started by

Figure 38. Traditional Jicarilla water bottle. Several vertical lines of overstitching add decoration. The carrying loops are made of braided horsehair. SAR B.163, three-rod construction, 12" high. (Photo by Vincent Foster.)

catching the fag end between two foundation rods, instead of perforating a rod and pulling the splint through the hole. Most fag ends are covered by stitching and show only as slight bumps on the surface of the baskets.

Jicarilla water bottles are coated with pitch only on the inside, unlike those made by most southwestern tribes, and the outside surfaces are coated with a thin layer of white clay (kaolin). The old bottles were usually made with globular bodies and fairly long necks that were straight or slightly flared (fig. 38). The necks of modern bottles tend to be shorter and more flaring, and the bodies have a distinctly angular shoulder. The two loop handles attached to the shoulders are made of braided horsehair thongs wrapped together with buckskin or cloth. Both old and new bottles are decorated with two, three, or four pairs of short buckskin strips that sometimes have large beads strung on them. Modern bottles often have a small rectangle of red splints at the base of the strips. Old bottles and some modern ones are decorated with one or two vertical lines of overstitching, and some old baskets have a strip of braided horsehair or cloth caught under every fourth or fifth stitch in the coil around the shoulder (fig. 38). In some cases the strips become part of the carrying straps. Unpitched bottles, sometimes made with decorations in the coiling, were used to hold seeds or corn instead of water.

Basketry is still a lively art among the Jicarillas. The women continue their work because they enjoy it, because they appreciate its contribution to the family income, and because they like the routine and companionship of the museum workshop. Most of them have reached or passed middle age. They are concerned about the future because, as they say, the young women are not interested in becoming basketmakers. They tell about three young women who came to the craft center in 1982 to learn basketmaking: two of the girls gave up after a few lessons; the third finished a small basket and then disappeared. The girls were discouraged because it was "hard work and it hurt their hands." The older women laugh when they tell such stories, and remind each other of how they learned to make baskets while sitting in the hills taking care of the family sheep.

The situation is not completely bleak, however, because some young women are being taught how to make baskets at home by older relatives. Those interested in basketmaking will not become productive until they have finished their formal education — a process that is strongly supported by the tribal council. For example, Melanie (Molly) Pesata, from the basketmaking family of Tanzanita Pesata, learned the craft from her mother, Lydia. In 1985 she was attending college in Santa Fe and could make baskets only during vacations. Already showing some originality in her designs (fig. 39), Molly uses slightly spaced stitching on a fine three-rod bunched foundation. Other girls of her age will become basketmakers, she says, and as long as this fourth or fifth generation of women continues to be interested in the craft, basketmaking will not disappear among the Jicarilla Apaches.

Figure 39. Melanie Anne (Molly) Pesata with a basket she made in 1984 while attending the College of Santa Fe. The design and open technique on this basket are original with her. SAR 1984-6-1, three-rod construction, 12" diameter. (Photo by Deborah Flynn, 1984.)

THE MESCALEROS AND CHIRICAHUAS

As neighbors, the Mescalero and Chiricahua Apaches shared many cultural traits, and they will be discussed together here. They were nearly destroyed by the various white governments that invaded their lands, and the two groups ultimately joined.

The early Mescaleros were mountain hunters and gatherers who periodically moved into the adjacent plains to hunt buffalo. Like the Jicarillas, they were similar to the Plains Indians in their use of skin tipis, fine buckskin clothing, and rawhide parfleches. Also like the Plains tribes, they used peyote, and the men wore their hair in long plaits. Other aspects of their lives were influenced by the Pueblos, from whom they learned the basic aspects of agriculture, the use of turquoise and other materials, and possibly their masked ceremonial dances. But the core of their culture was Athapaskan.

The Mescaleros hunted deer, antelope, mountain sheep, and all small game except coyotes, wolves, bears, snakes, and owls, which were regarded as either sacred or unclean. Fish were not eaten, but almost every kind of nut, seed, fruit, berry, and root was. They derived their name from one of their most important foods, the mescal *(Agave americana)*, also known as the century plant or maguey, from which pulque, tequila, and mescal are produced in Mexico. When the thick stalk began to grow from the center of these desert plants, the Mescaleros dug out the hearts and baked them in deep pits with heated stones. When they were ready, the hearts were excavated and eaten immediately or prepared for storage. When everyone was full, the remaining mescal was stored in parfleches or hidden in caves for future use. The beans of mesquite, locust, screwbean, and other trees were used to expand their menus, and in good times the early Mescaleros lived well.

The Mescaleros fought hard for their home territory against the Spaniards, the Mexicans, and the United States, only to be defeated in the end. In 1863, five hundred of them were rounded up by the U.S. Army and imprisoned with nine thousand Navajos at Fort Sumner (Bosque Redondo). Two years later they fled into the mountains, and little attempt was made to recapture them. A small and inadequate reservation was established for them in 1873, but they were decimated by smallpox and victimized by warring settlers. Since 1922, when they were finally given title to their land, conditions have slowly improved. A little farming, timbering, and herds of sheep and cattle provided a meager economic base, but unemployment continued to be high, and the tribe tried to attract sportsmen and other visitors to their beautiful land. While attempting to preserve their ancient ways, they have also adapted to the changing cultures around them.

Unfortunately, the art of basketry as once practiced has not been preserved. In 1984 none of the women on the reservation were making the traditional coiled baskets, and only three Chiricahua women were still making twined carrying baskets. At least five or six other women said they had made coiled baskets at one time, and two of them had taught basketmaking in the craft center, but eight or ten years had passed since any of them had coiled a basket. In the craft workshop of the community center, a few elderly people were doing beadwork on cloth and skin, making dolls, and cutting old coffee cans to make conical dangles for dress fringes, but the only evidence of basketry was a small demonstration piece with colored wool yarn sewn around a coil of rope "to show the young people how it used to be done," as one elderly informant said.

Even in the halcyon days of the great basket collectors, traditional Mescalero coiled basketry was not highly esteemed. In 1902 George Wharton James illustrated a Mescalero coiled bowl with the comment,

> This is a typical Mescalero Apache coiled basket. In weave coarse and crude, in color neither striking nor harmonious, it represents a low stage of the art. Not until the commercial aspect of basketry presented itself to these people did they attempt to do much at it, and the result is their efforts are neither skillful nor pleasing. (James 1902:107)

The baskets that provoked such disdain were not brightly colored with aniline dyes like those of the Jicarillas nor as tightly woven as Navajo baskets, but they were distinctive to say the least, and James must have been mistaken in his belief that the Mescaleros never made baskets until the "commercial aspect presented itself." The history of Mescalero basketry is not clear, but we know that they were producing characteristic baskets as early as the 1880s. Examples from this period are preserved in collections. It is possible, however, that baskets and basketmaking may never have been as important to the Mescaleros as to the other Apaches, and the comparatively limited number of their baskets that have survived reflects a relatively low level of production.

COILED BASKETS. Baskets were important to the Mescaleros for many of the same reasons they were important to other Apaches. The women gathered and carried mescal and many other roots, fruits, and nuts in deep twined burden baskets similar to those of other Apache groups, or in large, circular coiled trays. Water was stored and transported in pitched basket jars and bottles.

The coiled baskets of the Mescaleros were distinct in several ways. The coils were built on two or occasionally three sumac rods stacked one on top of the other. On top of the rods was a thin bundle of yucca fibers or beargrass (*Nolina microcarpa*). The flat, rather wide coils were sewn together with strips or splints of yucca leaves, producing a thin, flexible basket wall.

The sewing method contributed to this uniquely flexible structure. The stitches were passed through part of the fiber bundle in the previous coil instead of one of the rods and partially interlocked. As each new coil was sewn in place, each stitch split the one below it and interlocked with half of the old stitch (fig. 40). The loose structure of Mescalero coiling can be felt when the baskets are handled, and when they are held up to the light, the spaces between the coils and the delicate fibers which hold them together are easily seen.

The colors of Mescalero coiled baskets are also distinctive — subtle, delicate, some would say dull. The base, or ground, is khaki tan with designs in mottled yellow, amber, or yellow ochre, often outlined with chestnut or maroon red. The basic colors are derived from the materials used in sewing or stitching the coils: slender splints made from the leaves of the soaptree yucca (*Yucca elata*). The various colors are derived from different parts of the plant or produced by bleaching the leaves. The red accents in the designs are strips of yucca root (*Yucca* sp.). The surfaces of Mescalero coiled baskets are usually uneven because little care was given to the preparation of materials. Some of the foundation rods were slender and straight, but many, whittled flat on one or two sides, were as much as 1/2 inch in diameter and did not even have the bark removed.

The fag ends of the stitches were clipped to leave slightly protruding butts, or were left uncut and laid along the coil. Both techniques were sometimes used on the same basket. The moving ends of the stitches were generally left quite long on the nonwork surface and laid diagonally along the coil to be covered by the stitching or incorporated into the fiber bundle. The baskets were usually started by coiling the thin end of one of the rods and the end of the fiber bundle very tightly, leaving no opening; the second rod was added when seven or eight coils had been sewn in place. The work always moved from right to left. The rims were often finished with a single heavy rod, which was carved to give it a flat surface on both the inside and outside of the basket. The finishing stitches were always parallel lashing, sometimes with alternate stitches of tan and ochre.

Mescalero coiled baskets were made in three basic shapes: shallow, circular bowls or trays; deep, vertical-sided "boxes," often with fitted lids; and water bottles. The bowls or trays are by far the most numerous. Having served many purposes in the early days, they became the most popular shapes to sell to visitors. They are generally 14 to 21 inches in diameter and rarely more than 4 or 5 inches deep. Their designs are usually simple, broadly lined in execution and centripetal in conception. Long-armed stars or petals with triangles or diamonds between their projections are the most common motifs. The stars may have almost any number of arms, but the most common number is five (fig. 41). According to Farrer (1982), the baskets with star or petal designs that have more than four arms were always produced for sale to outsiders; the Mescaleros themselves used only four-pointed-star designs for ceremonies (fig. 41). Star designs with points in multiples of four were acceptable, but quite rare. Baskets were occasionally decorated with frets; arrangements of diamonds; triangles, identified by the Mescalero medicine man Bernard

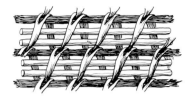

Figure 40. The Mescalero Apache coiling technique: two stacked rods and fiber bundle with split stitches. (Drawing by Arminta Neal.)

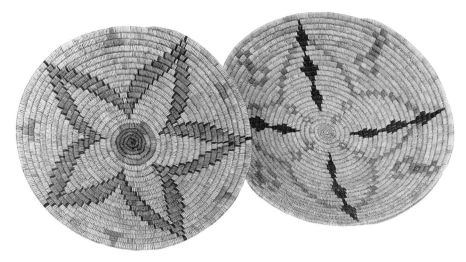

Second as "Old Man Lightning"; spiral "whirlwinds"; simple geometric motifs; and rarely, with human and/or animal forms. Characteristically, the designs extend to the edges of the baskets, and the points of many stars are truncated, as if the design were meant to continue beyond the final coils.

Mescalero coiled baskets of the second shape are unique in the Southwest: cylindrical or oval, with nearly straight vertical sides, flat bottoms, and often, a fitted lid (fig. 42). The type of coiling is also unknown in other tribes. It looks like the flat, broad coiling used in the trays, but it is made with very thin, wide slats of wood instead of stacked rods, and with the usual slender bundle of fibers along their upper edges. The slats are about 1/2 inch to 1 inch wide and 1/8 inch thick and are split from Gambel oak (*Quercus gambelii*) or willow and smoothed with abrasives. The flat bottoms of these baskets and the tops of the lids are usually made with two or three stacked sumac rods and a fiber bundle. Some lids are slightly domed, but most are flat and fitted to the basket by vertical wooden flanges around their edges. Some baskets were made with slightly flaring sides or rounded bottoms, but all have

Figure 41. Old Mescalero Apache coiled baskets. *Left,* a five-pointed star of ochre-yellow yucca outlined with deep red yucca root. SAR B.162, 18" diameter. *Right,* an open four-pointed star with red yucca-root diamonds and ochre coyote tracks. SAR B.323, 20" diameter. (Photo by Vincent Foster.)

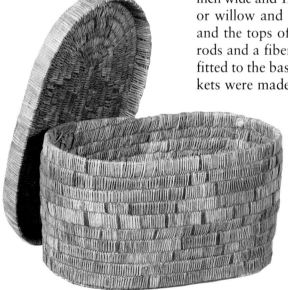

Figure 42. Mescalero Apache lidded box with slat coils. The faint, zigzag design is ochre-yellow with red spots. SAR B.127, 8" high. (Photo by Vincent Foster.)

similar designs of zigzag lines, diamonds, and crosses. Most of these unusual baskets were created for sale to outsiders. Some cylindrical baskets are 12 to 14 inches in height, but 7 to 9 inches is more common. The oval baskets are 12 inches or more long and about 8 inches high.

Ollas and water bottles were coiled with stacked rods and a fiber bundle, pitched inside and out, and made in several shapes. Most of them were globular with flat bottoms and short, flaring necks (Opler 1969:70); others had vertical sides and cylindrical necks. Mason (1904:pl. 227) illustrated an early bottle (U.S. National Museum 204651) pitched only on the inside and of unusual form: straight, flaring sides and a broad, flat shoulder. Some unpitched, vase-shaped baskets were decorated with geometric designs and embellished with pitcher handles for the commercial market. A few small, unpitched ollas were made by plaiting or twining rather than coiling (Opler 1969:70).

THE ORIGINS OF STACKED-ROD COILING. Why were Mescalero coiled baskets so different from the baskets of other southwesterners? Did they invent stacked-rod-and-bundle coiling and yucca-splint sewing? If not, where did they get them? Some early Mescalero baskets were sewn with willow splints instead of yucca (San Diego Museum of Man 9495), and Mason illustrates "an old bottle-shaped basket, made, according to Dr. Hough, long ago by the Mescalero Apache, before they adopted the present wide variety [of coiling]" (Mason 1904:513, fig. 193). This basket was sewn with splint stitching identified as willow or cottonwood — stitching materials used by other tribes in the region and in most prehistoric baskets. The Mescaleros may have sewn their baskets with willow splints at an undetermined time before the 1890s, adopting yucca splints later because they were easier to use than willow or sumac.

The origins of Mescalero stacked-rod-and-bundle coiling are even more mysterious. This distinctive type of coiling seems to have occurred at various times in southwestern prehistory. A few examples of two-rod stacked basketry were uncovered at Ventana Cave in Arizona, but there is no evidence that the technique continued into historic times. In the eastern Great Basin, however, "single rod and stacked variants of coiling dominated from 4500 B.C. until historic times" (Adavasio 1974:116). Even in 1985, the Idaho Shoshonis were making baskets with two or three stacked rods. This technique was also common in the baskets of the Southern Paiutes in 1880, and they still use it for some utility baskets (Whiteford 1985:20). The eastern Navajos used stacked-rod coiling in the 1930s, and in 1985 the western Navajos were using it again for pitched ollas.

Neither the temporal nor the geographic distribution of stacked-rod coiled basketry explains how it came to be the major technique of the Mescalero Apaches. There is no evidence that they had contact with the other tribes that made baskets in this way, and the technique has no viable antecedents in the

Southwest. Difficulties in obtaining and processing the materials that their neighbors used or their own diminished use of baskets may have induced the Mescaleros to adopt new methods. Perhaps baskets made in the old way were no longer worth the time and effort. Yucca sewing splints were much easier to procure, process, and use than sewing materials made from wood. Yucca is much less durable, but that would not discourage its use if the baskets were being produced for sale. Similarly, basket walls could be made more quickly with stacked rods than with bunched rods. Yucca-splint sewing, stacked or slat coils, and split stitching resulted in mediocre baskets that might not attract premium prices or selective collectors, but could be produced with relative ease. Like some of the modern basketmakers of other tribes, the Mescaleros may have discovered many of these features by themselves.

TWINED BASKETS. In any case, the Mescaleros ceased to make their peculiar coiled basketry, and there is little reason to suppose that it will be resurrected. However, twined basketmaking survives, although by a narrow margin.

Twined burden baskets must have been common at one time, but few have been preserved or identified. Some may have been made with U-shaped corner reinforcements, like the baskets of the Western Apaches. The more common type was nearly cylindrical, closely twill twined with split sumac splints with the warp ends lashed around a single rim rod (fig. 43). They lack reinforcing rods in the corners, and instead of being decorated with strips of fringe

Figure 43. An old Mescalero burden basket, twill twined with sumac splints. These baskets lack the reinforcing corner rods and fringed buckskin strips of some Western Apache carriers but were decorated with encircling rows of color and conical tin dangles. SAR B.326, 15" high. (Photo by Vincent Foster.)

they have rows of conical tin dangles encircling the rim and sometimes the bottom edge. They were decorated with bands of red and black dyed splints and some three-strand twining to create textural variation.

Among the most interesting twined sumac baskets were deep bowls collected in the 1930s, decorated with contrasting bands of twilled and plain twining and brown bands made by twisting the bark sides of the splints to the outside. Although these twined baskets are attributed to the Mescaleros, most of the documentation is dubious, and the early history of Mescalero basketry remains obscure.

CHIRICAHUA BASKETS. Of all the Apache tribes, the recalcitrant Chiricahuas suffered the most. They were driven from their land, slaughtered, and finally deported to prisons in Florida. "Before the end of 1889, 119 of the total of 498 Chiricahuas who had been sent to Florida had died" (Opler 1983b:408). In 1894 they were transferred to Fort Sill, Oklahoma, and finally given their freedom in 1913, when the government decided that the 271 survivors were not a serious threat to the republic. Some remained in Oklahoma; others moved to New Mexico and joined the Mescaleros.

Very little is known about Chiricahua basketry. Considering their sufferings, it is a miracle that any of their traditional ways survived. Opler (1941) described coiled bowls stitched with yucca, similar to those made by the Mescaleros. The twined burden baskets of the Chiricahuas were also very similar to the Mescaleros'.

In 1984 two Chiricahua women living on the Mescalero reservation, and a daughter of one of them, were twining deep baskets that resembled old-time burden baskets (Mauldin 1984:43). They used sumac rods for the warp elements and sumac-splint twined wefts with the white inner section of the splints turned to the outside of the basket. The twining on most of the basket was twilled (over two, under two), but several encircling bands were executed in plain twining with long twists (over three, under three). They did not use reinforcing corner rods, but attached three vertical strips with buckskin fringe — probably in imitation of the Western Apaches' use of fringed strips on the outside of the reinforcing rods. The Chiricahua women made their rims with two rods bound together and fastened to the body of the basket by a lashing of sumac splints. They also decorated their baskets by coloring the bands of plain twining red and blue. Each stitch was colored separately with a felt marking pen, taking great care that the color did not show on the interior and showed very little on adjacent stitches. The application of colored designs by painting exterior stitches is an old Apache technique; only the implements are new.

The Chiricahuas may have made other kinds of baskets at one time, similar to Mescalero baskets or those of their western neighbors, the San Carlos Apaches. We may never know.

THE WESTERN APACHES

The dislocations and hostilities that engulfed all the Apaches in the middle of the nineteenth century affected the Western Apaches less than the Mescaleros and Chiricahuas. The Western Apaches adapted to military subjugation, thereby avoiding the displacements and crushing defeats suffered by the other groups. They also preserved much of their traditional culture, and their fine basketry, featured in museum collections, exhibitions, and books (Roberts 1929; Robinson 1954; Tanner 1982), is the best known Apachean art.

The Western Apaches were not organized into a single tribe, but consisted of five separate and completely independent divisions or subtribes:

> Although the five Western Apache subtribal groups — the Cibecue, San Carlos, White Mountain, and Northern and Southern Tonto — intermarried to a limited degree, they considered themselves quite distinct from one another. Open conflict between them was not uncommon, and they never formed anything like a united political entity. The territorial boundaries of each group were clearly distinct, and it sometimes happened that trespassers were forcibly expelled or killed. (Basso 1970:5)

The present reservations in the mountains of central Arizona cover about 90,000 square miles. The Western Apaches have lived in the region since before their first contact with the Spaniards sometime around the beginning of the seventeenth century. The White Mountain Apaches are the most numerous, with between 1,400 and 1,500 people in 1985. Agriculture is most important among the Cibecue Apaches, followed by White Mountain, San Carlos, and Tontos.

Traditionally, hunting and gathering provided seventy-five percent of the Western Apaches' food, and agriculture twenty-five percent. Their small groups moved in a seasonal cycle. In April they moved to the river valleys and planted crops in family fields. In May everyone but the elders and some children moved out to harvest and process mescal crowns (Basso 1983:fig. 2). In late June and July, they gathered the ripening fruits of saguaro and prickly-pear cactus. Late July and August was the season for mesquite beans, yucca fruits, and acorns from the emory oaks. In September everyone returned to the valleys to harvest the field crops, and late fall was a busy time for hunting and gathering piñon nuts and juniper berries. As winter closed in, the Apaches settled down in sheltered valley camps. The women tanned hides, sewed clothing, and wove baskets, and the men raided white settlements and even some towns in Mexico for cattle and corn. Within the seasonal schedule, raiding was an important segment of the Apache economy, and they regarded it as no more than another kind of gathering.

Gold was discovered in Tonto Apache territory in 1863. The Western Apaches fought the invading miners and settlers effectively until Fort Goodwin was occupied by the army, when further resistance became futile. Many Apaches, especially the Cibecues, joined the Apache Scouts and helped the army subdue the Chiricahuas. In spite of their cooperation, they were rounded up with the other Apaches and confined to a small reserve at San Carlos for two years. Many were shipped to Florida with the Chiricahuas in 1890. "From the beginning, the Cibecue and White Mountain Apache were the least disturbed and responded to reservation conditions with only a moderate amount of social upheaval. But the awful truth remained that a way of life had been destroyed, and Apaches everywhere knew that it could never be restored" (Basso 1983:482).

Although farming and ranching are the most important economic activities for the Western Apaches, they still hunt and gather wild produce. The old ceremonial system declined because it was too expensive to maintain in a cash economy, but curing rites and rites of passage are still performed. Traditional costumes, fine beadwork, cradleboards, and certain kinds of baskets continue to be produced. Many of their baskets are finely constructed and attractively decorated, but they represent only a meager remnant of what was once a very highly developed tradition among these people.

TRADITIONAL BASKETS. During the final decades of the nineteenth century and the early years of the twentieth, the magnificent coiled baskets of the Western Apaches were eagerly sought by collectors. Because the early history of the Apaches has not yet been written, it is difficult to reconstruct the early phases of their basket tradition, and studies of their recent history have been concerned almost entirely with warfare and economic change. Even the most detailed study of early Apache basketry (Roberts 1929), based mostly on the collections of the American Museum of Natural History, does not say when the baskets were made or collected, nor does it name the collectors. Scattered information does exist, however, and some future scholar will have the pleasure of examining the old collections and attempting to correlate the structural and decorative features of these Apache baskets with the date of their manufacture or at least the date of their collection.

Because the Western Apaches made little if any pottery, they needed baskets for transporting everything from grain to firewood (fig. 44). Baskets were also used as serving dishes, food bowls, and containers for storing grain. Pitched basket jars were the only vessels they owned for storing and carrying water. Contact with whites severely disturbed this traditional pattern, but baskets began to gain a new importance with the development of a market among occupying troops and steadily encroaching settlers. A number of basketry innovations developed in response to the cash market, but most of the changes were modifications of traditional shapes and designs.

Figure 44. A Western Apache woman with a pitched water bottle. The horses carry typical burden baskets. (Courtesy Museum of New Mexico, neg. 76955; photo by Edward S. Curtis, about 1910.)

Before the end of the nineteenth century, scholars such as O. T. Mason believed that Apache basketmaking might soon vanish. Referring to the White Mountain Apaches, he said,

> The art of basket making is not actively practiced at present, the younger members of the tribe finding it difficult to learn and saying it injures their hands. Some of the old women, however, retain the ancient skill, and even superior work may be procured from the reservation. It may be said that the carrying baskets and the pitched water bottles are as frequently made as ever and are in constant use, whereas the finer bowls which were formerly common, as among the Pueblo tribes for storing meal, etc. are growing rarer every year and command high prices. (1904:511)

The many fine baskets being made on the White Mountain reservation at the turn of the century are well represented in museum collections. In contrast, the number of baskets documented from either of the Tonto tribes is extremely small, in spite of evidence that they were skilled in the craft at one time:

> On the authority of Mrs. J. S. Newman [not identified] there are five tribes on the Apache reservation . . . to class as basket makers. Of these the Tonto should rank first, making chiefly ollas, which require more skill than plaques or bowl shapes, and their work is universally even and good. Their specimens are nearly always marked with the arrow point, the pattern running vertically from the center. Their proficiency is accounted for in the fact that the land allowed them on the Gila River is the least productive of any on the reservation, hence their dependence on basket making for a living. (Mason 1904:510)

Unfortunately, Mason does not illustrate any Tonto baskets or describe them in further detail. Other studies such as Roberts (1929), Robinson (1954), and Tanner (1983) say very little about them, and they are rarely identified in museum collections. As a result, the baskets of these two tribes and early coiled baskets of the Cibecue Apaches have been lost in collections identified only as "Western Apache." Western Apache baskets in museum collections are generally identified as White Mountain or San Carlos, and even these are difficult to distinguish from each other.

In an attempt to define the distinctions between San Carlos and White Mountain basketry, Clara Lee Tanner (1983:140) examined the important Guenther collection, gathered by two generations of a missionary family at Fort Apache and donated to the Arizona State Museum. Her conclusions refer almost exclusively to design, and considering the subtlety of the distinctions, it is apparent that there were many more similarities than differences in the

Plate 1. The colored butterflies on this basket were an original idea with the young Paiute weaver Marilu Lehi, although the butterfly motif was used by the Havasupais, some modern Navajos, and several California tribes. SAR 1986-7-88, three-rod bunched construction, 27" diameter. (Photo by Vincent Foster.)

Plate 2. Sally Black of Medicine Hat, Utah, who made this basket, has been one of the foremost innovators in modern Navajo basketmaking, especially with her *yei* figures derived from sandpainting patterns. SAR 1982-5-4, five-rod construction, 24" diameter. (Photo by Vincent Foster.)

Plate 3. Jicarilla Apache baskets made for sale. In the early 1900s, white women appreciated the strength and beauty of Jicarilla baskets. Large laundry hampers (*left*) were popular, as were laundry baskets with distinctive loop handles formed by bending up a section of the rim coil. *Hamper*, SAR 1978-1-129, five-rod construction, 19" diameter, 27" high. *Laundry basket*, MNM 23488/12, 23" diameter, courtesy School of American Research collections in the Museum of New Mexico. (Photo by Vincent Foster.)

Plate 4. The traditional patterns on Jicarilla baskets made during the first half of the twentieth century were bold geometric figures in aniline red, blue, yellow, and brown. SAR B.288, three-rod construction, 20" diameter. (Photo by Vincent Foster.)

Plate 5. Modern Jicarilla basket with complex geometric designs and bright aniline colors. Coiled with three finely scraped sumac rods in a bunched foundation. Made by Bertha Velarde of Dulce, New Mexico, in 1983. SAR 1984-3-1, 14" diameter. (Photo by Vincent Foster.)

Plate 6. Western Apache ollas, or vases, coiled with three-rod bunched foundation and sewn with willow. The decoration is sewn with splints of black devil's claw and red yucca root. *Left*, SAR 1978-4-26, 15" high. *Right*, SAR 1978-4-25, 13" high. (Photo by Vincent Foster.)

Plate 7. A typical Western Apache radial design with various geometric and life figures in black devil's claw. SAR B.383, coiled with three-rod bunched foundation, 23" diameter. (Photo by Vincent Foster.)

Plate 8. A modern version of the Western Apache burden basket, made in 1983 by Evelyn Henry of San Carlos, Arizona. The leather trimmings are of commercial suede. SAR 1983-8-2, 16" diameter at rim. (Photo by Vincent Foster.)

Plate 9. Three unusual Pima baskets. *Left,* design of five large H-shaped figures. SAR B.22, 19" diameter. *Center,* eight expanding vanes containing "coyote track" crosses. SAR B.415, 13" diameter. *Right,* four dark expanding vanes with open insectlike figures edged with hooks (legs). SAR B.40, 12" diameter. (Photo by Vincent Foster.)

Plate 10. A colored Pima basket with a low ring base. The two bands of interlocking scrolls are dyed magenta on a green background. SAR B.68, 15" diameter. (Photo by Vincent Foster.)

Plate 11. Modern Papago yucca-sewn baskets decorated with plant and animal figures. Yellow and green splints of yucca leaves contrast with the bleached white, along with black devil's claw and red yucca root. *Left,* saguaro cactus design. SAR B.303, 11" high. *Center,* turtle. SAR 1981-2-20, 6" diameter. *Right,* deer design. SAR 1981-2-22, 14" long. (Photo by Vincent Foster.)

Plate 12. Hopi basket plaques from Second Mesa. *Left,* large tray with narrow coils. SAR 1984-4-27, 18" diameter. *Center,* a full kachina figure—possibly the Long Billed kachina—with overstitching on the headdress. SAR B.305, 12" diameter. *Right,* a traditional symmetrical design expanding from the center. SAR B.182, 17" diameter. (Photo by Vincent Foster.)

Plate 13. Hopi coiled bowls. *Left,* four figures of antelopes. SAR 1981-6-1, 10" diameter. *Right,* antelope heads above a zigzag band of checkers. SAR 1979-6-57, 9" diameter. (Photo by Vincent Foster.)

Plate 14. Plaited wicker tray from the Hopi town of Oraibi, decorated with a bird with spread wings. SAR 1983-6-2, 14" diameter. (Photo by Vincent Foster.)

baskets of these two Apache neighbors. Consequently, the baskets of the San Carlos and White Mountain Apaches will usually be treated without distinction in what follows.

Materials and Coiling Techniques. The Western Apaches used twining almost exclusively for the production of deep, bucket-shaped carriers, or burden baskets; all their other baskets, from large, shallow platters to deep ollas, were made by coiling. Traditional Western Apache coiled baskets were made with coils of three rods arranged in a trianguloid bunch. Since the baskets were sewn with fine wooden splints, they were constructed entirely of wood except for the materials used for decoration. Western Apache baskets are generally hard and stiff, with surfaces that are markedly corrugated — usually more on one surface than on the other. The positions of the rods were shifted to create the curves of the basket.

Various woods were used for coiled baskets, but the long, slender shoots of willow *(Salix lasiandra* and *nigra)* and cottonwood *(Populus fremontii)* were the most common. Debarked, scraped, and smoothed to serve as foundation rods, they were also split into three strands to provide sewing splints. Willow is slightly more flexible, but cottonwood splints have an attractive white matte surface. In time they both turn the yellow-tan characteristic of most old baskets in collections. The coiled baskets are always decorated with black designs created with splints from the outer surface of the tough, horn-like seed pod of the black devil's claw *(Martynia proboscidea parviflora)*. Very hard, this material is almost always used for the center of the bottom of bowls and the binding around the rim — the two areas that receive the most wear. Depending on the time of year the pods are picked, it is generally pitch black, but some pieces are brown. Sections sometimes get worn to a shiny, ivory-like surface. In some baskets, red designs or details were created with root sections from the yucca (pl. 6). These designs seem to have appeared about the turn of the century, when decoration was becoming increasingly complex in response to the preferences of tourists arriving on the railroad. In a few cases, commercial dyes were used to create brilliant designs in blue, green, and red. Distinctly untraditional, baskets with polychrome designs apparently did not catch on with tourists, and they disappeared. Tanner (1983:96, fig. 4.11.d) illustrates a good example of these baskets.

The coils in Western Apache baskets are invariably worked from right to left. The stitches are usually close, but not actually compacted; tear-shaped; and slanting slightly down to the left as they wind around the foundation rods. When the Apache basketmaker reached the end of her sewing splint, she usually passed it through the basket and cut it off. This moving end was sometimes cut very close so the protruding butts are not apparent, but they were often left sticking out far enough to be felt easily, providing one way to identify the nonwork surface. Some women left the protruding moving ends until the basket was finished and dry, then trimmed them all at once. New splints were threaded through the awl holes, with the fag ends left protruding. To keep them from marring the finish, they were usually clipped short and pulled down between the stitches, so they cannot be seen or felt. In addition, they were often covered by the following stitches, making them difficult to detect. In some cases, both the fag ends and the moving ends were laid along the rods in the new coil and covered by the following stitches (Roberts 1929:157). This seems to occur more frequently on White Mountain coiled baskets, and there are cases in which the basketmakers clipped some of their splices and laid others under the stitches, using both procedures on the same basket.

The texture of Western Apache coiled baskets is fine, especially compared with those of the Jicarillas and Paiutes. Many of the slender foundation rods have a diameter of no greater than 3/32 of an inch. The coils are rarely more than 3/16 inch wide. Baskets have from four to six coils per inch, but usually five, making the stitches about 3/16 inch to 1/4 inch long. The sewing splints are generally less than 1/8 inch wide, and most baskets have eleven or twelve stitches per inch. The thickness of the basket walls depends upon the width of the coils: most tend to be slightly less than 1/4 inch thick at the rim. The rims are finished with stitches of devil's claw passed through the upper rod in the final coil and wrapped around the three rods of the rim. In some baskets, particularly those made in recent years, the rims were finished with alternating stitches of devil's claw and cottonwood. Where the rim coil ends it is tapered to a point, making it hardly noticeable. The starts in Western Apache coiled baskets are tightly wound and look like a rosette of black devil's claw (see fig. 45). To begin, the basketmaker sharpens the ends of the first foundation rods, wraps them with a splint, and bends the slender end into a tight circle. The tip is sewn to the contiguous bent rod, and stitching continues from the center.

Shapes and Designs of Coiled Baskets. The coiled baskets made by the Western Apaches had two basic shapes: wide, shallow bowls; and ollas, or urns, of various sizes. When baskets served many functions around the camp, they made bowls of a convenient size for serving food and deep bowls for mixing foods or cooking with heated stones. As in other tribes, shallow bowls or trays were used for winnowing and parching seeds. Most of them were probably undecorated, and because such simple utility objects were rarely collected or preserved, they are almost completely absent in museums.

By the 1880s, the Western Apaches were designing most of their baskets to please and attract Anglo customers, and the shallow bowls, with their large, highly visible designs, became their most popular products. They are gently

Figure 45. These two Western Apache bowls illustrate the range in designs from very simple to extremely complex. *Left,* the common five-petaled star. SAR B.175, 21" diameter. *Right,* two concentric seven-pointed stars with black triangles containing negative crosses and coyote tracks. SAR B.18, 19" diameter. (Photo by Vincent Foster.)

curved, slightly flat on the bottom, and from 1 foot to more than 2 feet in diameter — much too large to have served any function in a traditional Apache camp.

The designs on these shallow bowls were boldly executed, almost exclusively in jet black, against the white or varied shades of tan stitching. Because Roberts (1929) and Tanner (1983) have described the patterns and motifs extensively, and Tanner has illustrated them in great detail, the present study limits itself to the collection of the School of American Research.

All the designs relate to two ubiquitous traits: the black circle of the rim and the black disk at the center. Between these two boundaries, some designs are quite simple, while others incorporate a number of motifs to create complex results (fig. 45). Tanner suggests that baskets with "simpler," more lightly executed designs were characteristic of the years between 1860 and 1890. Thereafter the decorations became progressively more complex until about 1940. According to her sequence, curvilinear "floral" designs and all-over patterns were popular between 1890 and 1910, but continued in use long after this time.

The baskets in the collection of the School of American Research support Roberts's (1929:177) conclusion that the most common designs in coiled bowls radiate from the center to the rim (fig. 46). Some radiating elements are straight, with additional design elements between the spokes (pl. 7); or a variety of spokes may be depicted, with curved, radiating lines producing whorls or whirlwinds (fig. 45, right) and converted into zigzag lightning motifs. All these designs produce a feeling of explosion, even in the common star or petal motifs, which are basically centripetal. Many of these designs are composed

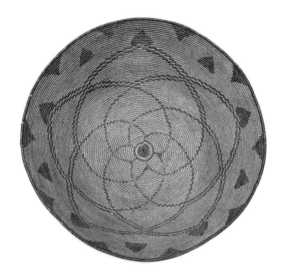

of curved, radiating lines that intersect at various points (fig. 46). The feeling of movement becomes subdued in more complex or heavier star or petal designs.

Simple encircling bands are rare in Apache designs (Roberts 1916:180), but more complex zigzag bands and bands of open diamonds do occur, which sometimes look like parts of star designs (fig. 47). Other bands are terraced or crenelated at the edges, some with such deep indentations that they resemble cogwheels. The basic motifs in these patterns are diamonds, triangles, and rectangular checkers. Western Apache basketry decorations are especially noted for the incorporation of crosses and life-forms such as dogs, deer, and men and women (see fig. 11, pl. 7). Such designs are highly conventionalized.

Ollas, also called urns or vases, represent the other major form in coiled basketry. Some ollas were very large and beautifully decorated. Guy (1977) and Tanner (1982:113) note that large ollas did not appear in descriptions or illustrations of early Apache encampments and agree with Roberts that they were made for sale. This was certainly the case with the very large and elegant specimens that are still eagerly sought by collectors, but it is also clear that olla shapes were produced long ago for water jars and deep containers for storing seeds and corn.

Some large ollas were collected before the turn of the century (Roberts 1929; Mason 1904), and photographs taken by A. Frank Randall in 1884 depict fairly large coiled ollas (fig. 48; Worcester 1979:4). These baskets indicate that if large coiled ollas were commercial products, they developed within the decade following the Western Apaches' impoundment at San Carlos (1875–77), probably from traditional water jars.

Figure 46 (left). A common Western Apache design of overlapping and interlocked petaled figures composed of curved lines radiating from the center. SAR B.176, 24" diameter. (Photo by Vincent Foster.)

Figure 47 (right). Banded designs, geometric figures such as these open diamonds, and plain or zigzag lines were all used by the Western Apaches. SAR B.173, 18" diameter. (Photo by Vincent Foster.)

Figure 48. Studio photograph of a San Carlos Apache man taken in 1884 by A. Frank Randall. The baskets shown here and in other Randall photographs indicate that fairly large ollas were being made as early as 1880. (Courtesy Arizona Historical Society, neg. 12560.)

Around the turn of the century, Western Apache women briefly made coiled ollas in many shapes and sizes, but the production of large baskets declined soon after 1900 because smaller baskets were more profitable. They also introduced the use of red yucca root about this time, generally in bordering lines and for bright spots in the designs. Many of the large ollas are about 20 to 24 inches high, and some are as tall as 36 inches or more. Their shapes vary as widely as their dimensions. Tanner (1983:77) shows nearly forty different outlines ranging from a few with almost cylindrical bodies to squat, globular shapes and tall, slender forms with straight sides expanding from flat, narrow bases. Most olla forms are decorated with all-over patterns: frequently, vertical, interlocking rectangles, rows of triangles or diamonds, bands of zigzags and terraces, or crossed diagonal lines forming networks of diamonds. The largest olla in the School of American Research collection (fig. 49) is decorated with animal and human figures, vertical lines of triangles, and large, open diamonds. Large coiled ollas were made also by the women of some other tribes, but for grace of contour and elegance of design, none equaled the baskets of the San Carlos and White Mountain Apaches.

The range of coiled-basket forms created by the Western Apaches is less extensive than that of some other tribes. In addition to shallow bowls and the olla-shaped jars, they made only a few deep bowls, oval bowls, and pitched water jars. Some of the deep bowls have vertical sides and flat bottoms, but straight, flaring sides were more common. Oval bowls, which are quite rare, were probably made to be sold. Ranging from about 6 inches to nearly 2 feet in length, they all have low, vertical sides, and the coiling starts around three straight rods bent back on themselves (Tanner 1983:fig. 4.26e).

The coiled water jars are ollas of medium size with a coating of piñon pitch to hold water and lugs or handles. The application of pitch seals both the interior and exterior surfaces, which are usually prepared by rubbing red ochre and/or crushed juniper twigs into the coils. The carrying loops, sewn into the coiling, are made from braided horsehair or vegetal fibers, leather or buckskin straps, or elbow-shaped twigs. There are usually two handles on the same side of the shoulder of the jar so that a long line can be attached to or passed through them for carrying the vessel on a person's back or hanging it from a tree. Such coiled water jars are relatively rare in collections, but they must have been common in Apache camps for water storage.

Figure 49. A large, coiled olla, or vase-shaped basket, a form that was among the most distinctive creations of Western Apache women. It is sewn with willow and devil's claw. SAR B.301, 29" high. (Photo by Vincent Foster.)

Twined Water Bottles and Jars. The majority of Western Apache water bottles and jars were made by twining, the preferred technique for baskets used by the Apaches themselves, but rarely used to make baskets for the outside market. Some twined water baskets were similar in shape to the coiled water jars of the Navajos and other Apaches, with wide, flaring necks, flat or recessed bases, and handles on the shoulders (fig. 50). They were probably used to carry or store water in camp; filled, they would have been too heavy for use on the trail. Smaller pitched baskets were made, often rounded or slightly pointed on the bottom. Specialized, double-bodied, dumbbell-shaped bottles could be carried conveniently on the hip by a cord around the waist or slung over or around the shoulders. With a stopper made from a corncob or a twisted wad of yucca fiber or juniper bark, they were ideal canteens for a traveler on foot or horseback. Pitched water bottles or jars were rarely decorated, but occasionally a black line of soot was drawn around the shoulder or some other simple pattern was applied. Usually, the heavy coating of pitch darkened with age, and designs in the basketry were obscured.

Because the surfaces of the pitched vessels were to be hidden by the pitch, little attempt was made to produce a smooth or attractive surface. The warp elements consisted of osiers, or shoots, usually with the bark remaining, crossed and tied to form the start and then bent up for the walls of the basket, where they were held in place by the twined wefts (Tanner 1983:figs. 2, 3, 4, 5). The San Carlos Apaches usually used willow for pitched vessels, while at the higher altitude of the White Mountain reservation, sumac was the customary

Figure 50. Western Apache twined and pitched water jars. *Left,* an old specimen with globular body, narrow neck, and three twig handles. SAR B.79, 12" high. *Center,* a form generally slung on the hip and carried on the trail. SAR B.2, 12" high. *Right,* a household jar in a shape possibly derived from white people's jugs. Coated with red ochre, two twig handles. SAR B.447, 15" high. (Photo by Vincent Foster.)

material. Long, slender shoots must be found, especially with sumac. Such growth occurs only when the mature bush has been cut down or burned, and basketmakers often burned certain areas during the winter to encourage spring growth (Bohrer 1983).

There has been some confusion regarding the actual materials used by the White Mountain Apaches in twining. Tanner (1983) and Collings (1976:5) repeat Roberts's (1929) identification of "squawberry" or "squaw huckleberry" as *Vaccinium stamineum. Vaccinium myrtillus* is identified by Francis H. Elmore (1976:182) as mountain huckleberry and described as a "low, sprawling, deciduous shrub with myrtlelike leaves, usually about 6 to 8 inches tall." Nothing is said about its use for baskets. "Squawberry" or "squawbush" (also called lemonade berry, skunkbush, lemita, etc.) is identified in most sources other than Roberts and Tanner as threeleaf sumac *(Rhus trilobata;* Elmore 1944, 1976; O. Stewart 1938; Bohrer 1983; Watahomigie, Powskey, and Bender 1982b). The sample shoot which the Reverend Arthur A. Guenther cut for me in 1983 as a specimen of the materials used at White Mountain was identified as *Rhus trilobata,* suggesting that the squawberry so frequently referred to in this context was sumac. To avoid confusion, perhaps it should be referred to as squawberry sumac.

A distinctive feature of these Western Apache twined water bottles was the thickened rims, usually formed with a ring of grass or bark fibers held together with splints like the wefts in the body of the vessel. Instead of being simply wrapped around the rim, the wefts were braided back and forth in a "false braid" or herringbone pattern, a method rarely used in other kinds of Apache baskets, and one that produced a casual, rather sloppy effect.

Twined Burden Baskets. The twined burden baskets of the Western Apaches are efficient and attractive. No other people in the Southwest gave as much attention to the construction and decoration of these useful containers. To Western Apaches, they were not just containers to be carried on one's back or hung from a saddle, but also important elements in such rituals as the Sunrise Ceremony.

Even when other kinds of baskets were supplanted by commercial containers such as metal buckets and gunny sacks, the production and use of traditional burden baskets continued. The burden baskets used by most tribes were conical, but the carriers of the Western Apache are shaped like deep buckets, with slightly rounded bottoms and nearly straight sides (fig. 51). Many are constructed on a stiff frame formed by two heavy rods bent into U-shapes, which cross at the bottom of the baskets, with the four straight sections forming the corners. The curved sections are usually left exposed on the bottom of the basket to protect the twined base. The vertical corner rods are sometimes enclosed in the wefts or partially exposed and tied into the basket with occasional weft twists. These burden baskets are almost always decorated with encircling bands of color and embellished with vertical strips of colored and fringed buckskin. Additional fringes are often added around the base.

The fine and varied twining techniques employed in these burden baskets were the most sophisticated of any southwestern basketmakers in historic times. Cottonwood and willow were used for both warp and weft elements. In earlier times, mulberry *(Morus microphylla)* was preferred by the White Mountain people for their finest baskets because of its golden-brown color. In recent years they have sometimes used the local salt cedar *(Tamarix pentandra;* Arthur A. Guenther, letter to author, 1985). Whole sections of stems about 1/8 inch in diameter, smoothed and usually debarked, were used for warps. Two groups of six or seven were laid across each other, and their ends were spread apart and fastened with twined weft splints. When a rectangle approximately 2 inches square had been formed, additional warp rods were inserted and twined in place. The weft strands were twined around each other with a Z-twist, enclosing one or more warps in each turn. The bottoms of these baskets were often inverted or concave, a feature that saved the area around the start from excessive wear and provided stability when the container was placed on the ground. When U-shaped reinforcing rods were used, they were added after the bottom of the basket was completed; their upright sections were then incorporated into the twining in the manner of extra warps set into the corners.

Several twining techniques were used, sometimes for reinforcing, but generally to create textural variations in the surface of the baskets. Simple twining — with the weft twists directly above each other in vertical columns,

Figure 51. A classic Western Apache burden basket in plain twining, with a double rim and two U-shaped rods to reinforce the base and corners. It is decorated with four fringed bands, a fringed buckskin base patch over red cloth, three bands with pendant triangles of devil's claw, and a red painted encircling band. SAR 1978-1-55, 17" high. (Photo by Vincent Foster.)

each enclosing one or more warps — was most common, sometimes combined or mixed with twill-twining, which produced a pattern of diagonal ribbing, the weft twists in each row enclosing a different group of warps from the twists above and below them (fig. 52). Three-strand twining was also used, generally for reinforcing areas of heavy wear, but also to create a raised line on the surface of the basket.

The rim of a basket is almost always its most fragile part, and burden baskets receive especially heavy and rough use. The Western Apaches finished their rims with double rods, one directly above the other and lashed together with willow or some other kind of splint and bound with strips of buckskin or rawhide. Before the end of the nineteenth century, the Apaches began to replace the upper rim rod with a circle of heavy-gauge galvanized steel wire. To avoid breakage in another critical area, the carrying straps were attached to two of the thick reinforcing rods, or the load was distributed over several warps and wefts with flat wooden pegs on the inside of the basket wall.

Some Western Apache burden baskets were decorated by applying vertical buckskin strips with fringes and coloring the strips with yellow ochre. Some baskets had four fringed strips, one on each corner; some had five; and some as many as eight. The bottoms of many baskets were covered with a large, circular buckskin patch, usually scalloped around the edges and hung with long, supple fringes of white or yellow buckskin that swayed gracefully as the bearer walked. In typical Western Apache fashion, the basal patches were also perforated with cut designs of diamonds and/or triangles and backed with bright red or green woolen cloth that showed through the perforations.

Baskets were also decorated with colored bands of diagonal bars or, less frequently, pendant triangles and checkered diamonds (Robinson 1954:pl. 39). The designs, distinctive for burden baskets, are often brightly colored. Black and red are the most common colors, and red, blue, green, yellow, and even orange are used as dyes or paints. The black elements may be devil's claw or wood splints colored with natural or commercial dyes, or they may be painted. The Western Apaches made by far the best painted designs on baskets in the Southwest, painting individual stitches with such care and precision that they are sometimes hard to distinguish from those made with dyed wefts. The paint almost never appears on adjacent stitches, and never on the inside of the basket. Native materials were used to produce soft red, ochre yellow, and black, but most of the other colors were commercial dyes and paints.

According to Goodwin (Ferg and Kessel 1987:73), burden baskets made with U-shaped reinforcing rods and decorated with buckskin fringes were used to carry the personal goods of a family when they moved from one camp to another. Other burden baskets, used to gather and carry food such as corn, mescal beans, and seeds, were similar in shape and materials but lacked U-shaped rods and were more flexible. Also, their decoration was simpler, usually consisting of bands of checks or diagonal lines. Often they were coated on the

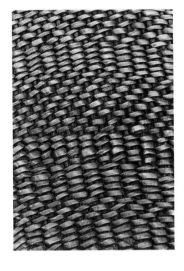

Figure 52. Detail of burden basket showing alternating bands of plain and twill twining. (Photo by Vincent Foster.)

inside with mescal juice. The elaborate, reinforced baskets may have been more highly prized because of the time and labor that went into making them. To avoid wearing them out with food transportation and gathering, they may have been replaced by the simpler, unreinforced baskets, which could be more easily replaced when broken or worn out.

MODERN BASKETS. In the rapidly changing world of the late twentieth century, the lives of the Western Apaches have not remained static, and their basketry has also experienced important changes. The superlative coiled baskets for which they were justly famous almost disappeared during the 1940s, while twined baskets — both burden carriers and water bottles — survived and flourished. While coiled baskets became commercial products, the Western Apaches continued to make twined baskets for their own use.

Twined burden baskets are still produced by the San Carlos Apaches and to a slightly lesser extent by the White Mountain Apaches, but differ from traditional baskets in both form and function. Modern burden baskets are no longer made for the transportion of corn or firewood, but for many years they continued to be important for ceremonial events. In the Sunrise Ceremony (fig. 53) gifts were placed in baskets which marked a course for the girls to run during the ceremony. This custom is still observed, but today the baskets are often replaced by cardboard boxes and other cheap containers (Quintero 1980:262–71). Most of the twined burden baskets made today are conical, with straight, flaring sides and constricted, almost pointed bottoms.

As in so many cases where native crafts have been kept alive, one or two families are responsible for the continuation of basketry at San Carlos. Evelyn Henry learned to make fine burden baskets (pl. 8) from her mother-in-law, Cecilia Henry, who was still making twined baskets in 1986. The conical baskets made by Evelyn Henry and a few other women are twined with willow splints over warps of cottonwood. Shifts between plain twining (usually over more than one warp) and diagonal twilled twining create textural variation in the baskets, and designs are produced by using willow splints with the brown- or ochre-colored bark retained. Because the weft strands are colored on only one surface, they are arranged carefully to keep the bark on the outside of the basket. Thus, a negative reflection of the design is produced on the inside surface. When the basketmaker wishes to change color she twists the wefts so the bark surfaces are turned to the inside, and the white willow splints come to the surface. In recent years, the colorful banded designs have been abandoned, and images of deer and birds have become popular. Reinforcing rods are no longer necessary, but vertical buckskin bands and fringes have been retained, and long fringes usually hang from the bases of the baskets (pl. 8). Most of the leather is now commercially prepared. The use of metal cones on the ends of the fringes was probably copied from Mescalero/Chiricahua baskets. The rims usually consist of a whole or split rod lashed together with

a ring of heavy steel wire and wrapped with leather thongs. Miniature burden baskets are now one of the most popular items being sold. They are made in a variety of sizes from 2 inches to approximately 1 foot high, and subminiatures about 1/2 inch high are sold for earrings.

Cecilia Henry also made twined ollas of various sizes, but it is impossible to know if these shapes were derived from the old coiled ollas, which some of them resemble, or from the twined water containers of the past. Some of the ollas she made in the 1960s had slender bodies and angular shoulders, while some of her later ollas had globular bodies, more like the old water jars. She also made smaller jars and replicated the old double-bodied canteens, which she decorated like the jars. Her skill, imagination, and energy have helped to keep twined basketry alive among the San Carlos Apaches, and she has transmitted her interest and some of her skills to younger relatives.

It is somewhat ironic that one of the least aesthetically appealing forms of twined baskets has persisted and is being produced in some quantity: the ancient and traditional pitched water bottle. Because they were practically indestructable and continued to serve a practical function in the home and in the fields, the old ones were preserved, and the art of making them never died out. Now they are being made for use and for sale, especially by Cibecue women. Few are made at San Carlos, although they are sold there. Several of the

Figure 53. In the Apache Sunrise Ceremony, which celebrates a girl's change from childhood to womanhood, burden baskets traditionally held the many gifts given to the girl's godmother. They also marked the ceremonial course around which the initiate ran to avoid all evil. (Courtesy Museum of New Mexico, neg. 68730, about 1915, photographer unknown.)

women, like Ramona Beatty, say they learned to make water bottles in a program sponsored by the tribe and the University of Arizona in about 1973 (Mauldin 1984:46).

Twined basketry persisted at Cibecue in the weaving of water bottles, revived about 1980 by a young weaver, Linda Guzmán, and her husband. The Guzmáns use wefts of mulberry and devil's claw and stiff warps of cottonwood because shoots of squawberry sumac are not long enough.

The majority of the pitched baskets produced at this time are vase shaped rather than bottle shaped (fig. 54). The bodies are globular, or have slightly angular shoulders around the midline, the necks generally quite wide and slightly flaring. Unlike traditional water bottles, which were usually finished with a herringbone stitch, the thickened rims are finished with lashed parallel stitching. Both the warp rods and the weft splints are made of sumac. The twining is generally plain over-one-under-one with a Z-twist, and the splices protrude prominently on the inside surface. Many have loop handles of braided horsehair inserted in the shoulders, but they are very slender and obviously nonfunctional. As with older water bottles, these jars are rubbed with crushed cedar leaves and powdered red clay before the melted pitch is applied. Most of the jars made today are about 12 inches high and 9 or 10 inches in diameter at the shoulder. Melted pitch is applied so heavily on both the inside and outside surfaces that it usually becomes opaque and turns a tan-amber color. This tendency does not enhance the appearance of these ordinary but increasingly popular little basket ollas.

The coiled baskets of the Western Apaches did not follow the pattern of continuous production and use that characterized their twined baskets. After reaching their height of quality and quantity in the 1930s, coiled baskets declined rapidly when the tourist market dried up during World War II. Eventually, they disappeared entirely. According to Evans and Campbell (1952:14), "Western Apache coiled basketry began to die out about 1930 and is now [1952] completely lost, with little likelihood of ever being revived." Fortunately, coiled basketry has recently shown some signs of revival, though the recovery is slow. Mrs. Joyce Montgomery, whose family has owned the Peridot Trading Post on the San Carlos Reservation for many years, estimated that no more than eight or nine coiled baskets were brought to the post for sale in 1983. However, even these few baskets showed some interest on the part of a new group of younger basketmakers, who were drawing at least to some extent on the skill and knowledge of older women.

This new phase of San Carlos Apache coiled basketry has not yet achieved the high level of artistry that once existed, but improvement can be expected if a market can be developed. Most of the new baskets are small, shallow bowls, approximately 12 inches in diameter and about 2 inches deep. They are generally sewn with white cottonwood stitching over coil foundations made

Figure 54. Modern pitched water jar made by Dicey Lupe of Cibecue, Arizona, in 1983. The jar is twill twined on the body and plain twined on the neck, with pitch applied over a coating of red ochre. The two bent wood handles are too thin to be functional. SAR 1983-8-4, 13" high. (Photo by Vincent Foster.)

of three scraped and smoothed willow or cottonwood rods arranged in a triangular bunch. The coils are approximately 1/2 inch wide, and the stitches tend to be quite even and slightly separated from each other. On the nonwork surfaces, the stitches are frequently split, the moving ends of the splices protrude as sharp butts, and vagrant loose ends detract from the finished appearance. Devil's claw is used in most of the baskets, reflecting designs of the past. Mary Porter, one of the younger basketmakers, has used the classic star motif in its open-work linear mode and in solid black (fig. 55), as well as incorporating other motifs such as simple crosses, checkered diamonds, and little animal figures. She uses devil's claw to make solid black rims and alternates stitches of black and cottonwood to produce a ticked effect around the rims.

Personal designs are likely to become more common if the craft continues to develop and younger artists are encouraged to make coiled baskets. Among others, Charlene Tuffley makes baskets with nontraditional designs of birds with open wings and distinctive wishbone motifs derived from some source other than the classic coiled baskets of her tribe (fig. 55).

Contemporary weavers have become increasingly sensitive to the aesthetics of other peoples and conscious of other basketmaking traditions. Already accomplished in beadwork and making dolls and cradleboards, Katherine Brown decided to try her hand at basketry in about 1978. She learned coiling from an elderly lady who had been forced to abandon the craft when her eyesight failed, and she began to experiment with different designs and colors. One of her distinctive baskets was awarded a prize by the Heard Museum

Figure 55. Modern San Carlos Apache coiled baskets. *Left,* a simplified version of traditional design motifs, made by Mary Porter. SAR 1982-5-6, 11" diameter. *Right,* an original design by Charlene Tuffley. SAR 1982-5-1, 13" diameter. (Photo by Vincent Foster.)

Figure 56. Katherine Brown has produced some of the most colorful modern coiled baskets on the San Carlos reservation. Some of her designs are traditional; others, such as this example, derive from such sources as the pictures in *Arizona Highways*. (Courtesy MelJoy Indian Traders, Globe, Arizona; photo by A. H. Whiteford.)

(fig. 56). Rather than copying designs, she draws upon many sources and produces entirely new patterns. Asked about the source of one of her designs, she ventured that it might have been suggested by something she saw in *Arizona Highways* magazine.

Although Katherine Brown uses innovative designs, her basket techniques and materials are traditional. She uses White Mountain willow for the three scraped rods in the coils and some willow splints for their ivory-pink color, which contrasts with the stark white cottonwood and the deep black of the devil's claw. Her sewing is quite close and her work surfaces are smooth, with the fag ends cut short and usually covered. Split and uneven stitches and protruding splice ends make the nonwork surfaces of her baskets less smooth. Never garish, the designs of her attractive baskets are integrated and smoothly executed. As her innovations provide satisfaction and recognition, other artisans will be encouraged to refine their skills and open their minds to new ideas in designs and colors. In this way, there may be a real and enduring renaissance in the once-famed coiled basketry of the Western Apaches.

5

The Yuman-Pai Tribes

For thousands of years, a number of distinctively different tribes who speak the Yuman language have lived in the area now known as western Arizona, occupying a broad band that generally borders on the Colorado River and stretches from the Gulf of California to the Grand Canyon. Much of this enormous territory is desert and semidesert, but the Colorado and the Gila-Salt river systems made it possible for these people to farm. Simple farming methods provided auxiliary sources of food, but other systems were very sophisticated, with complex networks of dams and canals for irrigation, and fairly dense populations developed in some areas.

The cultural patterns shared by all Yuman tribes indicate that they are descendants of the desert Archaic people. The northern tribes in particular closely "resembled the Paiutes . . . in low intensity [of development] and lack of specialization" (K. Stewart 1983a:1). Their political and social structures were generally simple and remarkably informal, but their farming and crafts produced a lifestyle that was more settled and probably more secure than that of the Paiutes.

There are four branches of Yuman-speaking tribes: one in California, one in Mexico, and two in western Arizona. The River Yuman branch includes the tribes along the lower Colorado between Arizona and California and on the middle fork of the Gila River — the Quechans (formerly called Yumas), Mohaves, Cocopas, and Maricopas. The River Yumans practiced floodwater farming, living in scattered family units along the banks of the rivers (K. Stewart

1983b; Spier 1933). Because they were primarily potterymakers, they will not be dealt with in this study. They all practiced cremation, and their baskets, undecorated utilitarian forms, were generally burned with them at death. The Quechans and Mohaves still make some pottery for sale, and the Maricopas produce a considerable amount of decorated ware; but most River Yuman baskets have long since disappeared, and the few preserved in museum collections are unimpressive compared to those of other tribes.

Separated from the River Yumans both culturally and geographically, the tribes of the Upland Pai branch — the Yavapais, Hualapais, and Havasupais — live on the upper Colorado River in the highlands of northwestern Arizona. Although they shared many features in their basketry, they also developed very distinctive styles.

THE YAVAPAIS

The coiled baskets of the Yavapais and Western Apaches are so similar that they are often confused. The two tribes have long been neighbors, friends, and relatives by marriage, but each has a unique and complex history (Khera and Mariella 1983; Gifford 1932, 1936). The Yavapais were always a people of the wide open spaces. In pre-contact times, they occupied an area of twenty thousand square miles (approximately ten million acres) in the great bend of the Colorado River. This area provided excellent hunting and gathering, and water was almost always available from the streams, springs, and ponds. In addition to gathering a great variety of seeds and fruits, including mescal, piñon nuts, and mesquite beans, they also cultivated corn, beans, and squash in the valleys.

In spite of their linguistic affiliation with the other Upland Pais, the Yavapais were constantly at war with the Hualapais and the Havasupais. They also fought their neighbors to the south, the Pimas, Papagos, and Maricopas, but maintained friendly relations with the Navajos and Hopis, trading mescal, buckskins, and baskets in exchange for woven blankets and silver. They were generally at peace with the Mohaves and Quechans, but their most enduring friends were the Western Apaches. Khera and Mariella (1983:40) suggested that this friendship resulted from the similarities in their two cultures, products of the environment and of traits acquired from the Pueblos. However, the two tribes were also very different from each other in sociopolitical structures and ritual complexes. When subjugated by the U.S. military, they were literally forced into each other's company.

In spite of early contacts with the Spaniards, the Yavapais had little trouble with invaders until gold was discovered in their territory in 1860 and miners began to arrive. When the Indians resisted the attempts of the newcomers to drive them away, the army subdued them and confined them to a small reservation on the Colorado River. In the winter of 1875, they were forced to march

180 miles to imprisonment at San Carlos. More than one hundred died on the trail. The tribe was broken up, and for fifteen years most of the Yavapais lived with the Apaches. Many married Apaches, and in addition to cultural similarities, the two tribes have many kinship ties.

When the Yavapais were set free in 1890, further fragmentation of the tribe occurred. Those who left San Carlos split up into three separate groups, most of whom were immediately involved in water disputes with white farmers who had moved onto their land. These disputes, which were still going on in the 1980s, were usually settled to the disadvantage of the Yavapais, most of whom were forced to give up farming and turn to wage work in the mines or become servants in the towns. In spite of fragmentation and poverty, they maintained a sense of tribal unity, and some traditional customs were preserved — especially basketmaking (fig. 57).

Figure 57. Yavapai basketmaker. Her large twined carrying basket holds trimmed stems of willow and/or cottonwood tied in rings for future use. (Courtesy Southwest Museum, neg. 32369; photo by C. C. Pierce, early 1900s.)

For many years, baskets made by Yavapai women were essential to their survival, and they continued to make them even in the concentration camps. None of their utility baskets have been preserved or identified, but a picture of a Yavapai camp taken before 1888 (Khera and Mariella 1983:50) shows several Apache-style pitched water bottles and a large conical twined carrying basket similar to those made by the Havasupais. At the turn of the century and well before, Yavapai coiled baskets were regarded by such connoisseurs as George Wharton James as among the finest in the Southwest. Commenting on the baskets of a small group of Yavapais called "Palomas," whom he mistakenly identified as Apaches, he wrote, "Apaches are all basket makers, but the so-called Yuma Apaches — this Palomas band — surpass all the others. Their work is characterized by finer stitches, more beautiful shapes, better colored splints and greater beauty and quality of design" (1903:153). James's misidentification is typical of the confusion that resulted from the use of such names as Yuma-Apaches, Palomas, Tonto-Apaches, Garroteros-Apaches, Walapai-Apaches, and others. The confusion complicated the Yavapais' attempts to gain tribal recognition and contributed to the erroneous identification of many of their baskets. Undocumented Yavapai coiled baskets are generally identified as "Apache." Some museums and collectors feel that it is impossible to distinguish Yavapai from Apache baskets, and classify them as "Yavapai-Apache." This practice tends to perpetuate the terminological confusion of the past and compound the problem of identifying Yavapai baskets.

YAVAPAI VS. APACHE BASKETS. In light of the long-enduring friendship between the Yavapais and the Western Apaches, their enforced proximity to each other, and intertribal marriage, it is not surprising that their baskets resemble each other. Edward Gifford (1932), an ethnologist who studied the Yavapais for many years, was convinced that the Yavapais acquired their basket designs and many of their techniques from the Apaches; but Bert Robinson (1954), a knowledgeable collector, believed the Apaches learned from the Yavapais. In conversations with basketmakers of both tribes, he found that the Apaches very rarely identified or interpreted any of the basket designs he showed them, while the Yavapais recognized many of them by name. Some elderly Apache women told him that their tribe had learned basketmaking from the Yavapais during the fifteen years the two tribes lived together at San Carlos. In any case, there seems to be little doubt that both tribes were making coiled baskets before 1875 and that each was later influenced by the techniques and designs of the other.

The problem is to determine which, if any, features distinguish Yavapai from Apache coiled baskets. They look the same in both form and decoration, and the materials and technical processes employed in their manufacture are the same. Some collectors distinguish the baskets of the two tribes with one or two diagnostic traits; others depend on a "feeling," and there have been few attempts to define the distinguishing features with sufficient clarity to serve as a guide for collectors and curators. Robinson (1954:79) commented, "In spite of the many likenesses existing between them, there also are differences which identify their tribal origin." Unfortunately, his presentation of these differences did not dispose of the problem. He observed that the star design was common on Yavapai baskets, but the Apaches used it too, and both tribes also used naturalistic motifs such as humans and dogs. Designs of eagles, diamonds, and swastikas were "sacred" to the Yavapais, but they also appeared on Apache baskets. In a more specific observation, he notes that the star design appeared at the center or on the bottom of most Yavapai baskets and that deep bowl shapes were more common among the Yavapais than the Apaches. Although he noted that crosses were not used on Yavapai baskets, some of the specimens he illustrated have crosses in their designs.

Clara Lee Tanner attempted to define the differences between Yavapai and Apache basketry in various publications. Because her concern was largely with decorative patterns, she searched for distinctive designs and attempted to define the motifs and arrangements that produced them. For example, she saw Yavapai designs as "more clean-cut, more organized, more evenly spaced and better arranged" (1982:178) than Apache designs — a result of spaces left between the elements in their designs — while the Apaches tended to join theirs together. Yavapai designs also left more blank space and were more evenly and regularly placed. Although both tribes used the same motifs, the Apaches tended to include more of them on a single basket, sometimes giving their baskets a cluttered appearance, with various elements included simply to fill space.

The two baskets in figures 58 and 59 illustrate some of these features. Figure 58 is an Apache basket combining human figures, animal motifs, and encircling bands of geometric elements. The life figures are grouped somewhat irregularly — some singly, others in pairs — while in the documented Yavapai basket (fig. 59) collected at Fort McDowell between 1943 and 1953, the pattern is very regular. Figures are used singly and in groups, and the open spaces left between the design elements are regular. This basket also illustrates the central star mentioned by both Tanner and Robinson, as well as heavy black lines, solid triangles, and other motifs within which negative (white) animals and humans are frequently included. These features are all typical of Yavapai baskets.

Before 1950 Yavapai and Apache coiled baskets were both of high quality. Yavapai baskets collected by June Steele while she was teaching at Fort McDowell between 1945 and 1953 are excellently made, with even stitching and smooth foundation rods. Like Apache baskets of the same period, the surfaces are smooth, the fag ends covered, and the moving ends clipped very short. After mid-century, the Apaches practically stopped making coiled

Figure 58 (left). Fine example of complex Western Apache design collected in the 1920s. Compare with fig. 59. In the Apache basket, some of the spaces are slightly uneven, the sequence of figures is irregular, and the use of negative space is less effective. SAR B.382, 23" diameter. (Photo by Vincent Foster.)

Figure 59 (right). Yavapai bowl collected at Fort McDowell between 1943 and 1953, believed to have been made by Lucy Smith. Although the same motifs are used as in the basket in fig. 58, the treatment of the Yavapai basket is more precise, and absolute symmetry is maintained throughout. 18" diameter, 7" high. (Private collection; photo by Vincent Foster.)

baskets, and the quality of Yavapai baskets declined sharply. Their surfaces were rough; the moving ends of sewing splices protruded sharply; there were many split stitches; and vagrant fibers, split from both the splints and the foundation rods, were left to mar the appearance and texture of the baskets.

In most southwestern tribes, including San Carlos, Jicarilla, and others, the moving end of a new splint was pushed through a perforation in the upper rod of the preceding coil, and the splint was pulled through until only a short section of the fag end was left protruding. This fastened the splint in place before it was bound around the new foundation rods. In contrast, some Yavapais (for example, Bessie Mike) laid the fag end of the new splint under the upper rod of the new foundation coil, inserting it from the back so only a short section protruded. The splint was then drawn over the rod and pulled down to be inserted in a perforation in the coil below. In the process, the fag end was tightly bound between the rods of the new coil and usually covered by the following stitches. This procedure is difficult to detect in finished baskets.

There is no single, reliable key to distinguishing the baskets of the Yavapais and the Western Apaches except specific information about the tribal affiliations of the women who made them. Even this can be confusing, because many of the basketmakers were of mixed Yavapai and Apache descent, and some of their baskets combined characteristics of both tribes. For example, the well-known basketmakers Kate Austin and Josephine Harrison were sisters whose father was Yavapai, but whose mother was Apache; and Viola Jimulla, a famous Yavapai basketmaker, learned the craft while her family was living at San Carlos (Barnett 1968).

Defining the more or less distinctive features of Yavapai coiled basketry may help curators and collectors identify baskets, and it represents a step towards the adequate description of Yavapai coiled basketry. There are risks involved, however. "Diagnostic traits" may be applied uncritically in the identification of undocumented baskets, with the added danger of a self-fulfilling prophecy: all the baskets thus identified will demonstrate the features used to establish their arbitrary identification. It is essential that records include not only all the documentation available, but also information about the critical features upon which identification was based and the identity of the person who made the identification. Classification on the basis of typology must always be distinguished from identification based on solid documentation, and both must be taken into consideration.

DESIGN CHANGES. In spite of the difficulties in identifying Yavapai baskets, the number of documented specimens is sufficient to delineate the pattern of changes they have undergone since the beginning of the twentieth century. Early baskets, baskets made between 1925 and 1965 by Viola Jimulla, and baskets collected at Fort McDowell between 1940 and 1955 by June Steele are all represented. During the 1960s and 1970s, a number of Yavapai basketmakers became known, and their work appears in several collections: Kate Austin, her sister Josephine Harrison, Bessie Mike, Lillian Shenah, Lola Dickens, Nina Smith, Jocelyn Hunnicut, and others.

Shapes and decorative designs of Yavapai baskets remained relatively unchanged for more than three-quarters of a century. The typical ollas made by the "Palomas" in 1900 had sloping shoulders and broad bases (fig. 60). These forms seem to have died out, but ollas with rotund, globular bodies made about the same time (James 1903:146) lasted much longer before being displaced by the slenderer, vase-like shapes the Yavapais shared with the Apaches and other tribes. Even in later times, Yavapai ollas tended to be shorter and broader than those made by the Apaches (Tanner 1982:178). The last large Yavapai ollas were made by Mable Osife in about 1950 (Robinson 1954:pl. G), but shallow bowls and circular trays continued to be made almost as they had been in 1900.

Designs were always rendered in black devil's claw splints, with occasional touches of red yucca root. Early patterns were often open and linear, but some baskets were decorated with bands of checkered rectangles and solid black triangles similar to later Yavapai and Apache designs. Large areas of solid black and negative designs, which later became almost diagnostic for Yavapai baskets, were not used at the beginning of the century. These features, along with earlier designs, appear in the baskets collected by Gifford in 1930 (Khera and Mariella 1983:50). Some baskets made by Viola Jumilla about the same time were decorated with black diamonds or triangles with white (negative) figures (Barnett 1968:36–38). Lighter, more linear designs,

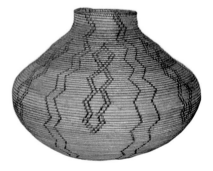

Figure 60. Some of the Yavapais, known as Paloma Apaches at the beginning of this century, made ollas with distinctive sloping shoulders. Three-rod bunched coils, willow and devil's claw stitching, 15" high. (Courtesy Smithsonian Institution, catalogue 209289; photo by A. H. Whiteford.)

Figure 61. This bowl exhibits Yavapai characteristics very clearly: simple clarity of design, absolute symmetry, fine workmanship, extensive use of black devil's claw, and negative figures of humans and animals. The central star is also typical. Collected in the 1920s. SAR B.386, 18" diameter. (Photo by Vincent Foster.)

Figure 62. Basket made in 1983 by Bessie Mike of Fort McDowell, Arizona, one of the few remaining Yavapai basket-makers. She explores unusual design concepts, as in this "eagle" pattern. Three-rod bunched construction, sewn with willow and devil's claw. SAR 1983-8-1, 17" diameter. (Photo by Vincent Foster.)

which often produced netlike patterns, continued in use. Black rims remained fairly constant, although some later baskets had ticked rims with alternate stitches of black and white. The star or petal motif also survived as a basic design element, and between 1940 and 1960 it was often used as a frame for negative and positive figures of animals, humans, and swastikas (fig. 61).

Animal motifs were used in the 1960s by Josephine Harrison, with an all-over pattern of "ants" and eagles with spread wings. Robinson (1954:97) noted that the eagle motif was "very sacred." At least one eagle design is attributed to the early part of the century (Heard Museum NA-SW-Ya-8-18), and a rather crude "eagle" was incorporated in a unique "leaf" pattern by Bessie Mike in 1983 (fig. 62). She also used the common star motif and is shown (Khera and Marilella 1983:49) making one with six points and heavy outlines in 1975. Lillian Shenah, another of the few remaining Yavapai basketmakers, made a basket in 1983 with one eight-pointed star inside another, both of them in white (negative) on a black background (Mauldin 1984:53).

Khera and Mariella (1983:48) reported that the production of traditional baskets "continued in the 1980s to be a highly skilled craft that was practiced by women in all the Yavapai reservation communities." In 1984 it was difficult to find any basketmakers except at Fort McDowell, where fewer than a dozen women were known to be weaving, and the few baskets offered for sale were well below the quality typical of only fifteen or twenty years before. Some of the most accomplished basketmakers died in recent years, and only a few of the younger women have learned the craft.

On the Prescott reservation, Viola Jimulla taught a basketmaking class in 1935, and for a while the students participated in fairs and demonstrations. Their skills were widely recognized, but enthusiasm waned, and only three basketmakers were left in 1946 (Barnett 1968:35). In 1986 the single remaining basketmaker, Effie Starr, was trying to arouse interest among the Indian students at Prescott Community College. Basketmaking remains alive, but it is practiced almost exclusively by a few elderly women at Fort McDowell. There are some signs of a basketmaking revival among the San Carlos Apaches, and there is hope that the same thing will happen among the Yavapais.

THE HUALAPAIS AND HAVASUPAIS

Traditional enemies of their relatives the Yavapais, the Hualapais and the Havasupais were a single people at one time, but there is disagreement regarding the date of their separation. On the basis of archaeological excavations, Schwartz (1956a, 1956b, 1959, 1983) argues that the two tribes separated in prehistoric times and that the present Havasupais developed directly from the ancient Cohonina culture, which first appeared in the region of the Grand Canyon about A.D. 600. Other research (Euler 1981; Euler and Dobyns 1984) suggests that these two Pai tribes descended together from the Cerbat branch of the prehistoric Hakataya culture and separated only recently. According to this view, the Havasupais and the Hualapais were a single tribe until the U.S. government arbitrarily designated them as two distinct tribes and gave them separate reservations in 1882. There is no doubt, however, that the Hualapais and the Havasupais are closely related to each other, intermarry with each other, and share many aspects of a common culture. As Schwartz (1959) points out, each tribe responded to the distinctive ecological pressures and resources of the area in which it lived, resulting in the present differences between them.

The region occupied by the Hualapais is similar to the home territory of the Yavapais: arid chaparral and desert grassland, mesquite, creosote bush, and palo verde, with juniper and piñon trees in the higher altitudes. Their territory is bounded by the canyons of the Colorado River on the north, the once-hostile Mohaves on the west, their enemies the Yavapais on the south, and their friends the Havasupais on the east. At the beginning of the twentieth century, there were fewer than six hundred Hualapais. There is evidence that dams and irrigation systems were known to the Hualapais and that they raised corn, beans, and wheat when the usually adequate supply of wild foods was scarce, but the U.S. Army destroyed this agricultural pattern.

Havasupai life was quite different. Possibly from as early as A.D. 600 (Schwartz 1983) until today, they have lived in the fertile and sheltered environment of a tributary valley of the Grand Canyon. In this oasis along the banks of Cataract Creek, the Havasupais enjoyed a settled agricultural life pattern. But they were not confined to the canyon, and long before whites entered the area, the Havasupais farmed in the valley during the summer months and spent the fall and winter seasons hunting on the surrounding plateau. Although they now have more than 250,000 acres of land, they are still a small tribe: their numbers increased from about 200 in 1860 to only 350 in 1985. Changing conditions have led to a decline in farming and the development of services for the ever-increasing flow of tourists as a source of tribal income. The continued production of baskets has been one of the significant responses to changing opportunities in their traditional homeland.

THE HUALAPAIS

The post-contact history of the Hualapais closely resembled that of the Yavapais and many other tribes. Settlers, miners, and the U.S. Army suddenly entered their lives in the middle of the nineteenth century. Within thirty years, their tribal life was destroyed, and they were rounded up and moved away from their homeland. They were allowed to return later, only to find that the country had been occupied by ranchers during their absence and that cattle grazing had completely destroyed the ecological base they depended on. Unable to sustain themselves in their traditional way, most of the Hualapais moved to the growing white towns in search of jobs and schooling for their children. They also began raising cattle, and by the 1970s the tribal herd had grown to about four thousand head. With an award of nearly three million dollars from the Indian Claims Commission in 1968, they developed some light industry, a forestry program, and other projects which helped to improve their standard of living.

TRADITIONAL BASKETS. Traditional Hualapai basketry waxed and waned within this context of rapid changes and abrupt dislocations. In the old days, when the people sustained themselves with food that could be gathered from the land and produced in their gardens, their basketry was well developed and almost exclusively utilitarian. In forms, techniques, and functions, their baskets were very similar to those of the Southern Paiutes. There were four basic shapes: conical burden baskets, flat circular trays, small bowls, and pitched bottles of various forms. They also made cradleboards, sandals, and racquet-shaped seed beaters. According to Bateman (1972), the Hualapais stopped making burden baskets, biconic water bottles, and seed beaters about 1910, but circular trays continued to be used as household implements, especially for parching piñon nuts, as late as the 1950s.

Hualapai burden baskets were made of closely twined splints. Cottonwood, willow, and mulberry were sometimes used, but squawberry sumac and catclaw were preferred. At least two members of the Leguminosae family are called "catclaw." The Hualapai distinguish between New Mexican locust

(*Robinia neomexicana*) and acacia (*Gleditsia triacanthos*), but refer only to the acacia as "catclaw" (Watahomigie, Powskey, and Bender 1982b). Most of these carriers were made in twill or diagonal twining, with bands of plain twining for textural decoration. Bands of simple designs were created with black splints of devil's claw, the black often being used as background for lighter colored zigzags or rows of diagonal slashes (fig. 63). The rims are generally double, and short sticks were often used on the inside of the basket wall as reinforcements, to which the ends of the carrying straps were attached.

Many of the carriers were conical. Both the Hualapais and the Havasupais made a rather distinctive shape with a constricted nipple-like base. Other Hualapai carriers had rounded sides and bottoms and were almost hemispherical, while some had relatively straight and slightly flaring sides. The bottoms of all the burden baskets were protected with patches of rawhide. They ranged considerably in size, from about 27 inches in diameter at the rim to about half that size. To keep wheat and even smaller grass seeds from leaking out of the carriers, their interior surfaces were often smeared with the pulp of stewed peaches, mescal pulp, and yucca fibers, which filled the openings between the wefts and dried to a hard and durable coating.

Shallow circular trays were usually treated in the same way to seal them for winnowing seeds and to protect them from burning when used with hot coals for parching. They were closely twined and decorated like carriers with bands of devil's claw and three-strand twining, in which the slightly raised stitches produced a textural change. The trays were between 12 and 24 inches

Figure 63. Hualapai burden basket, twill twined except for a band of plain twine and bands of three-strand twine at the base and below the rim. The base is covered with rawhide. SAR B.390, 16" high. (Photo by Vincent Foster.)

in diameter and about 1 1/2 inches to nearly 5 inches deep and were made with a double rod around the rim. The twined bowls, which were used in early times for serving food or cooking mush and stew with hot stones, were made in the same way and with the same materials. Although they were noted by Cushing in 1882, Spier (1928) reported that they were no longer being used in 1928.

The Hualapais' twined water bottles were coarsely woven and heavily coated with pine pitch. Most of them were globular or pear-shaped, with flat bottoms. Some were biconical bottles with pointed bases, which were sometimes protected with separate caps of twined yucca fiber (fig. 64). The biconical bottles usually measure approximately 15 inches in height and 10 to 12 inches in maximum diameter, while the globular bottles are only 8 or 9 inches high. Before being coated with pitch, the bottles were rubbed with peach mush or dried yucca root and then coated with a red mineral clay. The thick coat of pitch was commonly mixed with yucca fibers as a binding element. Like most Hualapai twined baskets, water bottles were finished by cutting off the excess sections of the warp elements and bending the protruding ends into a bundle that was wrapped between two splints or withes to form the rim. In some cases, the wrapping stitches of the rim were finished with a herringbone design. Carrying loops of braided horsehair or yucca fiber were usually worked into the bottles at the shoulders.

The racquet-shaped seed beaters of the Hualapais were very simple and completely undecorated. Those collected by Kroeber in 1935 were narrow, elongated spoon shapes made of sumac rods bent into a tight arc and brought back upon themselves to be bound together into a rough handle. Some rods did not extend to the end but were bent across the beater and plaited in and out of the warps. The wefts were bent to form a shallow concavity about 3 to 4 inches deep. The beaters were generally about 14 to 20 inches long and 3 to 6 inches wide. Sumac and catclaw were the materials most frequently used.

Figure 64. Hualapai twined biconical water bottle collected before 1930 by A. L. Kroeber. Such bottles were also used by the Havasupais, but the fiber cap on the base was a Hualapai custom. 14" high. (Courtesy School of American Research collections in the Museum of New Mexico, catalogue 10915/12; photo by Vincent Foster.)

MODERN DEVELOPMENTS. As the Hualapais were forced to change their lifestyle, they abandoned their traditional utilitarian basketry almost completely and adopted new forms and techniques. For the most part, new developments at the beginning of the twentieth century were the usual responses to the development of a market for baskets among non-Indians. Between 1900 and 1930, Hualapai women produced finely coiled baskets with foundations of three bunched rods of sumac or willow, sewn with splints of the same materials (fig. 65). These baskets were decorated with simple designs of black devil's claw, and the splints were colored with commercial dyes or natural colors. For a short period at the beginning of the century, commercial raffia was used in decoration.

Coiled basketry continued to develop among the Havasupais, but the Hualapais gave up coiled baskets for a particular style of twined basket that has become the hallmark of the tribe. These twined baskets are generally deep bowls with slightly rounded sides and flat bottoms (fig. 66), but small vase or olla forms were also produced in limited quantities. Squawberry sumac and sometimes willow are used for both the warps and the wefts. The general effect is usually much rougher than that produced by the old twined baskets. Robinson (1954:110) noted, "The Walapai women probably give less time to the preparation of their basket material than other Arizona weavers. I have seen them gather twigs from the sumac bushes and immediately start weaving them into baskets, with an occasional leaf still clinging to the twig." He goes on to say that the baskets are extremely stout: he had seen them support the weight of a man without collapsing.

The method of construction and decoration of these twined baskets was designed to catch the eyes of tourists and other potential buyers, and in this they have apparently been consistently successful. Robinson says that a basket he bought in 1926 was almost exactly the same as some he purchased twenty years later. Apparently this uniformity was not always the case, for Bateman's (1972:46) informants told him that many different shapes and sizes were made to sell at the Hackberry railroad station between 1900 and 1915, including "twined bowls, hourglass shapes, wastebaskets, goblets, ollas, baskets with lids, oval shapes, and miniature utility baskets." Probably in response to the dictates of the market, this diversity disappeared some time around 1918–1920, and Hualapai basketmakers began to devote their efforts almost exclusively to the production of deep twined bowls.

These modern twined baskets are started in the traditional fashion, by crossing two groups of three sumac warps and binding them together with splints split from other sumac shoots. Pairs of similar splints are then twined around the warps, generally in a Z-twist, which makes each stitch or twist slope slightly upward to the right. Diagonal, or twill, twining is the rule, with occasional courses or narrow bands of three-strand twining. For decoration, splints colored with commercial dye are woven into simple bands of zigzags

Figure 65. Hualapai shallow coiled bowl collected before 1930 by A. L. Kroeber. The devil's claw has been intensified with black dye. Coiling became rare in recent years. 11" diameter. (Courtesy School of American Research collections in the Museum of New Mexico, catalogue 10964/12; photo by Vincent Foster.)

Figure 66. Haulapai twined bowl collected in 1912. It is twill twined with split sumac wefts over unsplit sumac warps. The flat rim is made by enclosing the warp ends between two splints bound with a flat sewing splint. Decorated with aniline dyes. SAR B.347, 4" high. (Photo by Vincent Foster.)

and diagonal slashes (fig. 67), usually in black, red, brown, green, and russet. One of the distinctive features of these baskets is the rim — thick and usually very flat on the upper surface, resulting from the custom of trimming the warps, placing a rim hoop on each side of their ends, and binding the two hoops together with smooth sumac splints. In most cases, the rim hoops are split rods with the flat sides fitted against the vertical warp ends. Some other tribes finish their baskets with thick rims, but only the Hualapais make their rims so broad and flat.

Between 1940 and 1967, Hualapai basketmaking declined sharply because of low return and the shortage of basketmaking materials. Bateman (1972) found that sumac, the primary material, became scarce because the bushes were not trimmed and/or burned to make them produce the proper kind of shoots. Devil's claw, which had once been raised in local gardens, had died out; willow had to be brought from Havasu Canyon; and basketmakers were forced to travel nearly one hundred miles to find sumac near Prescott, Arizona (Bateman 1972). Ethnic pride among young Hualapais was very low during this period, and the elderly basketmakers were disdained as reminders of the unhappy past.

Toward the end of the 1960s, interest in tribal traditions revived. Basketmaking suddenly became a prestigious activity, especially after it was recognized that outsiders approved of and admired Hualapai baskets. The dozen or so elderly ladies who made baskets had long been sustained by their relationships with each other and pride in their creations. One of them, Mrs. Tim McGee, organized a basketmaking class in 1968, and several women learned the craft from her. About this same time a new store keeper arrived in Peach Springs. He and his wife were both interested in collecting baskets, and more important, he began to pay better prices for them. In 1967 only six baskets were offered for sale, but in 1970 more than one hundred were brought to the store (Bateman 1972:62). In five years the number of active basketmakers increased from four to thirteen, even though some of the older women died during this period. With increases in basket prices and personal prestige, some of the women revived old techniques. Basket forms which had not

Figure 67. Twined bowls made by Elnora Mapatis in 1983, similar to the bowl in fig. 66 that was made seventy years before. The unscraped surfaces of the weft splints can be seen on the interiors. *Right*, decorated with orange and ochre yellow. SAR 1983-17-2, 4" high. *Left*, decorated with bands of dyed red, blue, and maroon. SAR 1983-17-4, 6" high. (Photo by Vincent Foster.)

Figure 68. Elnora Mapatis of Peach Springs, Arizona, one of the women who preserved traditional Hualapai basketmaking, starting a twined bowl. (Photo by Deborah Flynn, 1983.)

been seen for half a century reappeared: water bottles, conical burden baskets, and circular parching trays. Some baskets were smeared with peach mush as in the old days, and some women experimented with natural dyes. Nevertheless, basketmaking was still considered an activity for old ladies. A few young women showed some interest, but most of the basketmakers were over fifty.

Interest in basketmaking continued into the 1980s. With tribal support, the Peach Springs Elementary School brought skilled basketmakers such as Elnora Mapatis (fig. 68), Eva Schrum, Annie Querta, Beth Wauneka, and Jennie Lee Imus into the classrooms to teach students the traditional craft.

Figure 69. A young Havasupai woman drinking from a traditional biconical pitched water jar. A burden basket and a coiled bowl lie on the ground. (Courtesy Southwest Museum, neg. 30874; photo by George Wharton James, early 1900s.)

They demonstrated both coiling and twining techniques and discussed the selection and processing of raw materials. Fine baskets made by earlier experts such as Mrs. Tim McGee and Maude Sinyella and preserved by the tribe were used as examples.

In addition to deep twined bowls — the only baskets made by the Hualapais for many years — weavers began making conical burden baskets in various sizes, coiled trays decorated with stars and animal figures (Watahomigie, Powskey, and Bender 1982a:16), water bottles, twined trays like those once used for serving food and parching nuts, and deep, open bowls. A series of excellent booklets written in Yuman, with summaries in English, described manufacturing techniques in detail and included excellent pictures of many kinds of Hualapai baskets (Watahomigie, Powskey, and Bender 1982b). With these resources, as well as the skill and enthusiasm of the teachers, it seems certain that Hualapai basketmaking will continue to flourish in the twenty-first century.

THE HAVASUPAIS

Although the Hualapais and the Havasupais are similar in many ways, there are also substantial differences between them, largely a result of where they live. While the Hualapais struggled to preserve themselves against the pressure of settlers and soldiers, the small band of approximately 250 Havasupais was hidden away in a verdant canyon of the Colorado River, 2,400 feet below the surrounding plateau. Along the green banks of Havasu Creek, a tributary of the Grand Canyon, they were almost completely undisturbed by outside influences before the twentieth century. Even now, of the few trails into their canyon, the best requires twenty-six miles of hard hiking.

TRADITIONAL BASKETS. Baskets were not only the Havasupais' "most important domestic utensils" (Spier 1928:124), but also their major craft. In function and shape, their traditional baskets were similar to those of the Hualapais. They made deep conical twined burden baskets; many shallow bowls and trays, both twined and coiled, for parching and winnowing seeds; a variety of smaller bowls for serving and holding food; deep baskets for boiling food; and biconical pitched water bottles (fig. 69). Acacia was the preferred material for twining, but willow and cottonwood splints were also used. The rim rods were made with serviceberry (Amelanchier alnifolia), Apache plume (Fallugia paradoxa), or mesquite (Prosopis).

Although the Havasupais acquired some modern trade items in the nineteenth century from the Hopis and other tribes, they remained isolated, and continued to make traditional baskets into the 1930s. The baskets of 1918–1921, described by Leslie Spier (1928), were almost identical to traditional

Hualapai utility baskets. Havasupai burden baskets were more frequently decorated with bands of devil's claw, and water bottles and small ollas were generally decorated with bands of three-strand twining. Spier (1928:132) noted, "The last row in both trays and burden baskets is almost invariably three strand twining," and the various textures produced by different kinds of twining were important decorative features (Herold 1982:15). In the late 1950s, Smithson (1959:143) saw twined trays still being used for "winnowing seeds, parching corn, pinyon nuts, or seeds, and for drying peaches, figs, or other fruits."

The arrival of eastern visitors to the Southwest and the development of a market for native goods affected the Havasuapis as well as the more exposed Hualapais, and the women of both tribes began to create new kinds of baskets. Although both tribes expanded in coiled basketry at first, their paths diverged. The Hualapais turned to their characteristic heavy twined bowls, and the Havasupais refined their skills in coiling. Before 1880, twined baskets were much more important than coiled baskets among the Havasupais, and Whiting (quoted in Herold 1979:44) believed that they acquired coiling about that time from the Yavapais. In technique (three-rod bunched), materials (willow, sumac), designs (geometric and life forms in black devil's claw and some dyed colors), and forms (bowls, circular trays), their coiled baskets closely resemble those of the Yavapais and many made by the San Carlos and White Mountain Apaches. For this reason they are often misidentified and can be distinguished only on the basis of a few significant traits in their manufacture and decoration. Fortunately, Joyce Herold of the Denver Museum of Natural History has thoroughly described these characteristics and traced their historical developments in several well-documented collections (McKee, McKee, and Herold 1975; Herold 1979).

Cushing (1882) was impressed by the beauty of Havasupai baskets and illustrated a type of coiled "boiling" jar (Cushing 1886:fig. 503) that James found still being used in 1899 (James 1903:163). When Voth collected some of these early coiled baskets at Hopi between 1893 and 1899, and Hough between 1901 and 1903, some of them were old and well worn, many had been repaired many times, and most of them were so impregnated with the remains of mush and other food that they had become hard and rigid — almost like pottery. Their coils were thin (less than 1/2 inch in diameter), with foundations of three slender, bunched rods. The sewing material is difficult to identify, but they were often decorated with designs in devil's claw. In shape, designs, technique, and texture, they were very similar to the decorated three-rod baskets that Powell found among the Southern Paiutes, and they may have been acquired by the Hopis from the Havasupais.

THE TWENTIETH CENTURY. In the early years of the twentieth century, the popularity of Havasupai coiled baskets with tourists and Indian neighbors often resulted in their misidentification. Many collectors bought them from the Hopis or the Navajos, who were using them in dances and ceremonies, knowing only that they had not made been made locally. Havasupai baskets were esteemed by collectors and Indian trade partners as comparable in the refinement of their coiling and the clarity and sophistication of their designs to any coiled baskets being made in the Southwest at that time (fig. 70).

Herold (1979:46) wrote, "Design motifs are generally more massive and limited in number than those of later baskets . . . diamonds, multipointed centers, radiating lines, encircling bands of double fret-lines, triangles and zig-zags. Life-forms include human beings, deer and horses" (fig. 71). The herringbone rim finishes often used on early baskets differed from the lashed rims on Apache and Yavapai baskets, and Havasupai rims were often sewn with light-tan willow splints instead of the dark devil's claw preferred by the Apaches (fig. 70). Unique knotted starts also set Havasupai baskets apart.

In the early commercial period, the Havasupais made some unusual coiled baskets that disappeared later from their inventory of forms and designs. For a while, they made double-bodied "compote" shapes of non-Indian origin.

Figure 70. Havasupai coiled bowls from the first half of the twentieth century. Three-rod bunched coils sewn with willow and devil's claw. *Left,* old basket with sharply curved sides. SAR B.212, 15" diameter. *Right,* basket with tan rim and common design of curved radiating arms with serrated edges. SAR B.213, 11" diameter. (Photo by Vincent Foster.)

Figure 71. Early Havasupai coiled bowl with typical encircling design, black lashed rim, white center, and knotted start. SAR B.216, 16" diameter. (Photo by Vincent Foster.)

Small, vase-shaped baskets with broad, flat bottoms, narrow necks, and flat lids were notable for their unusual shapes and the use of red and green aniline dyes in addition to the usual black devil's claw. They may have disappeared because George Wharton James, among other respected collectors and writers, regarded them as "non-Indian aberrations" and refused to buy them. Today they are rare and eagerly sought.

After 1900, the quality of Havasupai coiled baskets gradually improved. Unusual forms and bright colors were abandoned, coils became thinner, and stitching became finer and smoother (fig. 72). Because they were now being made exclusively for sale instead of use, the baskets were generally smaller. Changes in designs appeared constantly as basketmakers copied motifs from other groups or invented new ones themselves. Greater complexity in geometric patterns and increased use of plant designs and other life forms were typical. As quality improved, prices rose.

By the 1930s, the craft seems to have reached its apogee, with the finest coils, the tightest stitching, and the most complex and delicate designs in Havasupai history. According to Herold (1979:47), most baskets made at this time had "six to seven coils and fifteen to nineteen stitches per inch. Some weavers achieved fine and superfine textures, with as many as eight to ten coils and twenty-two to twenty-four stitches per inch in small . . . bowls." Stitching was generally passed under the upper rod in the previous coil instead of penetrating it. New splints were inserted from the back between two rods in the new coil, a method used by the Yavapais. Fag ends were covered by the stitching or left protruding until the basket was finished, and then trimmed

Figure 72. Two small bowl/trays showing variants of Havasupai decoration. Both were collected before 1930. *Left,* MNM 1027/12, 9" diameter. *Right,* MNM 971/12, 11" diameter. (Courtesy School of American Research collections in the Museum of New Mexico; photo by Vincent Foster.)

to short butts. Moving ends, usually dealt with in the same way, were often left hanging loose — a feature that gave many baskets a shaggy, unfinished appearance on the nonwork surfaces (fig. 73). Herringbone rims have been regarded as diagnostic of early Havasupai baskets, but many later baskets were finished with lashed rims: black, white, or ticked with alternating colors.

Circular trays were the most common form after 1930, but the Havasupais also made oval bowls and a few olla shapes. The designs of these baskets were largely geometric, with many radiating elements, central stars, and petaled motifs with six or seven points. Motifs taken from nature were also popular at this time: deer, eagles, ducks, butterflies, flowers, and people (fig. 74). Red yucca root was sometimes used in designs, and a yellow dye was made from Oregon grape. The beauty and diversity of these baskets are well represented in the McKee collection (McKee, McKee, and Herold 1975).

By the 1930s and 1940s, the Havasupais were making very few twined baskets, but some twined trays were still produced, and small conical baskets and some vase shapes were being made for sale to tourists (McKee, McKee, and Herold 1975:59). Some of the twined ollas were brown because the bark

Figure 73. Detail of untrimmed moving ends on the nonwork surface of a Havasupai coiled basket. SAR B.213. (Photo by Vincent Foster.)

Figure 74. Havasupai basket decorated with figures of butterflies. 7" diameter. (Courtesy School of American Research collections in the Museum of New Mexico, catalogue 941/12; photo by Vincent Foster.)

had been left on the catclaw wefts and turned to the outer surface. Most ollas and water bottles were woven with distinctive Havasupai bands of three-strand twining, and sometimes the entire surface was covered with three-strand twining (fig. 75). At the rim, warp ends were usually gathered into a bundle and lashed together with additional fibers. Thickened rims were also used on some cylindrical twined jars and deep bowls, which are similar to typical Hualapai baskets, except the rims are not flat and bound between two hoops. Twined water bottles, which were finished in the same way, were made in several shapes, including the distinctive biconical bottles with pointed bases. They are often identified as Paiute in collections, possibly because the Havasupais called them "Paiute water jugs" (Bateman 1972:18). Recent research indicates that biconical bottles may have been made not by the San Juan or Kaibab Paiutes, but by western Paiutes, or more likely, by the Havasupais.

At mid-century, the lives of the Havasupais changed drastically, bringing comparable changes in their basketry. As with the Hualapais and many other Indian people, the modern world entered their lives for the first time after World War II. Isolation was broken, never to be restored. Electricity was brought into the canyon, the mail began to be delivered (sometimes) by helicopter, jobs became available in tourist-oriented businesses, incomes increased, and in many respects, the quality of life improved. As in other tribes, women discovered that basketmaking was hard work and comparatively unrewarding in both prestige and financial return. In spite of the continuing demand for fine baskets and the increasing prices they commanded, the number of basketmakers declined drastically. In 1950 Carma Lee Smithson (1959:145) found only "half a dozen" women making baskets of any kind, and only three making decorated coiled baskets. Even the older women found other more profitable activities, and few younger women were inclined to learn the craft.

Figure 75. Havasupai twined ollas, woven of squawberry sumac or catclaw. *Left,* plain twine with several bands of three-strand twill twine. SAR B.273, 8" high. *Right,* three-strand twill twine with three bands of plain two-strand twine and banded designs in devil's claw. SAR B.128, 8" high. (Photo by Vincent Foster.)

Nevertheless, it seems unlikely that Havasupai basketry will disappear. As the beauty of Cataract Canyon has been increasingly recognized and advertised in recent years, thousands of tourists hike or ride down into the home of the Havasupais, buy food from the residents, admire the scenery, and look around for Indian souvenirs to take back with them. Baskets are waiting for them at the Havasupai Restaurant and Trading Post — but not the great baskets of the past, which would be too expensive and cumbersome for the casual tourist. Instead, the Havasupais make small coiled trays and bowls and toy or model twined burden baskets and bottles (Herold 1984:fig. 3). Many of the old designs are preserved, but the baskets rarely equal those of the past.

Joyce Herold's (1984) assessment of the situation gives at least some reason for hope. By 1979 quite a number of women, including some young women, were coiling or twining baskets for the tourist trade, and some more experienced basketmakers were once again producing relatively fine coiled trays. The prices were high and the demand was constant, but the quality of work produced in the mid-1970s never attained the level of the fine baskets made in the late 1920s. However, some young women were introducing new designs and ideas. If buyers are willing to pay the price for really fine baskets, the Havasuapis may fall back on their own tradition.

Figure 76. Aloisa Juan, a Papago woman from Bigfields, Arizona, coiling a basket with beargrass foundation. She has wrapped a bundle of raw materials in cloth, possibly to keep them clean as well as soft and damp. (Courtesy Arizona State Museum, neg. 51274; photo by Helga Teiwes, 1979.)

6

The Piman Peoples

The Pimas and Papagos of the southwestern Arizona desert are really one people. They speak the same language, visit and intermarry with each other, and possess regional variations of the same basic culture. The two names were first used by the early Spaniards, who found the Pimas living on irrigated farms on the Gila River. They called themselves the "River People" and referred to their relatives to the south, the Papagos, as the "Desert People" or the "Bean People." As is usually the case, the names by which these people became known to missionaries, soldiers, and administrators and by which they are known today bear no relation to their own names for themselves. They call themselves *O'odam,* meaning "we, the people."

The Pimas and Papagos constitute the two divisions of Piman-speaking peoples and are referred to together as Pimans. The Piman language belongs to the Uto-Aztecan linguistic group, as do Hopi and Southern Paiute. This does not mean that these languages are mutually intelligible, only that they share a common ancestral root.

The Pimans' traditional ways of life were very different from the Hopi and Paiute cultures. The territory they occupied for centuries includes the western two-thirds of southern Arizona, a region called Upper Pimaría (Pimaría Alto) to distinguish it from the adjacent area in Mexico, Lower Pimaría (Pimaría Bajo), which is also occupied by Piman peoples. Upper Pimaria is mostly in the Sonoran Desert. This difficult region compelled its inhabitants to develop life patterns that were flexible enough to cope with the unpredictably changing weather. Floods occur, as well as droughts, and erosion changes the contours of the land with amazing rapidity. In spite of, or perhaps because of these conditions, the Piman people developed a broad and adaptive subsistence pattern, including agriculture, and at a later time, livestock raising.

Tribal organization was always loose among the Pimans. They lived in rancherías — small, scattered, extended-family groups — and came together only for warfare against the Apaches, Quechans, and Mohaves and for periodic ritual celebrations. The settlements of the Pimas were larger and closer together than those of the Papagos because their rich lands were watered by irrigation canals along the Gila and Salt rivers, and more than a single crop of corn, beans, squash, and pumpkins could be raised in a single year. At the end of the seventeenth century, they acquired wheat from the Spaniards, and it became their most important trade crop.

Agriculture supplied more than sixty percent of the Pimas' food. In contrast, the Papagos derived only twenty-five percent of their subsistence from farming, depending upon a wide range of wild beans, roots, seeds, and fruits, and to a much lesser degree, upon hunting. The Papagos practiced *akchin* farming: planting corn and other crops along the lower edges of slopes where runoff water would be concentrated. The prospects for a successful harvest were always uncertain. During dry periods, many Papagos could not grow enough food and were forced to take refuge with the Pimas or other agricultural neighbors. They worked for their hosts, and were usually allowed to plant a plot of land for themselves.

The Pimas suffered hardships of a somewhat different nature. At times, the spring floods were not adequate for a full season of irrigation, or else floods would sweep away their homes and silt up their irrigation systems. Also, both the Pimas and the Papagos had to maintain constant watch to protect themselves against raids by the Apaches. Fortifications and stockades were built, and the settlements were clustered together as closely as possible for mutual protection. After the Apaches were subdued in the 1870s by the U.S. military, both groups spread out into wider territories.

The Pimas enjoyed a brief period of prosperity in the early twentieth century by expanding their production of wheat, but it ended with a long drought and increased use of the diminished water supply by white farmers settling along the river valleys. In spite of the establishment of reservation lands, no effort was made to protect the Indians' water rights. In 1887 a large canal diverted all the water from the Gila River to the farms of white settlers, resulting in poverty for the Pimas, and in 1895, government food rations. The people dispersed in search of wage work, chiefly to the rapidly growing towns around them, and their traditional social structure withered.

The subsequent history of the Pimas was one of prolonged, complex, expensive bureaucratic programs intended to provide water for this rich but dry region. The twenty-five-million-dollar San Carlos Project, completed in 1934, produced so little water that the Pima Tribal Council refused to pay for the operation of the project. Although many Pimas continued to farm, water shortages resulted in disagreements that weakened tribal unity:

> The Gila Pimas probably were the most nearly culturally assimilated of all Indians in New Mexico or Arizona. The Pima Tribal Council continued in operation but it did not function as a political institution for Pimas as a whole. The tribe as a unit of social organization or culture had ceased to exist in the Arizona milieu. (Spicer 1962:151)

But the Pimas, like other Indians, survived. In 1961 there were 11,246 "living descendants from the ancestral populations of the Gila and Salt River reservations," and sixty percent of them were still living on the reservation (Hackenberg 1983:176). In recent years their standard of living has improved, primarily because of their increased legal sophistication in dealing with the various offices of the federal government and other outside forces that have victimized them in the past. Although many Pimas were forced to give up farming, a number of small industries provided employment on the reservation. The Pimas also built an arts and crafts center, improved roads, and modernized housing and educational facilities. The old way of life is almost gone, but living conditions are now generally better than they were at the beginning of the twentieth century.

The Papagos experienced different kinds of changes because their basic subsistence pattern was different. In the early days of contact with the government, they were able to maintain their tribal solidarity. For a while their lives actually improved as the government helped them to develop cattle herds and dug wells for them, but the long-range development program was sabotaged by the antic weather. Unusually heavy rainfall between 1905 and 1920, which allowed the Papagos to expand their cultivation of traditional crops and wheat, was followed by forty years of drought. The government increased its efforts to provide water with wells and other projects, but nothing could be done to sustain the Papagos' herds and fields. The population continued to increase after the 1950s, while resources continued to shrink. Most Papago families were forced to sustain themselves with wage labor in the cities and towns and with seasonal work on other people's land. In 1960 nearly 5,000 Papagos still lived on the reservation, but more than 4,000 had moved to towns and cities in Arizona, and about 1,000 had left the state in search of work — conditions that were destructive to the traditional customs of the tribe. It is within this pattern of declining opportunities that their surviving arts must be considered.

PIMA AND PAPAGO BASKETS

Although the historic Pimas and Papagos never equaled the beautifully wrought stonework and pottery of their probable ancestors, the Hohokam, they were accomplished artisans. They wove cotton textiles, made weapons and agricultural implements of wood, and produced distinctive and attractive pottery. Some pots were decorated with flowing geometric patterns, and their large water jars were notable for their graceful shapes and their usefulness. They also made unique carrying nets, or kiahas (gi'hos), of looped agave cord, decorated with red and blue painted designs and tied to a rod ring fitted to a cross frame of poles made from saguaro ribs. Kiahas were used to carry many kinds of loads: pottery vessels, firewood, mescal hearts, and baskets of grain or seeds (Bahr 1983:188, fig. 7).

The baskets of the Pimas and Papagos surpassed their other creations and equaled the finest basketry of any tribe in the Southwest. Their coiled baskets are easily identified by their materials and by their bold and complex designs. Traditionally, they were sewn with narrow splints of willow, like the baskets of the Apaches and the Pai tribes, but instead of coiling with a foundation of wooden rods, the Pimans used a tight bundle of vegetal splints: beargrass (Nolina microcarpa) for the Papagos, and cattail (Typha angustifolia) stems for the Pimas (fig. 76). While the materials were moist and soft, the walls or sides of the baskets were pounded between two stones. This flattened the coils and produced a very smooth, level surface that is quite different from the corrugated surface of Apache and other baskets coiled on a rod foundation.

In the old days and well into the twentieth century, baskets were used in every household. Carried on the women's heads, they transported everything from cactus fruits to household implements, and even water. Because they were practically impervious, they were used as sinks for washing and to brew and hold saguaro-fruit wine for annual ritual events. Pimas and Papagos also used baskets to mix dough for tortillas, prepare pinole, and parch and winnow wheat and grass seeds.

The most common baskets were large, shallow bowls or trays that ranged from 10 to 36 inches in diameter and 4 to 6 inches deep. Their interiors were invariably decorated with striking centripetal designs sewn with black splints of devil's claw. Most of the designs, as well as the shapes of the baskets and the techniques used in making them, were shared by the Pimas and the Papagos. Because they intermarried, traded baskets and other goods, and shared each other's traditions and language, it is not surprising that many of their baskets are difficult to tell apart.

Both tribes also coiled vase- or olla-shaped baskets of various sizes, small- and medium-sized bowls with flat bottoms and straight sides, large granaries of wheat straw, and some specialized baskets made by plaiting flat splints of agave or river cane. Kissell (1916:224) noted that the Pimas "greatly altered the shape of their baskets, so that curio shops are filled with the novel forms, waste-paper basket shapes, and large olla jars, besides a variety of smaller baskets." She did not illustrate any of them in her report. Because these changes were earlier observed by Russell in 1908, it is apparent that the process had been going on for some time in both tribes. Robinson (1954:32) wrote, "The Pimas make olla-shaped baskets in various sizes, but these are made almost exclusively for sale to the white trade. Under the white man's influence they have made waste-paper or scrap baskets of various sizes, but in the Indian's home one will find only the flat bowl-shaped baskets, which serve many purposes in everyday life of the family."

PIMA-PAPAGO BASKET STARTS

The starts of Pima and Papago coiled baskets were the most varied and complex of any in the Southwest. Pima basketmakers sometimes used spiral, or "normal" starts, but coiling was usually started around a distinctive four-square knot, also known as a swastika knot. To make a spiral start, the end of a bundle of well-soaked cattail splints was wrapped with devil's claw or willow splints for approximately 1/2 inch and bent into a U. The bundle of the first coil was then bent around the U and sewn to it to begin the spiral. The coiling continued outward from this point, building from right to left to form a counterclockwise spiral.

The four-square knot (fig. 77) was the distinctive start of Pima-Papago basketry. Although it has sometimes been said to occur only in Papago baskets, Cain (1962:29) described it as typical of Pima baskets. Breazeale (1923:47) found many baskets with spiral starts among the Pimas, but he also noted their use of the four-square knot and other starts: "Oftentimes a peculiar knot of devil's claw is made, which gives the center a checkerboard effect." In addition, he described "a center as large as three inches square . . . woven in checkerboard style before the regular coil weaving is begun." Kissell (1916), the only writer who not only described knotted and plaited starts but also explained how they were made, also found spiral starts, four-square knots, and plaited squares in both Papago and Pima baskets.

One confusing aspect of four-square starts is that the two sides are different. In some baskets, the four-square knot is on the outside (bottom) of the basket (fig. 77c), and a "double-S" knot appears on the inside (fig. 77b). In other baskets, a four-square knot appears on both sides, or there may be a four-square knot on one side and a small, rectangular "mat" of plaited splints in plain or twill plaiting (fig. 77d) on the other.

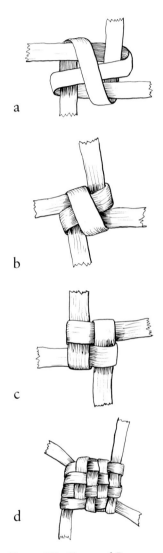

Figure 77. Pima and Papago starting knots. *a,* Expanded view of double-S knot. *b,* Closed double-S knot. *c,* Four-square or swastika knot on reverse side of double-S knot. *d,* Plaited rectangle. (Drawings by Arminta Neal.)

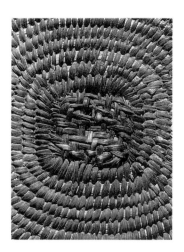

Figure 78. As an elaboration of the four-square starting knot, some Papago coiled baskets were started around a small plain- or twill-plaited rectangle. (Photo by A. H. Whiteford.)

How are the two sides related to each other, and how do they serve as a start for the coiling? The knots and mats are made in several ways: (1) Two bunches of devil's claw splints are tied into a double-S knot (figs. 77a, 77b); the obverse side of this knot is a four-square plait (fig. 77c). (2) If the weaver wants a four-square plait on both sides, she turns up the four bunches of splints on the double-S knot and weaves them into a plait, each passing over its neighbor, and the last passing under the first. (3) Josephine Thomas, a noted Papago basketmaker, sometimes plaits four bunches of devil's claw into a four-square center and then turns up the ends and plaits them over and under each other to make another four-square plait, as in the second procedure. (4) As an alternative, Mrs. Thomas turns up the bunches of splints, separates them, and weaves them into a plaited mat (fig. 77d). On some old baskets, the plaited mat at the center was worked in twill plaiting (fig. 78). All of these procedures seem to be used for starts in the modern yucca coiled baskets made by the Papagos.

Some old baskets have plaited mats on both surfaces of the start, accomplished by plaiting a small mat, bending the protruding strands up, and plaiting them again over the first mat. A mat of single thickness could serve as a start, but it might be fragile, and was rarely used.

With both four-square and plaited mat starts, the protruding corner splints are bent around the knot or mat (fig. 79; Kissell 1916:fig. 52a) to form the foundation for the first coil, which is stitched to the edges of the mat or knot. As a result, the first coils are often rectangular rather than circular, but subsequent coils are less so.

PIMA BASKETS

Because the early Pimas lived along the rivers, they had easy access to basket materials such as willow *(Salix nigra* or *gooddingii)* for sewing splints, and cattails for the foundations of their coils. Willow shoots about 18 inches long and as thick as a pencil were gathered in summer and carefully divided into narrow splints. Before the splints were dried and stored, or when they were moistened before sewing to make them soft and pliable, the bark was scraped off and they were smoothed and evened by scraping or by pulling them through holes punched in the lid of a tin can. When they were dry they could be stored almost indefinitely. Cattails once grew luxuriantly along the river banks and irrigation ditches. Their long, straight stems were split repeatedly, producing narrow splints which were tied together in bundles and stored to dry. The hooked seed pods of devil's claw, also used for baskets by the Western Apaches, grew wild and were gathered in the fall to be fastened by their own hooks into large bundles which the Pimas called "heads." The pods were soaked in water (sometimes heated) long enough to soften them, and two narrow black splints were stripped from each hook. Because devil's claw is much harder than willow, it was used for the parts of the basket that received the most wear: the base and the rim (see illustrations in Newman 1974).

The sewing of Pima baskets was similar to techniques used by other tribes except for the use of a splint-bundle foundation, which made stitching easier because the awl could be pushed through the coil without having to split a hard wooden rod. After the sewing splint passed through the bundle it was pulled tight to make the coil firm, and while the materials were still moist, the coils were pounded between two stones to make them flat and even (Newman 1974:61). Devil's claw was used for a central disk of black, which was followed by the willow stitching. At one time, the Pimas occasionally used cottonwood splints, but they preferred willow because it was less brittle (Kissell 1916:130). With any of these sewing materials, the surfaces of the baskets were always even and smooth, partly because of the pounding, but also because the bundle foundation made it easy to bury the splint ends. A new section of sewing splint was pulled through the coil until the fag end almost disappeared. The moving end of the preceding splint was clipped so closely on the nonwork surface that "in most good baskets it is almost impossible to find where one split [sic] ends and where another one was put in" (Breazeale 1923:47).

The fag ends of the sewing splints in Pima coiled baskets usually appear as small butt ends, almost hidden at the bottom of the final stitch of the preceding splint. This juxtaposition results from inserting the new splint in the same perforation that the terminal end of the old splint passed through. Less often, but sometimes in the same basket, the fag end was bent diagonally upward along the coil and held in place with one or two subsequent stitches. The completed basket was rubbed vigorously with a rough cloth to remove stray fibers and give the surface a smooth and almost polished finish.

The stitches in Pima baskets are extremely uniform in size and placement. Instead of interlocking with the stitches in the coil below, new stitches are inserted carefully between them, so they are very rarely split. Breazeale (1923:51) counted from twelve to more than thirty stitches per inch in the finest Pima baskets, but Tanner (1983) concluded that the majority had four, five, or six stitches per inch, and only the tightest baskets had as many as fourteen to sixteen stitches per inch. In the collection of nearly eighty Pima baskets at the School of American Research, fifty have between nine and twelve stitches per inch, and at least twelve others have between thirteen and sixteen stitches to the inch. The width of the coils in the collection ranges from slightly more than 5/8 inch to as little as 1/8 inch. The final coil, which makes the rim of the basket, is tapered so gradually that its termination is hardly noticeable. The entire rim is usually covered with stitching of tough devil's claw, either by alternating two splints in a diagonal lashing or by weaving a single splint in a figure-eight pattern to produce a false-braid or herringbone effect.

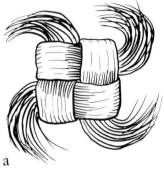

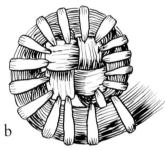

Figure 79. Pima-Pagago basket starts. *a*, The splint ends protruding from the starting knot are bent in the direction of coiling. *b*, Additional fibers are added, bent around, and sewn to the starting knot. (Drawings by Arminta Neal.)

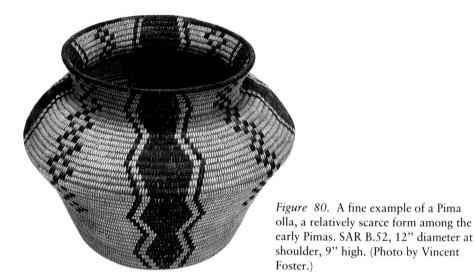

Figure 80. A fine example of a Pima olla, a relatively scarce form among the early Pimas. SAR B.52, 12" diameter at shoulder, 9" high. (Photo by Vincent Foster.)

BOWLS AND OLLAS. Most of the Pima baskets in collections are the large, shallow, bowl-shaped baskets that served so many purposes in Pima households, known variously as "wheat baskets" (Robinson 1954:30), "squaw baskets" (Breazeale 1923:5l), or "trays" (Tanner 1983). Deep, rounded bowls, some quite large, were used by both the Pimas and the Papagos to brew wine from the fruit of the saguaro cactus *(Cereus giganteus)* (Fontana 1983:fig. 5 top).

Between 1920 and 1940, when the Pimas were having particularly hard times, the women produced quantities of small and medium-sized bowls, ollas, and cylindrical "waste baskets" for the white market. They were generally decorated with adaptations of traditional designs, although there were modifications, and some new motifs were created.

Vase- or olla-shaped baskets of various shapes and sizes were probably used in Pima homes to hold grain, or perhaps sacred or valuable personal objects. Most of them are of medium size, from 6 to 15 inches in height. Some are distinguished by low, angular shoulders and slightly flaring rims (fig. 80), although others lack flaring rims or necks (Tanner 1983:159). It is characteristic of Pima ollas that the designs — vertical bands, all-over open diamonds, or bands of frets — cover the entire body and extend to the rim.

Although they were neatly made and decorated, Pima bowls from the mid-twentieth century were generally undistinguished commercial products. The most common form has a flat bottom and straight, slightly flaring sides (fig. 81). Fret designs, vertical bands, diamonds, triangles, and other geometric arrangements are common. A few have widely flaring sides, and some were

Figure 81. Three small willow-stitched Pima bowls. *Left,* five pairs of men and women holding hands. SAR B.292, 5" high. *Center,* four-pointed squash-blossom design. SAR B.319, 11" diameter. *Right,* four human figures spaced with coyote tracks. SAR B.359, 5" high. (Photo by Vincent Foster.)

decorated with complex derivatives of bowl-tray designs. Deep, cylindrical bowls, or wastebaskets, were quite common, and Russell (1908) noted that before the turn of the century, some were decorated with human figures. Like the smaller bowls, deep bowls were decorated with a variety of other designs, and one example has the pattern of concentric rectangles called "turtleback" or "shell."

The Pimas also made miniature bowl shapes and shallow trays with traditional designs during the first half of the twentieth century. Many were no more than 2 or 3 inches in diameter and less than 2 inches high.

DESIGNS. The distinctive designs on Pima trays or shallow bowls were the model for the decorations on other basket shapes. Almost without exception, they are geometric and abstract, with the motifs appearing in an endless series of combinations. The names of many of the designs — butterfly wings, shield, coyote tracks, and others — were invented by white traders or collecters, and were not used by the Pimas or Papagos. The designs tend to emphasize a centripetal concept, invariably with three, four, or five lines extending from the center toward the edge of the basket. When the lines curve, they form one of the favorite designs, the "whirlwind." The arms of the whorl are often narrow, parallel zigzags (fig. 82). Rectangular or trapezoidal blocks are some-

Figure 82. Miniature bowl decorated with the Pima whirlwind design of zigzag lines. SAR B.444, 4" diameter. (Photo by Vincent Foster.)

Figure 83. Pima whirlwind with rectangles forming curving vanes. SAR B.408, 18" diameter. (Photo by Vincent Foster.)

times added in the angles of the zigzags (fig. 83), or the whirling vanes may be formed by offset rectangles. In some designs, the lines are arranged in pairs, and the space between them forms the whirling elements. Often the lines or vanes in the whirlwind are embellished with triangles or fret-hooks on their edges. In some complex designs, the curving lines meld into motifs such as frets and swastikas.

The vortex and the fret, two other principal motifs in Pima decoration, also emphasize the whirling, centripetal concept. The term "vortex" is used here to describe a recurring black disk with three, four, or five points or vanes radiating from it. In its simplest form, it appears as a bold, black figure surrounded by three or four concentric lines that are frequently edged with small triangles, creating a serrated effect. On the ends and the edges (usually the left) of some points, parallel encircling lines and other forms create spiral effects. The famous Pima fret, commonly added to the vortex points, occurs in many forms. Robinson (1954:22) counted more than one hundred variations of this motif on baskets in his personal collection. Sometimes the frets are simple and bold (fig. 84), but more often, the vanes of the vortex are attached to

Figure 84. Designs built around a whirling petaled vortex were common on Pima and Papago baskets. *Rear,* SAR B.25, 21" diameter. *Left front,* SAR B.418, 10" diameter. *Right front,* SAR B.33, 15" diameter. (Photo by Vincent Foster.)

complex motifs such as cross/swastikas, rectangles, or vertical bars. These designs are often varied by enclosing them within a broad border, which usually repeats parts of the central design. The basic pattern of the vortex is varied when the vanes spreading from the central disk are formed by open lanes between the black lines or when they are attached at the center to an open circle instead of a solid black disk. In some baskets, three vanes or points instead of the usual four and occasional five emanate from the center of the design.

Whirlwind and vortex designs occur on most Pima coiled bowl-trays at the School of American Research. There seems to be almost endless variety in the use of these basic patterns. Designs of a different nature, also typical of Pima baskets, include the famous, complex squashblossom patterns used by the Pimas as their tribal emblem. They generally have five points or petals (fig. 85), but may have as many as twelve (Robinson 1954:24). A simpler version occasionally appears with only four petals.

Struck by the recurrence of certain features in Pima basket designs, Breazeale (1923:53) attempted to demonstrate that most of the designs had originated as variations of the fret and squashblossom patterns: "Even to a novice . . . there is a certain relationship in nearly all the geometrical designs. . . . I suspicioned that the whirlwind was a nephew of the squashblossom and a first cousin of the swastica . . . probably due to the fact that they originated from the same and simple patterns." His proposed developmental sequence points up a core of similarities in Pima (also in Papago) baskets that gives them their truly distinctive quality.

Figure 85. Two traditional Pima designs. *Left,* an old pattern that has been called "butterfly wings." SAR B.35, 16" diameter. *Right,* a five-pointed example of the famous squashblossom design that is used as the Pima and Papago logo. SAR B.31, 18" diameter. (Photo by Vincent Foster.)

Figure 86. Two old Pima designs. *Left,* a simple four-petaled star or squash-blossom. SAR B.23, 20" diameter. *Right,* an excellent example of the Pimas' use of narrow lines, here forming two circles of frets joined together by swastikas. SAR B.226, 19" diameter. (Photo by Vincent Foster.)

The most common designs in the School of American Research collection include one sometimes referred to as "butterfly wings" (fig. 85) that is clearly similar to the squashblossom. Other designs, also arranged in four or five segments or fields around the central disk, combine various elements to produce complex patterns in which the radiating paths or lines retain the general centripetal Pima pattern, but with a relatively static effect. Another, similar group of designs consists of floral patterns with three, four, or as many as six ovoid or triangular petals spread out from the center. The petals are generally hachured with cross lines (fig. 86), and the intervening spaces are similarly hachured or filled with blocks and/or crosses. A different kind of floral or "floret" pattern consists of curving lines of small blocks that form overlapping and interlocking star or petal designs.

Among the other, less common or even unique designs in the collection are several clear, bold designs based upon expanding, radiating vanes. Some have three arms or vanes; others, with four vanes, resemble open Maltese crosses. A variation on the latter design has eight radiating open vanes, separated by similar motifs (pl. 9). One unusual design has four slender vanes separated by strange figures, like tapered ladders edged with angled lines that make them look like decapitated centipedes (pl. 9).

A unique basket in the collection has a circle of five large figures similar to the letter H (pl. 9). A second unique basket exemplifies the rather rare Pima custom of painting baskets with colored designs (pl. 10). Well coiled, it is decorated with double bands of interlocking frets dyed green and purple, now badly faded. The colors and its strange shape (like a compote with an annular base) indicate that it was made for sale. Finally, a third design, although very different from the others, is regarded by the Pimans as traditional. They call it Elder Brother's House and say that it depicts the pattern of devious trails by which their legendary hero Siuu-Huki evaded powerful enemies (Robinson 1954:27). It is commonly called the Man in the Maze (see fig. 90). It was not recorded by Kissell (1916); Breazeale (1923:81) noted that "younger members of the tribe" were using it, but he had never seen it on old Pima baskets. Red sections, probably of yucca root, were occasionally worked into black designs in Pima baskets (Collings 1976:14; Robinson 1954:34), and beads were sometimes added, especially large, blue China beads around the rim.

The baskets in the School of American Research collection demonstrate the complexity and diversity of Pima designs. Many of the motifs such as stars, whirlwinds, radiating lines, and concentric circles are also found on Havasupai, Western Apache, and Yavapai baskets; but the complex arrangements of frets, crosses, and swastikas, as well as the centripetal and concentric arrangements embodied in designs such as the squashblossom, are unique to the Pimas and Papagos.

This tradition has flourished for at least a century and a half. A drawing by Arthur Schott for Major William Emory's survey report of 1855 (Trimble 1983:13) shows two Pima women with large basket trays identical in shape and decoration to those in collections of contemporary baskets. They are decorated with black linear designs, one of which is clearly a traditional arrangement of fret motifs. Baskets from a variety of collections — Russell's of 1901, Kissell's of 1910–11, Breazeale's of the early 1920s, Robinson's of between 1916 and 1950, and J. F. Collins's from "before 1920" — demonstrate continuity in design through the first half of the twentieth century.

Certain designs occur and reoccur in the time represented by the baskets in these collections. It is often said that no two Indian baskets are alike, but many Pima baskets are, to say the least, very similar. Two baskets collected by Collins have nearly identical "vortex" designs, and practically duplicate baskets were collected by Russell (1908:pl. 25) and Kissell (1916:fig. 62d). With only slight variations, the recurrent use of designs such as whirlwinds, butterfly wings, flower petals, and many varieties of frets with swastikas has also occurred. Although designs were duplicated to perhaps a greater extent than in the baskets of any other southwestern group, this is not to disparage Pima basketry in any way. The excellence of the baskets and the complexity of the decorative patterns give each one its own distinctive character.

Although many Pima designs are unique to the tribe, certain similarities to the baskets of other tribes do occur. The common whirlwind pattern with zigzag curving lines was also used by the Havasupais and Hualapais (see fig. 65) and by the early Navajos (see fig. 26). The Navajos and Jicarilla Apaches (see pl. 3) also used the four-vaned Maltese cross, and Pima petal designs were very similar to those of the Mescalero Apaches (see fig. 41) and

Western Apaches (see fig. 46). The pattern based upon three or four radiating, curved lines edged with solid triangles was very popular with the Havasupais (see fig. 70), and the San Carlos Apaches also used it. Some of these shared designs probably resulted from common coiling techniques, but others were undoubtedly borrowed.

WHEAT-STRAW BASKETS. Both the Pimas and the Papagos made baskets with thick bundles of wheat straw sewn in place with strips of mesquite bark, although the Pimas sometimes used willow bark. The most important such baskets were large, globose bins or granaries, similar to the granaries of their Yuman-speaking neighbors. Pima granaries were flat on the bottom, with rounded sides that sloped inward to a constricted opening. There was no neck or distinctive rim, but the top was generally covered with a flat, circular, coiled lid (Kissell 1916:184; Robinson 1954:33). They were worked from right to left, but because Pima women often found it convenient to work on them from the inside, they often appear to be coiled in the opposite direction (fig. 87).

Figure 87. Pima woman making a large grain storage basket with coils of wheat straw sewn together with spaced stitches of mesquite bark. (Courtesy Southwest Museum, neg. 24116, photo by Putnam and Valentine, about 1900.)

Figure 88. Minnie Marks of Santa Cruz, Arizona, was the last Pima woman to make the old-fashioned wheat-straw baskets, two of which are on the table in this photograph. (Photo by Thelma Heatwole, 1966.)

These large bins were kept in storehouses adjacent to the family dwellings to hold the harvest of wheat, corn, grass seeds, or other foods for the winter months. With care, they would last for eight or ten years (Kissell 1916:182). Smaller baskets — plain, rather crude in appearance, but strong and very durable — were sometimes made with the same technique and materials. At the age of eighty-eight, in the early 1970s, Minnie Marks was still making this kind of basket (fig. 88). She believed that she would be the last maker of "mesquite baskets" because the "younger generations . . . didn't want to learn" (Heatwole 1967).

The Pimas also made granary or storage bins that have been referred to as "bird's nests" to distinguish them from "real" baskets. In spite of their rough and haphazard appearance, they *were* baskets, but of a peculiar sort. Their mode of construction, which has been called a "coiled technique of twisted osier withes" (Kissell 1916:173, quoting Barrows 1900:52), consisted of weaving parallel twigs or branches of arrowbush *(Pluchea borealis)* so they were twisted together and into the branches below. The walls were thick and rough, but effective. Covered with a mat of branches that extended beyond the sides, the bins were placed on raised platforms or the roofs of houses, which served as the bottom of the granaries. Such storage bins were common among many tribes of north-central Mexico, where they probably originated.

Figure 89. Until mid-twentieth century, both Pimas and Papagos made plaited baskets of beargrass and river cane splints. This example, collected in 1957, was made by Mexican Pimans, who used *sotol* instead. (Courtesy Museum of New Mexico, catalogue 9883/12; photo by Vincent Foster.)

PLAITED BASKETS. The technique of plaiting baskets, another import from Mexico, was used by both the Pimas and the Papagos. The Papagos used flat strips of sotol leaves *(Dasylirion wheeleri),* while the Pimas plaited with split and flattened stems of river cane *(Phragmites communis),* which once grew wild along the streams.

Kissell (1916) described the plaiting procedure so well that it will only be summarized here. Almost all plaiting was twill, or diagonal, plaiting, which produces a braided or herringbone pattern. Two sets of splints cross each other at right angles, interlacing over two (or three), under two at staggered intervals (see fig. 9). Because the plaited matting was thin and flexible, it was excellent for deep bowls or small ollas. Plaiting started with a square or rectangular mat, the way ring baskets are started, but the bottoms of these baskets were flat, with angular corners. At the edge of the starting rectangle, the splints were turned up and plaited together to produce the sides of the basket. Towards the top, the sides were bent into a circular opening. At the rim, the splints were bent to form a hem and plaited back down into the basket (fig. 89).

Plaited baskets were almost never decorated. The deep bowls were used for holding tortillas and other foods, and many were fitted with lids that overlapped the rim by an inch or so. These baskets were rare among the Pimas by the end of the nineteenth century. In recent years, the Papagos used them primarily for holding ceremonial equipment. Long, rectangular baskets, with overlapping lids that could be tied in place with a cord, were the preferred forms. They were often known as "medicine baskets" (Cain 1962:30).

Basically a utilitarian technique, plaiting was used to make not only mats and containers, but also head rings similar to those worn by the Pueblos (Kissell 1916), brow bands for the tumplines used with their netted carrying frames (kiahas), and the rectangular mat that protected the back and shoulders of the woman carrying the load. The arched fenders or sunshades on cradles were twill plaited with colored splints to produce simple designs (Cain 1962:20).

The Papagos continued to make plaited mats and traditional square-bottomed baskets until the middle of the twentieth century. The baskets were often used to strain the liquid in making saguaro wine. However, in 1983, when old plaited baskets were shown to Anita Antone, a prominent Papago basketmaker, they seemed completely foreign to her. After examining them carefully, she said, "These were not made by our people." She could not remember having seen any being made.

CHANGES IN PIMA BASKETS. In spite of fine construction, elegant decoration, and high production, Pima basketry declined rapidly in the mid-twentieth century and almost became extinct. Although Breazeale had some qualms about the future of Pima basketry in the 1920s, he was certain that the craft had reached a level of refinement that surpassed that of any previous period. Only fifteen years later, in a report for the Office of Indian Affairs, Elizabeth Hart (1935) claimed that Pima basketry was dying out and would soon disappear. Bert Robinson, the superintendent of the Pima Agency from 1935 to 1951, mentioned the disappearance of some basket types but expressed no particular concern about the state of the art as a whole. An undated photograph of "Isabelle Johns" with a fine coiled squashblossom basket (Robinson 1954:23) probably refers to the Isabel Johns who wove the collection of nine beautiful squashblossom baskets that now adorn the Gila River Arts and Crafts Center. She began to weave when she was thirteen (about 1923), and made baskets until about 1940. The photograph was probably taken in the 1930s. Although these dates are not precise, they do indicate that Pima artisans were still producing fine baskets at that time (Wilson 1972).

The middle of the twentieth century may have marked the height of Pima basketry. Shortly thereafter, Cain (1962:23) reported that it was "definitely on the wane and almost inevitably will die out entirely within the next two decades unless something can be done to revive interest." Unfortunately, little was accomplished in this regard during the subsequent decades. In 1986, only a few Pima women — among them, Hilda Manuel (fig. 90; Mauldin 1984:48; Gogol 1982:5) — were still making fine coiled baskets. A few other women make miniature and horsehair baskets. Tanner (1983:165) viewed the situation with some optimism, but the great, traditional Pima coiled baskets are now jewels of the past.

Figure 90. Small basket made by Hilda Manuel, Pima, of Salt River, Arizona, in 1983. It shows the ancient Man in the Maze or labyrinth design used by both Pimas and Papagos, who named it "Elder Brother" after the culture hero associated with the legend about it. SAR 1983-17-3, 6" diameter. (Photo by Vincent Foster.)

PAPAGO BASKETS

The traditional coiled baskets of the Papagos, sewn with willow and devil's claw splints, were so similar to Pima baskets that they are often difficult, if not impossible, to distinguish from them. Almost everything that has been said here about Pima baskets could also be applied to Papago baskets. However, Papago basketry does have certain distinctive characteristics, and the history of Papago basketry is very different from the history of the craft among the Pimas.

TRADITIONAL BASKETS. Papago coiled baskets reflect the region in which they were made. The cattails used by the Pimas for splint bundles in the foundations of coiled baskets were not available in the arid country of the Papagos. Instead, they used fine splints of other plants, sometimes yucca, but most often beargrass *(Nolina microcarpa).* A member of the lily family, beargrass grows in thick clumps, with narrow, razor-sharp leaves and a flowering stalk. Also known locally as palmilla, it is so tough that it is harvested commercially to make brooms (Parent 1984:69). The Papagos trim the sharp edges and split the narrow leaves again and again to produce long, slender foundation splints for coiled baskets. Even when the beargrass is visible in the finished basket, it is difficult to distinguish from the cattail splints used by the Pimas. Beargrass, which is dark green but fades to yellow-tan, is somewhat coarser and more angular, often with a slightly shiny surface; while the cattail splints in Pima baskets are tan and more fibrous, with some very slender and almost thread-like elements.

The sewing splints in old Papago baskets were made of willow *(Salix nigra)* and devil's claw, as were those in Pima baskets. Even in the early days, willow was scarce in Papago country and often had to be traded or purchased from the Pimas. Wild devil's claw was also scarce, but it could be cultivated (the variant hohokamiana), and basketmakers could assure themselves of a supply if they had enough water to keep it alive. The three varieties of devil's claw grown by the Papagos produce sewing splints varying from 4 to 18 inches long (DeWald 1979:32). The Papagos tended to use more devil's claw stitches and fewer tan willow stitches than the Pimas.

The Pimas and the Papagos decorated their large trays with basically the same patterns, although Kissell (1916) felt that some were more common to one tribe or the other. The simpler, bolder designs belonged to the Papagos. She also pointed out that on Pima baskets, lines parallel to the rims were usually a single coil wide, while on Papago baskets, they were often two coils wide (fig. 91). Although not inevitably, the difference results from the greater use of devil's claw in Papago baskets — one of the features that often makes them look darker than Pima baskets with the same or similar designs. On

Figure 91. Papago baskets. *Left,* typical vortex-fret design, but with lines the width of two coils. SAR B.404, 20" diameter. *Right,* a very large black vortex with frets in negative relief. SAR B.21, 19" diameter, 7" high. (Photo by Vincent Foster.)

some Papago baskets, the black elements dominate the designs, and negative patterns were occasionally produced with entirely black backgrounds (fig. 91). Kissell (1916:251) commented that Papago designs had "a strong feeling for large masses of dark and light," while Pima baskets revealed "a feeling for line . . . which is expressed in a network of black."

Papago basketmakers also tended to prefer certain characteristics of form and sewing technique. Kissell (1916) and Tanner (1983) present many profiles of Pima and Papago baskets to show the differences between them: Papago bowls tend to be globose, with broad bases (fig. 92), while Pima bowls generally have sharper, narrower bases and flaring sides (see fig. 81; Kissell 1916:176). To a lesser degree, the same is true of trays: Papago forms have flatter, broader bases. They also differ in texture. Papago bowls and trays are quite solid and stiff because the coils are often thicker than those in Pima baskets. The sewing splints are pulled so tight that old Papago baskets, especially wine bowls, are watertight. Basket bowls were often inverted and used as drums. In contrast, Pima baskets are thin and flexible, with smooth surfaces resulting from very even stitching. These differences are all a matter of degree, and no single trait can be depended on for positive identification.

Basket starts were generally the same as in Pima baskets, although Papago baskets were more commonly started with a four-square knot or small plaited mat. Contemporary Papago yucca baskets invariably start in this way. The rim finishes in the old willow baskets of the two peoples were also similar, although the Pimas were more inclined to use diagonal stitches or herringbone patterns, while Papago baskets were generally finished with parallel lashed stitches. Pima stitching was generally more even and compact. More than the Pimas, the Papagos tended to bend the fag ends of the new sewing splints and tuck them into the coil or lay them along the coil to be covered by the following stitches.

Figure 92. A typical, large, semiglobular Papago bowl for saguaro wine. The design is an angular squashblossom. SAR 1986-9-4, 19" diameter, 8" high. (Photo by Vincent Foster.)

MODERN BASKETS. Through all their historical vicissitudes, the Papagos preserved many of their traditional ways and demonstrated an admirable degree of adaptability. Long after manufactured goods became available, many of them continued to use their basket trays and bowls for household functions (Robinson 1954:47). As soon as the new railroad began to bring tourists and other travelers into their land, however, they began to produce baskets for this market.

As the demand for baskets grew, other changes occurred in Papago life. Women were forced to decide between basketmaking and working in one of the growing towns, and some concluded that the income they could earn from basketmaking did not justify the work. They also seem to have concluded that white buyers did not know one kind of basket from another. As a result, they virtually abandoned the traditional, hard-to-make willow baskets ("tree baskets") and invented a new kind of basketry that was much less time consuming and yet appealed to potential buyers — Papago yucca coiled basketry.

In a swell of creativity that continued unabated into the 1980s, new shapes were produced, new designs created, new sewing techniques developed, and new materials brought into use. Most Papagos abandoned the search for willow and substituted the more easily available yucca for stitching. They also stopped packing the stitches tightly against each other, deliberately spacing the yucca stitches apart so the beargrass in the bundle of the coil was exposed. Formerly, this technique had been used only in coarse wheat-straw baskets. Spacing the stitches and using yucca instead of willow reduced the time and effort needed to gather materials and produce baskets. This basketmaking revolution was supported and encouraged by the tribal council, which in 1939 established a revolving fund to buy baskets. They were then sold through the Papago Arts and Crafts Board. By 1942 at least four hundred women were participating in the program (Shreve 1943:11).

Papago yucca-sewn baskets were being made in many new shapes by 1900 and possibly as early as the 1880s, when eastern settlers and visitors first began to arrive. The ollas, deep bowls, and cylindrical baskets, stitched with yucca splints and decorated with black devil's claw, parallel the early development of trade baskets among the Pimas, except the Pima baskets were always sewn with willow splints, never with yucca. Among the most impressive Papago yucca-sewn baskets are large ollas, generally decorated with geometric black designs (fig. 93). Some are quite large (15–18 inches high), but others are small enough to sit on a table. Flat-bottomed bowls with vertical or slightly flaring straight sides were also common, as they were among the Pimas. They were made in various sizes, some nearly cup sized, others large enough to serve as wastebaskets.

One of the most interesting developments in close-stitch yucca coiling was the introduction of life figures and action scenes. Some early baskets had pairs of highly simplified human figures around them. Later decorations included rows of flying birds, large saguaro cactus plants (pl. 11), and the popular scene of women picking saguaro fruits. Deer, horses, eagles, insects, snakes, and butterflies were also depicted. The Papagos use Elder Brother's House (see fig. 90) as their tribal symbol. Points or sections in many of these designs were often highlighted with yellow yucca splints or red yucca root. In about 1930, Papago women began bleaching the white inner leaves of the yucca in the sun (DeWald 1979:31) and using the outer leaves that had turned tan-brown with age (Castetter and Underhill 1935:58), producing polychrome baskets in various natural hues: green, white, red, and yellow-tan (pl. 11).

Some of the best modern Papago baskets are made with compact yucca stitching on beargrass coils and decorated with such complex traditional patterns as concentric frets, turtleback designs, and many-pointed squashblossoms (DeWald 1979:37). The creation of such baskets is still a time-consuming process requiring great skill, but apparently it is easier than sewing with willow, and yucca remains somewhat less difficult to procure.

About the middle of the 1930s, some women in the village of Kohatk deliberately and consistently began to split the stitches on their baskets — a technique they said had been copied from old granary baskets (Shreve 1943:14). This practice constituted a major change from traditional willow baskets, in which great care was taken to avoid splitting the stitches to keep from making the surface uneven. Split stitches, which added further interest to yucca

Figure 93. Large, yucca-sewn Papago olla. These baskets have become less common in recent years because they require so much time to make. Some are more rounded than this example. SAR 1978-4-47, 16" high. (Photo by Vincent Foster.)

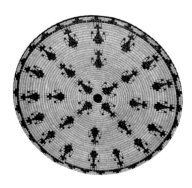

Figure 94. Modern Papago basket made in the old style with willow and devil's claw splints. This unique "bug" design was made by Gladys Antone of Chuichu, Arizona. 23" diameter. (Courtesy Dennis and Neva Kirkland; photo by Vincent Foster.)

baskets, may have originated with the Kohatk women, or the idea might have been stimulated by Washo or Miwok baskets seen at fairs, museums, and demonstrations.

Robinson (1954:51) noted that a few Papago women continued through the years to make willow-sewn baskets for their own use, and even in the 1980s, a small group of Papago women living in the village of Chuichu on the northern edge of the reservation were still making fine baskets, traditional in construction and materials, but often original in their decoration. Complex squashblossom patterns are quite common, and designs with rattlesnakes, butterflies, and insects are sometimes produced (fig. 94).

The finest examples of Papago spaced and split stitching are the relatively rare baskets sewn with willow splints, probably made for a short time during the 1930s. They are undecorated except for the pattern formed by the stitching. On one medium-sized olla collected in the early 1920s, the stitches are carefully executed and meticulously spaced about 1/8 inch apart. Another example (fig. 95) was made in a nontraditional globular shape and fitted with a lid. The precisely spaced split stitches wind up the sides in spiral lines to create a subtle and attractive design.

Baskets with split willow stitches are rare, but the style continued in yucca-sewn baskets, sometimes with attractive results. Often done quickly, split yucca stitching can produce a casual effect. Papago women were not satisfied with spaced and split stitches, and before long they produced a unique, fancy variation called the "wheat stitch," in which the usual spaced, split stitches are inserted and one or more long additional stitches are passed through them and carried diagonally to one side or the other (fig. 96). This variation not only creates an unusual and decorative appearance, but because the auxiliary stitches fill the intervening spaces, also makes it possible to move the stitches even farther apart.

Figure 95. This Papago basket is unusual for its almost spherical shape with a fitted lid, and for the precisely split willow stitching that covers it. SAR 1981-2-18, 13" diameter. (Photo by Vincent Foster.)

The variety of contemporary Papago yucca basketry seems to be almost infinite. Basketmakers today combine plain stitches, split stitches, and wheat stitches of various types with overstitching to create complex, attractive baskets, unlike anything done in the past. Many different forms are made, with designs ranging from depictive to completely abstract. The many stitching techniques that have been created are combined with great skill, and some young basketmakers such as Barbara Havier (Mauldin 1984:49) are producing complex, lacy patterns that seem like Papago dreams.

Figure 96. Papago wheat-stitched baskets. *Left,* a lacy design of white yucca stitches with different spacing between the rows. The center is plain compact stitching. SAR 1986-9-3, 12" diameter. *Right,* bowl with widely spaced rows of large stitches. Green beargrass coils show between them. SAR B.449, 11" diameter. (Photo by Vincent Foster.)

EFFIGIES, MINIATURES, AND HORSEHAIR BASKETS

Nontraditional forms such as pedestaled bowls were made in quantities by both the Pimas and the Papagos during the first quarter of the twentieth century as they tried to attract white customers. The Pimas did not carry this venture very far, but the Papagos created handbags, coasters, wall pockets, baskets with hoop handles, and an amazing variety of effigies: owls, ducks, cacti, turtles, animals, and humans. Because such baskets, especially effigies, were not made when Russell (1908) and Kissell (1916) were studying Pima and Papago baskets, these forms must have entered the market at a later, undetermined date. Douglas (1930) did not mention figurines in his survey of Papago basketry, but Shreve (1943) reported that many were being made in the early 1940s, suggesting that they became popular in the 1930s.

Figurines are made by bending and sewing coils of the same materials used in baskets into special shapes and adding pieces to represent legs, ears, and other features. Accents and designs are made with stitches of devil's claw

Figure 97. This Papago coiled bird effigy has a removable head so the basket can be used as a container. SAR 1985-8-4, 11" high. (Photo by Vincent Foster.)

or colored yucca, and occasionally by overstitching. Split stitches and spaced stitches are used to create textures. Many of the upright effigies such as owls, seated dogs, and women in long, full skirts were made as containers, with removable heads as fitted lids. In one bird effigy (fig. 97), the body is formed by a flat-bottomed, tapered basket sewn with rather broad yucca stitching and with dashes of yellow-tan stitching to represent breast feathers. The wings are oval-shaped coils of yucca edged with stitches of devil's claw. The final coils on the wings are pulled into three open loops on the lower edge. The head-lid is made separately, with two upright ears or horns and a flat, protruding beak, all formed by looping a section of coil and sewing the sides of the loops together. Devil's claw stitches are used for decoration and to form the claws and the eyes. The details of the eyes are oversewn with narrow strands of yucca.

The Pimas and Papagos made many miniature baskets stitched in willow or yucca (fig. 98). Some small bowls and trays are no more than 1 inch in diameter; other finely stitched pieces are about 6 inches in diameter. Almost every shape and design found in full-sized baskets was duplicated in miniatures (Cain 1962:pls. 4, 5, 6), and they have been collected enthusiastically. Most miniatures produced today are stitched with yucca by the Papagos.

The Pimas and Papagos also produced miniature coiled baskets made with strands of horsehair instead of yucca or willow for the foundation and stitching. The Pimas seem to have made them first, but the Papagos took over the craft, and recently they have developed it to a remarkable degree of artistry. The early baskets — plain, or occasionally stitched with white hair on a foundation of black or vice versa — were rarely more than 2 inches in diameter. The stitches were usually spaced so that the foundation showed. Finer stitching began some time in the early 1970s, and the first baskets with figures were created: the traditional Man in the Maze pattern (Gogol 1983a:8). In the 1980s, a number of dedicated young women, most of them from

Figure 98. Papago miniature baskets by Mary Thomas. *Left,* "friendship ring" of human figures, 7" diameter. *Right,* a version of the same design, 5" diameter. Both are sewn with willow and use black devil's claw and red yucca root in the designs. (Private collection; photo by Vincent Foster.)

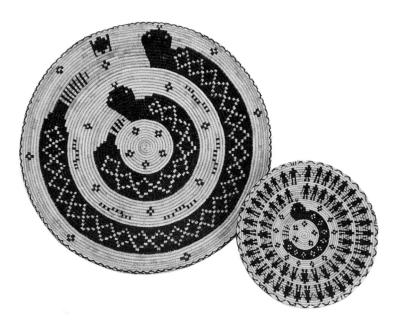

Chuichu, began making horsehair baskets as large as 12 inches in diameter, with tight, compact stitching and elaborate designs (fig. 99). Doreen García and Evelena Juan made rattlesnake patterns and circles of human figures, and Norma Antone created beautiful white baskets with three circles of black figures, like a Yokuts gambling tray. One of her creations includes more than 170 male and female figures holding hands in a circle.

The fine horsehair baskets produced by these young women are original creations. The basic techniques, forms, and some of the decorations may be based on traditional Pima willow baskets, but they have never been executed in horsehair before. New designs, derived from a variety of sources, make these baskets something altogether new and different. Future developments cannot be predicted. The basketmakers are enthusiastic about their work, which is now appreciated and avidly sought by collectors and dealers.

Today (1986) the Papagos are making more baskets than any other Indian tribe in the Southwest or elsewhere. Several hundred women participate in this flood of creative productivity. It is almost impossible to describe the many different kinds of baskets they have made in the past and are making at this moment; and it is beyond anyone's reach to imagine what they may be producing in the future. Many women draw upon the rich tradition of ancient designs, some convert recent concepts into something even newer, but others seem to be able to draw upon an unlimited supply of ideas and experiments, which enable them to combine old styles in new ways and create designs, techniques, and forms that have never been seen before. Such an approach to basketmaking keeps the ancient craft alive and flourishing among the Papagos.

Figure 99. Recent Papago horsehair miniatures. *Left,* double snake design by Betty Elizabeth, 9" diameter. *Right,* snake motif combined with a friendship ring, by Evelena Juan, 5" diameter. (Private collection; photo by Vincent Foster.)

Figure 100. Prehistoric Pueblo III coiled baskets found near Grants, New Mexico. Two-rod-and-bundle coiling, designs in natural dyes and possibly devil's claw. *Top,* 15" diameter, double coiled. Bottom, 9" high. (Courtesy Grants Chamber of Commerce; photo by Deborah Flynn.)

7

The Pueblos

The baskets made by the prehistoric Pueblo people are better known than those made by their descendants in historic and recent times. The great number of baskets and basket fragments unearthed by archaeologists reflects the importance of basketry in the lives of the early Pueblo people, but the relative scarcity of baskets in the records, photographs, and collections of the early historic period indicates that most of the functions served by baskets in earlier times were taken over later by pottery and trade vessels. Only among the Hopis have baskets continued to be produced and used to any great extent.

The skills of the earliest Anasazi were recognized by the archaeologists who called them the Basketmakers. Their tradition of complex coiled baskets came down to them from the earlier Archaic cultures, especially the Cochise-Mogollon and the northern Oshara. Among the many basket techniques invented by the Archaic peoples, the Anasazi used mainly plaiting and two kinds of coiling: one-rod and two-rod-and-bundle foundations. The Basketmakers produced a great variety of basket shapes, including large conical and pear-shaped burden baskets, bowls, and trays or platters of different sizes. Many of their earliest baskets were decorated with black geometric patterns. Red was introduced later, especially on large carriers. These people were also the first to make ring baskets, which were plaited with yucca splints.

During the subsequent Pueblo periods of Anasazi culture, pottery became common, but basketry continued to flourish in most areas until Spanish contact. The coiling of the Pueblos was generally finer than that of their predecessors, with tightly compacted stitching, complex designs in black and red, and patterns in featherwork and even mosaic. Among other new forms, cylindrical baskets appeared during the Pueblo III period (fig. 100), and a new technique using a foundation of three bunched rods became popular. This coiling technique occurred sporadically in early times (Ventana Cave, Danger Cave), but came into common use only with the late historic Pueblos, who may have acquired it from their Hakataya neighbors to the west. Coiled baskets with one-rod, two-rod, and three-rod-and-bundle foundations continued to be made and used by most of the Pueblos into historic times (A.D. 1700), but the quality of their baskets declined steadily from then on. The Hopis proved the exception: their basketmaking flourished, and they now produce coiled and plaited wicker baskets that do not resemble any Anasazi baskets of earlier times.

BASKETS OF THE HOPIS

The modern Hopis are one of the foremost basketmaking groups in North America. Their baskets have been extensively collected, described, illustrated, and exhibited (see, for example, Robinson 1954; Tanner 1968, 1983; Collings 1976; Breunig 1982; *Arizona Highways* July 1975), and a great deal is known about contemporary materials and techniques, as well as the many functions that baskets continue to serve in Hopi life. However, the ancestry of Hopi basketry is not well understood — where it came from and how its diverse forms and techniques developed. Hopi baskets are different from those made by any of their neighbors, and they are not clearly related to any prehistoric culture.

COILED BASKETS. The baskets coiled by the women of Second Mesa for sale and ceremonial use are unique in the Southwest for their designs and relatively thick coils (fig. 101). The coils are made with a foundation of a bundle of galleta grass (*Hilaria jamesii* Torr.; Wright 1979:66) or rabbitbrush (*Chrysothamnus nauseosus;* Dunnington 1985:22–25) and sewn with narrow splints of yucca leaves (*Yucca angustissima* Engelm.). In the past, none of the other Pueblos used bundle foundations to any extent. The Hopis probably acquired the technique from the prehistoric Hohokam people, and it is still characteristic of the probable descendants of the Hohokam, the Pimas and Papagos. In 1716 Padre Luis Velarde noted that the Hopis maintained close trading relations with the Piman-speaking tribes until the Apaches came between them (Wyllys 1931:139, cited in Di Peso 1953:5–6).

The prehistory of the Hopis is still vague, but archaeologists generally agree they descended directly from the people who lived in what is now northern Arizona between A.D. 500 and 600. During the fourteenth, fifteenth, and sixteenth centuries, this region became one of the three major centers of Pueblo life, along with Zuni-Acoma and the Rio Grande pueblos (Brew 1979:514).

Little evidence of Hopi ancestral basketry has been recovered, but there are suggestions that bundle-coiled baskets may have been made in northern Arizona for a long time. Nineteenth-century baskets are well represented by examples collected before 1890 by Voth (Field Museum), Keams and Fewkes (Harvard-Peabody), Cushing (Smithsonian), Rust (Logan-Beloit), and others. These baskets demonstrate that many aspects of Hopi coiling have been maintained with little change, while other aspects have been modified and some new features have been introduced.

Many of the coiled baskets made a century ago were flat plaques, with thick (1 inch in diameter), soft coils (pl. 12). Some of these baskets, probably made for ceremonial use (Wright 1979:67), were no more than 4 to 6 inches in diameter and undecorated. At the same time, women of Second Mesa were also making plaques and shallow trays or bowls with thinner, solider coils, similar to those being made today and often decorated with nearly identical

Figure 101. Before a wedding, the women relatives and friends of the bride gather at Shipaulovi on Second Mesa to make baskets to be given to the groom's family. Here they are making coiled baskets. (Courtesy California Historical Society, Los Angeles, Title Insurance collection, neg. 1083; early 1900s, photographer unknown.)

Figure 102. Modern Hopi coiled plaques with traditional designs from the villages on Second Mesa. *Left,* a typical design of stars and/or petals in natural black, yellow, and red. SAR 1981-25-3, 13" diameter. *Right,* Long Billed kachina, SAR B.305, 12" diameter. (Photo by Vincent Foster.)

designs, including kachina figures (pl. 12, fig. 102), radiating points or petals (fig. 102), curving volutes or whirlwinds, and bilaterally symmetrical figures in which the two sides are often different colors (pl. 12).

The base colors on Hopi coiled baskets are the natural shades of yucca leaves, from which the sewing splints are made: the outer leaves for olive-green; the tender inner leaves, which are frozen to make white; and others bleached in the sun for a golden-yellow color (Wright 1979:67). The yucca splints can also be dyed black by boiling them with sunflower seeds, piñon pitch, and ochre; and yellow-orange with a dye made from Navajo tea, or greenthread *(Thelesperma)*. Natural alum is sometimes used to set the dyes, and the colors are usually intensified by holding the dyed materials in the smoke of burning white wool. White clay (kaolin) and some other pigments were occasionally daubed or painted on the baskets, usually for ceremonial purposes. The same colors and materials are still used in modern coiled baskets. At the end of the nineteenth century, aniline dyes were used for a short time, but they had been abandoned by the turn of the century (Collings 1976:129).

The Hopis were more isolated from the white frontier than the other Pueblos were, but missionaries, traders, and soldiers reached them, influencing their lives well before the middle of the nineteenth century. In 1881 the Atlantic and Pacific Railroad passed through Winslow, Holbrook, and Flagstaff, Arizona. Within a few years, many adventurous tourists, teachers, and government agents were making the difficult trip across the desert to see the already famous Snake Dance and to buy pottery, weavings, kachina dolls, and baskets from these "interesting and primitive" people (Dockstader 1979:526).

Hundreds of articles were purchased from the Indians to be sold in eastern markets, and many of the famous museum collections of Hopi arts started during the 1880s. By the turn of the century, the Fred Harvey Company had gathered a large collection for display and sale in its hotel at the Grand Canyon. The company also filled orders from the Field Museum in Chicago, the National Museum, the Carnegie Museum in Pittsburgh, and the Museum für Völkerkunde in Berlin.

The active market in Indian goods that developed between 1880 and 1900 inevitably affected the Hopis' productivity and attitudes. Many traditional pieces and even some sacred objects were sold, and a great many items must have been produced for sale rather than use. However, Hopi workmanship was so consistent that it is nearly impossible to identify baskets or pottery vessels made specifically for the market. "Commercial" kachina dolls were being sold in the early part of the twentieth century (Harvey 1976:3), but Hopi basketmakers never stooped to the production of the bizarre shapes made by some other tribes, and their only concessions to commerce may have been deep wastebasket forms and the limited use of bright aniline colors. The new market did not seem to diminish the extensive use of baskets by the Hopis themselves, especially for ceremonial purposes, which was probably instrumental in their maintenance of technical quality and traditional designs.

Many of the large coiled baskets made between 1880 and 1900 were decorated with detailed kachina masks or full kachina figures (fig. 103), and

Figure 103. Old coiled basket from Hopi Second Mesa, decorated with cloud symbols and the Crow Mother kachina. SAR 1984-4-38, 18" diameter. (Photo by Vincent Foster.)

Figure 104. Joyce Ann Saufkie of Shungopavi, one of many fine modern basket weavers, holding one of the deep baskets for which she is famous. The designs and coiling technique have changed little since 1890. (Photograph by Deborah Flynn, 1983).

superb baskets of this type are still being made by artists such as Joyce Ann Saufkie of Shungopavi (fig. 104). Deep, bowl-shaped baskets were fairly common early in the twentieth century. Often, they were decorated with animal figures, deer or antelope heads, or geometric figures (pl. 13). Some deep baskets fitted with lids and bail handles may have been used to carry seed corn when the fields were being sown.

The coiled baskets being made today on Second Mesa generally have thin (1/2-inch), solid coils and fine, compact stitching. The slender yucca sewing splints are wound tightly around the foundation bundle of the new coil. They pass through such a small section of the preceding coil and fit so closely between its stitches that the stitches appear to be interlocked, but they are not. The narrow area in which the stitches of adjacent coils overlap provides a degree of strength to the baskets that testifies to the skill of the basketmakers. Hopi women achieve very smooth, even surfaces on the work face of their baskets, but close examination reveals diagonal ridges under the stitches formed by the long fag ends of the stitching splints, which are held down with the left thumb and covered by several following stitches (fig. 105). A feature typical of Hopi coiling appears on the nonwork surfaces: a series of triangular or diagonal spots where the moving ends have been twisted and then laid along the coil before being covered by stitching (fig. 106). Some of the moving ends are 4 or 5 inches long.

Coiled baskets are started with a tight spiral of yucca-leaf strands, and the more rigid galleta grass bundle is added after the second or third turn. Rims are almost always finished with simple parallel stitching, and the final coil is thinned to a point. Some baskets, usually small (5–6 inches in diameter), and probably made for ritual use, appear to be unfinished because the coiling ends with the bundle foundation protruding. With no further explanation, notes by Walter, Fewkes, and Keam at the Peabody Museum indicate that this unfinished end shows the basket was made by a "fertile woman."

Contemporary coiled baskets from Second Mesa equal or surpass any made in earlier times. Materials are carefully prepared, the baskets are tightly coiled and stitched, and large quantities of them are made as gifts, as ritual objects, and for sale to outsiders. The market for them is strong, and hundreds of coiled baskets pass through the sales outlet of the Hopi Culture Center every year. Most of them are made in the old shapes: plaques, trays, and bowls. Many of the old designs have been perpetuated and often elaborated with details of kachina headdresses, eyes of animals, and corn kernels worked in overstitching — a refinement of an old technique in which short sections of colored splints are sewn over the coiling when the basket is completed. Without question, these baskets represent the most elaborate and colorful coiling being done by any North American Indians.

PLAITED WICKER BASKETS. Distinctive plaited wicker baskets are specialties in the villages of Third Mesa: Old Oraibi, Hotevilla, Kyakotsmovi, Bacabi, and Moenkopi. They are made by plaiting slender stems of rabbitbrush over and under warps of squawberry sumac shoots *(Rhus trilobata Nutt.).* Of the several varieties of rabbitbrush *(Chrysothamnus nauseosus), graveolens* is used as well as the shorter variety, *bigelovii.* The traditional shapes made with plaited wicker are circular plaques of various sizes and shallow bowls. Deep bucket shapes, often with flat bottoms and slightly flaring sides, were probably developed for the non-Hopi market (Wright 1979:63). The Hopis name each type of basket according to its use or colored design (Breunig 1982).

Figure 105. Detail of Hopi coiling. On the work surface, the fag ends form diagonal ridges where they are covered by the following stitches. (Photo by Vincent Foster.)

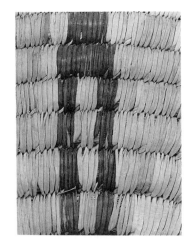

Figure 106. Detail of Hopi coiling. On the nonwork surface, the moving ends of the splints can be seen at the bottom of each coil. (Photo by Vincent Foster.)

Figure 107 (left). Hopi plaited wicker wedding plaque made on Third Mesa. A band of blue rectangles linked with a black and orange line symbolizes the links that will hold the bride and groom together. SAR B.92, 11" diameter. (Photo by Vincent Foster.)

Figure 108 (right). Third Mesa plaited wicker plaque showing the Crow Mother kachina with head and mask enlarged. SAR 282, 14" diameter. (Photo by Vincent Foster.)

Like coiled baskets, many wicker plaques are still used to hold corn meal, shelled corn or cobs, piki bread, fruit, and other dry foods, especially when they are to be carried into the kivas; the sprouted beans in the Powamu ceremony; and sacred objects in many other rituals. Early photographs of Hopi ceremonies taken by Vroman (Webb and Weinstein 1973), Mora (Smithsonian Institution 1979), and especially the unique pictures taken in the kivas by the Reverend H. R. Voth before 1900 (Waters 1963), clearly depict the extensive ritual and domestic uses made of various kinds of baskets. In the basket dance, women of the Lakone society carry wicker, coiled, and some non-Hopi baskets, giving them away at the end of the dance. Baskets are also required to be given to young girls at the Powamu ceremony and to be buried with ceremonially killed eagles (Wright 1979:64). During the long Hopi marriage rites, they are carried to the groom's house by women related to the bride. These baskets are made during a "plaque-making party" (see fig. 101) as repayment for wedding robes woven by the men of the groom's family for the bride. A special "wedding basket" (fig. 107) with a design of linked rectangles signifying "holding together" is given to the groom to be preserved and buried with him so he may be admitted to the Hopi underworld (Breunig 1982:10).

Hopi women decorate their wicker baskets with an enormous variety of designs. Some, like the wedding-basket pattern, are traditional, and many have been given names such as "caterpillar," "corn cob," and "striped blanket." Other designs depict kachina masks or complete kachina figures (fig. 108). Bird motifs (pl. 14), butterflies, and whorls are still popular, and old geometric patterns are common. The deep wicker baskets are generally decorated with terraces, bands of rectangles, or spiraling bands of color (fig. 109). Animal motifs appear on the deep wicker baskets (fig. 109), as they do on the coiled baskets of the same shape, and textile designs from sashes and robes are occasionally depicted (Breunig 1982:10).

The starts of Hopi plaited wicker baskets are often recessed. Two bunches of sumac warp rods are cut to the desired length, and four pairs of them are bound together at their midpoint by plaiting fine weft splints back and forth across them — under two, over two — for a space of about 2 inches. For baskets that are to be decorated at the center with a broad kachina mask or some other large motif, as many as fourteen pairs of warps are plaited together for the starting bunch. In a different kind of start, the warp rods are bound together by wrapping a splint around them. This flat wrapping is usually divided into two triangular sections, so smaller groups of warps are wrapped together within the bundle.

When two bundles of warp rods have been fastened together by either method, they are crossed over each other at right angles, their rods are spread

Figure 109. Deep, plaited wicker bowls have been popular in historic times with tourists, who use them as wastebaskets. *Left,* the most common shape, decorated with antelopes. SAR B.335, collected between 1912 and 1915, 10" high. *Right,* decorated with diagonal bands of green, black, and brown. SAR B.151, 8" high. (Photo by Vincent Foster.)

Figure 110. Hopi woman weaving a plaited wicker plaque with a kachina design on Third Mesa about 1900. The picture demonstrates the many elements a weaver must control in making a wicker basket. (Courtesy Southwest Museum, neg. 22828; photo by A. C. Vroman, about 1900.)

Figure 111. Hopi plaited wicker tray made with a central handle and a rim that is braided instead of bound with yucca. Such trays may have been lids for storage pots or baskets. SAR B.340, 11" diameter. (Photo by Vincent Foster.)

out like spokes, and the first weft splints are plaited over and under, encircling the starting bundles and binding them together (fig. 110). Additional sumac warps are added as the basket grows, and they are incorporated into the web of plaited wefts. The two plaited or wrapped starting bundles remain separate elements in the finished baskets. Occasionally, one of these bundles was bent up into a loop to serve as a handle (fig. 111).

Near the center of the basket, the wefts are plaited over and under two warps, and toward the rim, they cross three or more warps at a time. At the rim, all the warp rods are cut off except the long one at the left in each group, which is bent to the left and twisted into a bundle with two or three warps bent over from the adjacent warp groups. The twisted bundle of warps is then wrapped with a long splint of yucca leaf to fasten it together and attach the rim firmly to the web of the basket. Occasionally, a different kind of rim (fig. 111) was made by bending the ends of two of the three warps in each group and braiding them with adjacent warp groups. Two encircling bands of braided warps made a neat rim finish that required no yucca binding.

Although a few plaited wicker "peach trays" (fig. 112) were left undecorated, most of them are colored with a greater variety of brilliant colors than any other Indian baskets (pl. 14). In recent baskets, the ingredients are generally native plants and minerals, but some aniline dyes are still used with great delicacy to blend with the natural colors (Wright 1979:63). The sources and processes of the dyes have been well described and analyzed by Wright (1979) and Mary-Russell Colton (1965).

Burden Baskets. The Hopis used two kinds of carrying baskets, neither of which resembled those of their neighbors in form or technique. At one time, men made most of them using unscraped sumac shoots for warp and weft elements. Single weft elements were plaited around the basket, over and under groups of three or four sumac warp rods. One common form was large and rectangular or oval, with two thick, scraped, U-shaped rods of oak or juniper, parallel rather than crossed, shaping the bottom of the basket and extending up the sides and beyond the rim. These extensions were used as handles to lift the loaded basket onto someone's back to be carried with a tumpline, or more commonly, onto a burro. Their shape made them especially effective as panniers, with one balanced on each side of the pack animal. The rims of these heavy burden baskets usually seem unfinished, with the warps sticking out, and no special binding (Wright 1979:65).

Figure 112. A plain wicker Hopi peach tray—a type common at Hopi and Zuni before 1900, when baskets served many daily functions. In recent times most of them have been made on Third Mesa. SAR 1978-1-51, 18" diameter. (Photo by Vincent Foster.)

Figure 113. Carrying a well-worn, plaited wicker burden basket, the Ogre Maiden (Soyok'Mana) kachina and a Black Ogre (Natashka) kachina wait at the hatch of a kiva with a Heyheya kachina. They are demanding food during the Bean Dance (Powamu) on First Mesa. (Courtesy John R. Wilson; photo by Joe Mora, 1904–1906.)

The second type of burden basket was made in a deep bucket shape, rounded on the bottom, and roughly rectangular or square in section. They were plaited with multiple warps and single wefts of sumac shoots, usually with reinforcing rods to form and strengthen the four corners, although some were made without them. They are usually undecorated, but the bark was occasionally scraped off some wefts to produce a simple pattern of encircling bands. Because they were commonly used to carry fruit up to the villages, these baskets are called "peach baskets." Small ones might have been used by little girls, and they appear on the backs of certain kachinas during ceremonies (fig. 113).

Piki Trays. These square or rectangular trays, which are often quite large, have been referred to as a "portable working surface for Hopi women" (fig. 114; Wright 1979:60). They are used especially to hold rolls of paper-thin piki bread as it is stripped off the stone griddle and to carry it into the kivas. They are made with shoots of sumac and dunebroom (*Parryella filifolia* G.). The center section of the tray is usually worked in twilled plaiting, with single wefts passing over and under groups of four to six warps, and the broad rim border is in plain plaiting. The center section is often plaited with dunebroom, and the stiffer border with sumac, usually with the bark remaining. Attractive designs of diamonds, rectangles, and diagonal lines are sometimes added by splitting or scraping one set of the plaiting elements for a lighter color. At one time, shallow bowls employed the same technique, but these now seem to be obsolete (Wright 1979:60). Like the rims of plaited wicker plaques, the rims of piki trays are finished by bending the ends of the weaving elements into a bundle and wrapping it with a strip of yucca leaf.

Figure 114. A Hopi piki tray made by Dora Tawahonqua. SAR 1984-5-1, 24" long. (Photo by Vincent Foster.)

PLAITED RING BASKETS. The all-purpose plaited ring baskets of the Hopis and most other Pueblo people are the oldest kind of basket in the Southwest. They appeared first in the Basketmaker III period (about A.D. 500) and continued to be made and used without a break and almost without modifications by all the subsequent Anazasis: "The manufacture of ring baskets has continued for fully 15 centuries without interruption. No other product of Anasazi handicrafts has persisted so long or with so little change" (Morris and Burgh 1941:20).

The popularity of these rugged, attractive baskets endures over a large area because they are easy to make, they serve many functions well, and the materials they are made of can be obtained and prepared easily. It is difficult to understand why they were not enthusiastically adopted by any prehistoric tribes besides the Anasazi.

Their construction is basically the same as that of wicker plaited piki trays, except the materials are different, and a rod rim is used. Flat splints are prepared by stripping off the ridge that runs down the center of the leaves of the narrow-leafed yucca. The strips are plaited into a mat, and while the materials are still moist and supple, the fabric is pushed into a ring made of a sumac rod. The basketmaker then stands on the yucca matting and pulls the ring up to bend the mat into a bowl shape. The protruding edges are trimmed a bit, bent over the rod, and fastened by twining two yucca cords through the splints and into the wall of the basket. The sumac ring is practically hidden, and the ends of the yucca strips make a sort of fringe around the rim (see figs. 10, 119).

Yucca ring baskets are almost always circular, shallow bowls, varying in size from 6 or 7 inches in diameter to about 18 inches. They can hold or carry almost anything, but they are especially important as sifters for straining out the heated sand that has been used to parch corn. The plaited splints can be spaced apart for this purpose or compacted to make a smooth, tight surface. The variety of plaiting techniques used to create textures and designs is fully described by Adavasio (1977:99–123); generally, they are limited to plain plaiting and twill plaiting. Hopi sifters are invariably made with plain open plaiting, which gives a checkerboard effect. The plaiting may be one over one, two over two, three over three, or any consistent sequence. All other ring baskets are made in twill plaiting with patterns of concentric diamonds or squares, sometimes with added crosses and small figures; diagonal bands; meanders (Mauldin 1984:33); or all-over designs of small diamonds. Such patterns are produced by the diagonal nature of twill plaiting, but Hopi women are experts at shifting from one plaiting pattern to another to achieve variation (fig. 115). They also emphasize the designs by using yucca leaves of different colors (green, yellow, and white). In recent years, their designs have become increasingly complex, and bright colors have been introduced by dying some of the splints.

At one time, yucca-leaf baskets were also plaited in other forms. Diagonally twill-plaited deep bowls with square, flat bases, some with rod rims, were collected in the 1880s for the Smithsonian Institution by Powell, Stevenson, and Cushing. A small, vase-shaped basket in the School of American Research collection (B.271) made with twill-plaited yucca strips is catalogued only as "Pueblo," but it is probably Hopi.

Figure 115. Isabel Coochyump-tewa of Mishongnovi, Second Mesa, holds a yucca ring basket with the distinctive Hopi design of two interlocking rectangular scrolls or spirals. (Photo by Deborah Flynn, 1983.)

Since about 1940, plaited baskets with wire rims have been made in oval and rectangular shapes, mostly for sale to visitors (Bartlett 1949:38). Plaiting was also used to make back straps for belt weavers, pads for tumplines, and a variety of rings used for supporting and carrying pots. Some rings were woven in a twill-plaited cylinder 4 or 5 inches long, and while still moist and flexible, the ends were turned to the inside (Kissell 1916:159–64). Others were round in cross section, like doughnuts (Wright 1979:59). Both types are represented in the School of American Research collection.

BASKETS OF ZUNI, ACOMA, AND LAGUNA

Along with the Hopis, the people of Zuni, Acoma, and Laguna represent the Western Pueblos. Although they share many cultural features, they speak different languages, and their divergent histories and geographic separation make them independent of each other. Many years of archaeological and ethnological study in these villages have resulted in a wealth of information about them dating from early dealings with the Spanish to the economic and social problems of today. Many of their traditional crafts have waned, but a few have increased in importance. For example, weaving and potterymaking nearly vanished from Zuni, but silver and beadwork developed. Acoma pottery experienced a renaissance, and some women from this pueblo achieved fame in the craft.

Basketry, however, has suffered a marked decline. With the exception of an occasional yucca ring basket, no baskets have been made at these pueblos for years, and what little is known about the history of their basketry is confusing and frustrating. Morris and Burgh (1941:44) summarized the situation:

> The student of basketry might expect Anasazi culture in historic times to be represented by a wealth of good material in contrast to the prehistoric. Actually, the specimens are few, of dubious date and questionable origin, widely scattered in museums and private collections, and all of them only inadequately published.

There is no doubt, however, that like their neighbors to the east, the people of these pueblos once made baskets. One of Coronado's chroniclers noted many baskets at Zuni in 1540 (Schroeder 1979:252). In 1879 and 1880, Stevenson, Cushing, and Powell collected more than two hundred baskets there for the Smithsonian Institution (Stevenson 1883), and James and Matilda Cox Stevenson expanded the collection in 1888–89. The list of baskets acquired by the Smithsonian in 1881 includes trays and bowls for "sacred flour"; water baskets; small baskets for "gathering and caging locusts or their larvae"; small burden baskets for carrying fruit or parched corn; a "large basket for carrying peaches"; small, "loosely plaited baskets"; small willow trays; a "large basket tray of marsh grass for washing corn"; small basket sieves for parching or toasting corn and piñon nuts or for sifting parched corn; a "small ancient basket for medicine"; a "treasure basket in form of a water bottle"; a "small doublelobed and necked water vessel of wicker work"; a "basket cup with handle"; and a "corn-meal sieve of amole" (Stevenson 1884:576–80). The list gives the Zuni terms for each basket; the materials used in some (willow, grass, amole or yucca); occasionally, the technique of construction (wicker, plaited, coiled); some sizes and shapes (small and large bottles, double-lobed vessels, bowls, vases, trays, and canteens); and most informative of all, functions. More than fifty baskets were described as water containers, and at least forty-one as baskets for gathering or caging locusts or their larvae.

In spite of the large number of baskets he collected at Zuni, Stevenson commented, "Those made by the Zuni are so rude and coarse as not to entitle them to any merit" (Stevenson 1883:334). O. T. Mason (1904:506, 227) recognized that the Zunis made some plain plaited wicker "peach trays" and simple wicker carrying baskets, but concluded that the Zunis traded for all their other baskets from the Navajos, Apaches, and other tribes known for their basketmaking. Examination of the collection tends to support this interpretation. However, to avoid the risk of throwing out the baby with the bath, some baskets deserve further consideration.

There are not many of these "Old Pueblo" baskets, as they have been referred to in the literature. Morris and Burgh found "no more than a score" of them in their survey of collections, and they are difficult if not impossible to attribute to any of the tribes from whom the Zunis acquired most of their baskets. No Pueblo people were making baskets of this kind when the collections were made, so it was assumed that even though the Zunis used them, they could not have made them. Most anthropologists identified them as Apache, Navajo, Ute, or Havasupai, though none of these tribes made similar baskets.

The best known of these baskets are coiled in the shape of small ollas (fig. 116). They are often decorated with simple designs of open diamonds or spirals of small rectangles (Mason 1904:pl. 218) or narrow, separated lozenges (Peabody Museum 66522; Field Museum 103032). The designs are worked with splints dyed black or dark brown and are sometimes filled in

Figure 116. Two small, rod-and-bundle coiled ollas of the type collected at Zuni, Acoma, and other Pueblo villages before the end of the nineteenth century. *Left,* SAR B.236, 7" high. *Right,* SAR B.3, 8" high. (Photo by Vincent Foster.)

with red. The ollas usually have flat bases, bodies that are globose or tapered toward the neck, flaring necks, and flat rims finished with single-strand herringbone plaiting. In some cases, the lack of a flaring rim results in a slightly different shape. The most significant feature of these baskets is the two-rod-and-bundle foundation of their tightly sewn coils. This in itself eliminates all other tribes but the early Navajos from consideration. However, extensive search in museum collections indicates that small, olla-shaped baskets of any kind were so rare among the Navajos that there is little chance of their being responsible for the "Old Pueblo" baskets.

Besides the little ollas, Stevenson collected a number of other baskets coiled with two-rod-and-bundle foundations, including small, cup-like bowls; large shallow bowls; globular seed jars; and ollas of various sizes (U.S. National Museum 234–395, 40882, 41227; Mason 1904:pls. 214, 218). It is not known when they were made, but they are worn with age, coated from use, and often patched. Knowledge of their age would shed little light on their origins, however, nor would it give any reason to assume they were not made at Zuni. Morris and Burgh (1941:13) point out that two-rod-and-bundle coiling has a long history among the Pueblos, concluding:

> Two-rod-and-bundle basketry with uninterlocked stitches was made by the Anasazi from Basketmaker II until, we believe, about 1750–1800. The "Old Pueblo" baskets collected by Stevenson are probably heirlooms of the 18th century. . . . We may suppose that subsequently the Pueblo people found it much easier to obtain basketry from neighboring tribes than to make it themselves, and that in consequence the art died out among them.

Considering that most of these two-rod-and-bundle coiled baskets were collected at Zuni, that there were many of them in diverse shapes, that no one else except the Navajos made two-rod-and-bundle baskets in historic times, and that this technique had existed in the Zuni area for nearly fourteen centuries, it seems logical to conclude that the "Old Pueblo" baskets and the other two-rod-and-bundle baskets collected with them were made at an early time at Zuni Pueblo. The Zunis told Stevenson that some of these baskets were old and that they had been used to hold "sacred flour," "sacred meal," and "treasures" (Stevenson 1884:576–80). The evidence seems quite conclusive that they are indeed Zuni heirlooms.

Three excellent examples of "Old Pueblo" baskets are preserved in the School of American Research collection (fig. 116), and other fine, but usually misidentified, specimens are hidden in other collections (Peabody-Harvard 06-5-l0/66522; Southwest Museum 156-G-62; Field Museum 103032). Several baskets of this kind were collected at Zia Pueblo (Mason 1904:pl. 212), at least one came from Hopi (U.S. National Museum 68473), and another is catalogued from Acoma (Arizona State Museum GP52698). In 1959 Florence

Hawley Ellis and one of her students made a careful survey of the Rio Grande pueblos (Ellis and Walpole 1959) and collected nearly a dozen old baskets made with two-rod-and-bundle coiling. The owners believed they had been made in the villages of Zia, Santa Ana, Jemez, San Felipe, and Acoma, but some could be traced back three generations to the 1880s (Ellis 1959:50). Ellis (1959:10) concluded that these were the kind of baskets that influenced the Navajos and that they represented an old type lasting "from [Basketmaker] II to the present period, among the Keres of the Middle Rio Grande and perhaps elsewhere." Her interpretation agrees with Morris and Burgh (1941), who concluded that although two-rod-and-bundle coiling was extinct in the pueblos, it represented an Anasazi tradition that had persisted into the early part of the twentieth century. It is possible that the large two-rod-and-bundle baskets with unusual designs that I have called Navajo may represent rare examples of these early Pueblo coiled baskets (SAR B.266, 267).

PROBLEMATIC BURDEN BASKETS. Another group of baskets collected in the western pueblos possesses distinctive features that are difficult to explain. These bucket-shaped burden baskets look very much like the carriers of the Western Apaches, but differ from them in certain details (fig. 117). Like the Apache baskets and the plaited wicker peach baskets of the Pueblos, they are built on two U-shaped scraped willow rods that cross each other on

Figure 117. An old Pueblo twined burden basket showing distinctive designs and rim finish. SAR B.15, 12" high. (Photo by Vincent Foster.)

the bottom of the basket and form the vertical reinforcements for the corners. Like the Apache baskets, most of these carriers are twined with split-willow or sumac splints. Unlike the Apache baskets, they are almost never decorated with strips of buckskin fringes or basal patches; and perhaps of greater significance, their rims are quite different.

Apache burden baskets almost invariably have double rims made with a wooden rod and a ring of heavy wire, or a wrapped bundle of splints in which the ends of the warps are included. Roberts (1929:148) notes that the warps "are never bent back into the fabric when the basket is completed to insure [sic] a better edge which will keep the twining from working off, but are either cut off short or topped with a rim laid along their ends." It is a distinctive feature of the baskets collected in the pueblos that the warp ends are bent at right angles and plaited in and out of the adjacent two or three groups of warps as in Hopi plaited wicker baskets and many plaited peach baskets. This method creates a series of open loops around the rim (fig. 118). A single-rod hoop is laid across the top and laced to the warp loops with a strip of buckskin or a broad willow splint.

Figure 118. Single-rod rim and interwoven warp ends on a Pueblo burden basket. SAR B.15. (Photo by Vincent Foster.)

Although these baskets have not been documented beyond any doubt, they were almost certainly used, and perhaps also made, in the Pueblo villages. Two specimens in the Museum of New Mexico (MNM 45768/12, 45767/12) were discovered in a cache under the floor of an old house at Acoma that was destroyed in about 1963. The rims of both baskets are finished with plaited warp ends and a single rod. One of them does not have U-shaped reinforcing rods. Several other baskets of this type were collected at Acoma Pueblo, including one purchased by Kenneth Chapman before 1930 (MNM 1122/12). Several in the Arizona State Museum were acquired at Zuni by the resident trader, E. C. Kelsey, sometime between 1900 and 1923.

Some of these baskets are decorated. Simple geometric designs of bands or diamonds were created by using weft splints with dark bark on one side and twisting the light or dark surface in or out as desired. Textural changes were produced by mixing bands of plain and twilled twining and occasional courses of three-strand twining. Two of the baskets of this type in the School of American Research collection are decorated with bands of color: blue and red in one case, and black and red in the other. The colors may have been painted on, but color on the inside of one of the baskets indicates that the splints were dyed. Except for the rim treatment, both baskets look like Western Apache carriers, a similarity further emphasized by the remnants of four buckskin fringed strips on the corners of one, a true hybrid.

All the baskets of this type in the School of American Research collection are well worn, with breaks in various places, and with most of the interiors heavily coated with what appears to be organic matter. Even though they were all collected in the western pueblos, there has been a tendency to classify them as "Apache burden baskets," overlooking their unique features. The rim treatment closely resembles the technique used in Pueblo plaited wicker baskets and a few twined bowls. A fine example of the latter in the School of American Research collection, identified only as "Pueblo-Keres," has warp ends bent and plaited to produce a band of diagonal wicker plaiting just below the rim rod, which is lashed in place with yucca splints (SAR 1978–1–10).

There is historic precedence for this technique of plaiting the warp ends back into the basket. At prehistoric Lovelock Cave (Loud and Harrington:1929) and Humboldt Cave, Nevada (Heizer and Krieger:1956), where hundreds of basket fragments were discovered, the common rim finish on the large plaited and twined wicker burden baskets was a band several inches wide produced by plaiting the warp ends over and under their neighbors. The gap of 1,700 or 1,800 years between these prehistoric baskets and their Pueblo counterparts might seem to rule out any relationship between them. Yet information about prehistoric burden baskets is so meager that evidence linking the early and later examples may have decayed or gone undiscovered. In addition, Anasazi-Pueblo use of burden baskets seems to have declined over the centuries, and the techniques of twining and plaiting were largely displaced by coiling. These changes may also help explain the absence of a continuous sequence of materials that would link the early plaited-rim baskets with the later Pueblo examples. But even without these links, it is apparent that this particular finishing technique has deep historic roots in the Southwest.

BASKETS OF THE RIO GRANDE PUEBLOS

Because of the proximity of the Rio Grande pueblos to colonial administrative and religious centers during the Spanish period, it would seem reasonable to expect that their early history would be more thoroughly recorded than that of the other pueblos. Unfortunately, this is not the case, and it is extremely difficult to determine what kind of baskets they undoubtedly made and used. Today, yucca (*elata* and *glauca*) ring baskets and a distinctive type of plaited wicker basket are still being made in several villages, and a few coiled baskets are produced at Jemez Pueblo.

YUCCA RING BASKETS. Yucca ring baskets similar to those made at Hopi are now made chiefly by several Jemez women. Until recently, they were commonly used in several towns for winnowing wheat (Lange 1959:pl. 14b), washing grain (fig. 119), sifting flour and other fine materials, and in other domestic activities. Some are still used today. Yucca-leaf splints of white, yellow, and green, usually plaited in groups of two or three, are used to create simple designs of concentric diamonds. The plaited splints are generally stripped from the leaves of the narrowleaf yucca, but leaves of beargrass are sometimes used. The rim ring is made of willow. Like Hopi ring baskets, they range from about 12 inches to more than 2 feet in diameter, but they tend to be deeper and less

Figure 119. A woman of Jemez Pueblo washing grain with yucca ring baskets. (Courtesy Museum of New Mexico, neg. 42075; photo by Williamson, about 1930.)

varied in design than Hopi examples. In the late 1950s, a few yucca baskets were still being made at Cochiti Pueblo to wash grain and serve bread, and at that time the people said they had never made any other kind of baskets (Lange 1959:163). As in the other villages, many other kinds of baskets — especially Apache and Ute — were used extensively. At Santa Clara Pueblo, ring baskets were made until about 1940, but "in recent years all twilled yucca baskets have been imported from Jemez" (Hill 1982:92).

PLAITED WILLOW WICKER BASKETS. Plaited willow wicker baskets have been made for many years in several Rio Grande pueblos. They are so different from any other baskets of the Southwest that they are assumed to have been copied from European-style baskets made or imported by early Spanish settlers. An ethnologist at Santa Clara between 1904 and 1930 stated, "Basket making was also unknown excepting a large open weave basket, the technique of which was learned from Mexican neighbors" (Jeancon in Lange 1982:91). We do know that baskets of this style were made in several European countries and at various times and places in the United States (Teleki 1975:fig. 16, pl. 5). On the other hand, such baskets are related in basic technique, materials, and function to the entire range of Pueblo plaited wicker baskets described earlier, especially some of the simple "fruit trays" like one from Tesuque Pueblo in the Maxwell Museum (34.68.9), with warp ends bent and plaited back into the basket. The Pueblos seem as likely as any other group of people to have discovered the technique of making these baskets for themselves.

The most common shape for these plaited wicker baskets is a shallow bowl with a flat base and nearly straight flaring sides. Some are rather small, about 10 inches in diameter; others are 30 inches across. The largest one in the School of American Research collection, made by Pascual Martínez at San Ildefonso Pueblo, is 32 inches in diameter and 12 inches deep. It has stout loop handles woven into opposite sides of the rim (fig. 120). These baskets are made of willow shoots, usually with the dark red bark left on, but often scraped to show the white wood for decoration. The white designs are simple, consisting of light rectangles (fig. 121) or bordering lines in the lacy loops around the rim. On some small baskets the bark was removed entirely, making them completely white or light yellow.

Figure 120 (left). An unusually large plaited wicker basket made by Pascual Martínez of San Ildefonso about 1912. The body is plaited with flat splints of willow instead of the usual osiers. SAR B.123, 32" diameter, 12" high. (Photo by Vincent Foster.)

Figure 121 (right). Basket by Tomás García of Santo Domingo Pueblo, one of the most productive contemporary weavers of these plaited wicker baskets. In this 1981 piece, the technique of removing the bark for decorative contrast can be seen. SAR 1982-16-11, 19" diameter, 7" high. (Photo by Vincent Foster.)

Other shapes were less common. One of the most productive basketmakers of the area, Tomás García of Santo Domingo, makes deep bowl shapes. Cylindrical shapes with fitted lids have also been produced. Some of the most interesting baskets of this type are the large ollas with angular shoulders made by Pascual Martínez early in the twentieth century (fig. 122). I have not found any of these in museum collections.

The construction of plaited wicker baskets is quite complex. To start them, two bunches of heavy willow or sumac rods (1/4 inch in diameter) are crossed and lashed together, their ends are spread apart, and groups of slender willow wefts are plaited over and under them. In Tomás García's baskets, these thick rods cover the bottoms, and the bunches of four or five slender warps are introduced at the lower edge of the sides. Instead of using heavy starting rods, some basketmakers begin with four bunches of slender willow

Figure 122. Pascual Martínez of San Ildefonso Pueblo was one of the last residents of this village to make the large plaited wicker baskets with scalloped rims that were once made throughout the Rio Grande Valley. A few weavers still produce them. (Courtesy Museum of New Mexico, neg. 27982; photo probably by Kenneth Chapman, about 1917.)

shoots laid across each other with their ends spread out in a star or petal formation. Each bunch contains three or four warps, and others may be added as the basket expands. Many shallow bowls consist of a small plain-plaited base and curving sides of lattice-like diagonal plaiting. The distinctive lacy appearance of these baskets results from the way flat bunches of as many as seven warp strands are curved at the rim and plaited back through each other. The finish is a brilliant feat of basketmaking, in which the bunched warps are finally brought to the outside of the basket and worked into a flat three- or four-strand braid which fastens all the loose ends together and produces a reinforcing flange on the base of shallow trays or a decorative band around the sides of deeper bowls.

Regardless of the origins of these baskets, they are strong and decorative and have served many functions in several of the Pueblos. In 1972 one of the accomplished basketmakers from San Juan, the late Steve Trujillo, taught at least one woman at Jemez. He was also hired to teach basketmaking to some girls from Santa Clara, but the results were disappointing. As always, some of the older basketmakers are retiring, but Arnold Herrera makes baskets at Cochiti, and a few younger people are learning the art at Nambe, Pojoaque, and other villages. Overall, the production of plaited wicker baskets seems to be increasing.

RIO GRANDE COILED BASKETS. Rio Grande coiled baskets present another problem in Pueblo basket history. Although scholars usually assume that the late-arriving Jicarilla Apaches and Navajos learned to make baskets from the Rio Grande Pueblos, there is little solid evidence to support this interpretation, and few coiled baskets can be positively identified as having been made or used in the Rio Grande villages during the early historic period (1700 to 1900).

The meager but important body of information on Rio Grande coiled baskets was reviewed by Ellis (Ellis and Walpole 1959) and less intensively by Mauldin (1983). Ellis sought out basketmakers and knowledge of basketmaking in all the eastern pueblos. She also collected every available basket, and they are now housed in the Maxwell Museum of Anthropology.

Many of the baskets in the Maxwell collection could be at least a century old. Most of them have been broken or worn out and repaired several times. They show some diversity in coiling techniques, a variety of designs, and a number of links with the baskets of other tribes. Their exact ages cannot be determined, but one basketmaker, Isidro Shije of Zia, who died in 1957 at the age of eighty-five, was taught to make baskets by his father in the late 1800s.

Most of the eight Zia baskets in the collection were made with two-rod-and-bundle foundations stitched with sumac or willow. Several were decorated with faded red designs outlined with black: terraced bands, bands with serrated edges, and a band of nine thick, square crosses. The basketmakers used native dyes, but no splints of devil's claw. The rims of most of the baskets have worn or broken off. Shije said that he usually finished his baskets with plain lashing, although he used a herringbone finish for the final inch of a small "prayer meal basket" he made for his wife. This feature is found in some prehistoric Pueblo baskets (see fig. 100).

Ellis also collected two-rod-and-bundle coiled baskets at San Felipe and Nambe, and an especially interesting one at Santa Ana (Maxwell Museum 69.59.26) which the owner said had been made by his great-grandfather in about 1890. It is decorated with three large, red rectangular crosses outlined in black, and the rim is lashed with fine parallel sumac stitches. A similar basket, also decorated with crosses, was collected at Santo Domingo by Wesley Bradfield before 1912 (San Diego Museum of Man 10372[SD32]). At Acoma, Ellis was able to examine, but not to acquire, three old, undecorated trays coiled with two-rod-and-bundle foundations. She concluded that they were examples of "Old Pueblo" baskets that had persisted among the Keres Pueblos of the Middle Rio Grande into the historic period (Ellis and Walpole 1959:10). She also saw them as the basic types from which the Navajos had learned their "traditional" basketry techniques. No recent evidence refutes either of these interpretations.

Ellis also found a few coiled baskets with three-rod bunched foundations at Zia, and one at Santa Ana (Maxwell Museum 69.59.14) notable for its well-preserved herringbone rim and its fag ends, which were twisted before being caught under the stitches. She acquired three-rod baskets at San Juan and Jemez and, referring to Hill's notes, describes three-rod baskets with herringbone rims and black and red geometric designs from Santa Ana (Ellis and Walpole 1959:11). She ascribes this type of coiling to the prehistoric Anasazi tradition of the northern Tewa-speaking Pueblos and suggests that it influenced Jicarilla Apache basketmaking.

Relatively thick coils with four or five sumac rods distinguish yet another kind of coiling that Ellis found in the Rio Grande pueblos — the only kind still being made today. As she pointed out, these baskets have generally been identified as Jicarilla Apache, a conclusion justified by their herringbone rims and bright, aniline-dyed designs. Many Jicarilla baskets are still used in the Rio Grande villages today, but Ellis was convinced that some of the baskets that appeared to be of Jicarilla origin had actually been made by the Pueblos and represented another old tradition.

This tradition has continued to the present at Jemez, where the men of the Gachupin family have made coiled baskets for at least two generations. Ellis was told that Alcario Gachupin learned basketmaking from Felipe Yepa of Jemez. However, in 1983 Alcario's son, Rosendo, explained that he and his brother had learned to make baskets from their father, who, contrary to the idea that he was perpetuating an ancient Pueblo tradition, had learned his craft from the Jicarillas (conversation with author).

Figure 123. Coiled baskets practically disappeared from the Rio Grande pueblos many years ago. Today coiling is done only by the men of the Gachupin family of Jemez Pueblo. Their techniques resemble Jicarilla coiling. (Courtesy Heard Museum, catalogue NA-SW-Jemez-B-4; photo by A. H. Whiteford.)

The baskets Rosendo Gachupin has made in recent years are like Jicarilla coiled baskets in almost every way. The coil foundations are usually made of five scraped sumac rods, although three rods are occasionally used; the compact sewing is done with white splints of the same squawberry sumac; and the rims are finished with herringbone plaiting. Decorations usually consist of several separated geometric figures of terraces or triangles (Mauldin 1984:27). The baskets made by his father sometimes had original designs (fig. 123), but they were generally similar to Rosendo's. The colors of Rosendo's designs are produced by dyeing sewing splints with commercial red, green, lavender, and orange — a greater range than generally occurs in Jicarilla baskets.

All the Jemez baskets are shallow, curved bowls about 14 to 16 inches in diameter and 4 to 6 inches deep. The coils are approximately 1/2 inch wide, and the baskets are strong and rather heavy. Because of their scarcity, the baskets made by the Gachupins can be easily sold to collectors, but the makers sometimes give them to their relatives and friends at the pueblo.

The history of this single surviving example of Rio Grande Pueblo coiling, like the history of Pueblo basketmaking in general, remains obscure. The problems are fascinating, and it may never be possible to solve them completely. What are the origins of Rio Grande plaited wicker baskets? What was the origin of Jicarilla Apache heavy coiling? What happened to two-rod-and-bundle coiling, and where did the Navajos learn it? Although the time may have passed when it was possible to answer such questions with any degree of certainty, they will continue to fascinate researchers for long into the future.

Figure 124. Baskets decorate the dining room of Lorenzo Hubbell's residence at the Hubbell Trading Post, Ganado, Arizona. (Courtesy School of American Research collections in the Museum of New Mexico, neg. 15986; photo by Ben Wittick.)

8

The State of the Art and its Future

Besides being the oldest and most conservative native American craft in the Southwest, basketmaking is also the most widespread. Today, towards the end of the twentieth century, it is practiced by more tribes than any other single craft. Baskets are made in great quantities by the Papagos, followed closely by the Hopis; at a greater distance by the Jicarilla and Cibecue Apaches, San Juan Paiutes, Hualapais, Havasupais, Yavapais, San Carlos Apaches, and Navajos; and to a small degree by the Rio Grande Pueblos and Pimas. Unlike the other crafts, basketmaking was once important in all the tribes of the Southwest, and although it has waxed and waned, it has survived among them to a remarkable extent.

A major change in the production of baskets began around A.D. 500, when the Anasazi and Hohokam peoples became settled farmers, and pottery gradually displaced the baskets their ancestors had used for cooking and the storage of food and water. As the need for baskets dwindled, there was little incentive to improve their quality or beauty, and some groups practically stopped making them altogether. The arrival of European explorers in the Southwest and the stream of traders and merchants who followed resulted in further reductions in basket production. Iron cooking pots, cups, tin plates, and other implements quickly displaced homemade baskets and pots.

Basketmaking might have been abandoned entirely in the Southwest, as it was by Indians in other regions, if a new need for them had not developed. Soldiers took native crafts home to their families as souvenirs, and when the railroad arrived in the 1880s, the flow of visitors initiated a demand that has not abated. Even the earliest tourists were eager to purchase crafts as mementos of their adventures in the unknown Southwest, and within a few years some became avid collectors of textiles, pottery, and baskets. It became the vogue to decorate homes, particularly summer homes, with Indian crafts (fig. 124). On the reservations, many traders encouraged production, demanded improved quality, and developed markets for sale and distribution (Kent 1985). Old baskets sold quickly, and in some tribes, women began to make baskets specifically for sale. Old styles and techniques were revived, and many new basket shapes and designs were created to suit the tastes of the white customers. Some basketmaking tribes, especially the Hualapais and the Jicarilla Apaches, even created exotic shapes and colors to catch the eye, and the cash, of tourists.

TRADERS, COLLECTORS, AND COOPERATIVES

The traders' appraisal of the market and their personal tastes influenced the kinds of baskets that were made in the early twentieth century, but there is little specific evidence that they became as interested in baskets as they did in rugs and pottery. However, collectors such as George Wharton James and Grace Nicholson, knowledgeable connoisseurs and traditionalists, had lasting influence. They purchased only the finest baskets, searching zealously for the best old examples and brusquely rejecting any they regarded as poorly made or created specifically for sale. James reached many people through his publications and his enthusiastic development of basketmaking and collecting clubs and magazines. Nicholson collected widely for other collectors and museums. Their knowledge and taste established the standards by which southwestern Indian baskets came to be judged and purchased. In response, Indian basketmakers quickly learned which styles were acceptable and which were not.

Traders and collectors continue to have an important influence on the quality and quantity of Indian baskets. Most of the baskets produced since the turn of the century were made to be sold to non-Indians, so the quirks and foibles of this market are of great concern to the basketmakers and their families. The increasing number of shops selling "Indian art" and curios and the many dealers who invade the Indian villages in search of desirable baskets tend to confuse the artisans, who must choose between making many baskets that will sell quickly and making fewer and finer baskets that will bring higher prices. Some basketmakers solve the problem by doing some of each.

Most of the tribes have arts and crafts cooperatives of some sort, established to encourage the production of native crafts and provide a market that will bring fair prices. In some cases the cooperatives purchase supplies at wholesale prices, provide information about the kinds of designs and products that sell best, and often serve as the liaison between the artisan and the dealer or customer. Some cooperatives sell baskets or other products on consignment with an established commission; others buy baskets outright and sell them for the best price available. At the crafts center of the Jicarilla Apaches, basketmakers are provided with facilities and paid an hourly rate for their work, which then belongs to the center and is sold to cover expenses.

Tribal crafts cooperatives and traders play somewhat similar roles. As points of contact between the basketmakers and their market, they influence the shapes and styles of baskets by selecting those they can sell most readily. Basketmakers are quickly discouraged from producing baskets that traders and cooperatives are not eager to offer for sale. In many cases, this process discourages innovation. However, traders sometimes, and cooperatives generally, will support a fledgling artisan by buying her beginning efforts to keep her practicing until she develops into a good basketmaker; and the Papago tribe subsidized many weavers while they explored new types of basketry.

Often, a basketmaker depends on the local trader or tribal cooperative only until she perfects her skills and establishes a reputation. Once established, she frequently bypasses local outlets and takes her baskets directly to shops or dealers in urban centers, negotiating prices to suit herself and eliminating the percentage taken by the middleman. Many basketmakers among the Hopis, Papagos, and other tribes have taken a further step: a weaver whose name is known and whose baskets are in demand can sell them directly to customers as soon as they are finished, or she might choose to make baskets only on commission. At each step in this sequence, the basketmaker commands higher prices for her baskets. Unless the local trader or the tribal crafts cooperative succeeds in forging a strong bond of loyalty with the individual basketmakers, the best ones will eventually desert them for more lucrative outlets.

THE CURRENT STATE OF BASKETMAKING IN THE SOUTHWEST

In 1986, some basketmaking endures in almost every tribe, but the vigor of the craft varies greatly. Several Apache groups that once made fine baskets, such as the Mescaleros, Chiricahuas, and the White Mountain and Tonto groups of the Western Apaches, today make almost no traditional baskets. The Jicarilla Apaches, however, maintain an active culture center and produce large numbers of the kinds of baskets they have made since before the twentieth century. Coiled baskets, which once epitomized Western Apache

Figure 125. Sandra Black, a traditional Navajo basketmaker from Kayenta, Arizona, working on a Paiute-style Navajo wedding basket coiled with multiple bunched rods. (Photo by Deborah Flynn, 1983.)

crafts, are perpetuated by only a small group of women at San Carlos. Other San Carlos basketmakers have turned to the production of twined conical burden baskets of a recent style, introduced by Cecilia Henry and developed successfully by the younger women of her family. At Cibecue, similar twined burden baskets of superior quality are being made by Linda Guzmán and her husband, Mike, and the craft is being taught in classes to older women. Twined pitched baskets are still being made at Cibecue by Minnie Narcisco and her pupils. The basketmakers of Jicarilla and Cibecue seem to be the only Apaches making an active effort to train future basketmakers.

The far-flung Navajos, among whom basketmaking nearly disappeared early in the century, began to teach basketmaking in the 1960s. Since then, the craft has spread among them, producing many basketmakers and a wide array of baskets (fig. 125). Wedding baskets and pitched jars of various kinds are popular and in great demand by collectors and traders; coiled trays with colored designs of birds, *yei* figures, and other patterns are made on the western reservation near the Shonto, Oljeto, and Inscription House trading posts. On the extreme northern edge of the reservation, the women of Mary Holiday Black's family have been among the most innovative basketmakers. Some old-style baskets are made in the eastern part of the reservation, and Yenora Platero and a few other women make large coiled jars covered with smooth, amber-colored piñon pitch. The future of Navajo basketmaking seems assured, but the directions it will take are unpredictable.

The basketry of the San Juan Paiutes, neighbors of the Navajos, has undergone an even more radical revival. At one time, this small band made only wedding baskets for the Navajos and a few old-style utility baskets, but then they moved into the production of finely coiled baskets of various sizes, decorated with many-colored designs of great variety. The guidance and support of the trader at Sacred Mountain Trading Post was important in this remarkable development, but the Paiutes were ready for change, and they were probably influenced by the explosion of ideas and decorative styles taking place among the western Navajos. The San Juan Paiutes are now one of the most productive basketmaking groups in the Southwest.

Among the Yuman-speaking tribes, no such development has taken place. The Havasupais now make a few coiled baskets like the old ones, and some of the old-time basketmakers such as Caroline Putesoy and Minnie Marshall were working until the late 1970s. However, even skilled artisans make mostly small trays and models of old burden baskets for the many tourists who visit the canyon. Although the Hualapais do not have the tourists, their basketmaking has been strongly supported by an active school program, employing skilled basketmakers such as Elnora Mapatis and Jennie Imus as teachers. The characteristic colored twined bowls, as well as traditional berry baskets and shallow trays, are still made. Yavapai basketmaking is in severe decline. At Fort McDowell, only Bessie Mike, Lillian Shenah, and a few other women are still coiling baskets, and there is no program to encourage them or help them pass their skills to younger women. On the Yavapai reservation in Prescott, basketmaking was very active under the leadership of the tribal chief, Viola Jumilla, but in 1986 only one former basketmaker was trying to arouse interest among younger people, and with very little response.

At one time both the Pimas and Papagos made very fine coiled baskets, but in recent years Pima basketmaking has almost disappeared except for the work of a few women such as Hilda Manuel (fig. 126). Her daughters may continue the tradition, but Pima basketmaking does not seem to be economically feasible. The Papagos, with even fewer economic alternatives, found that income from the sale of willow-sewn baskets did not justify the time it took to make them. With the encouragement of the tribal council, Papago women turned to yucca-sewn baskets, which could be made more quickly, and which used materials that were easier to get. For greater efficiency, they spaced the

Figure 126. Hilda Manuel, Pima, holds a basket with the traditional design of Elder Brother, or the Man in the Maze, a depiction of an ancient legend. (Photo by Deborah Flynn, 1983.)

stitches apart and devised fancy stitching techniques for visual interest. They also bent and sewed the coils into a variety of human and animal figures. These nontraditional baskets have been very successful. Gradually, they have become more refined, with increasingly complex, lace-like designs.

At least until the 1950s, the Papagos coiled small baskets out of horsehair, but about 1970, some women in the northeastern area of the reservation began using hair of various colors and coiling it into tight baskets decorated with circles of human figures or coiled snakes. For Norma Antone (fig. 127), Elizabeth Julian, Evelena Juan, and Betty Elizabeth, these difficult creations are a challenge and an important source of income. Some of their older relatives, such as Matilda Thomas, Lola Thomas, Josephine Thomas, and Linda Hendricks, continued to make fine willow-sewn baskets long after they had become extinct elsewhere. In 1986, they were making fine, small (6–10 inches) willow baskets and some ordinary yucca pieces. At least one kind of basket or another is produced in almost every part of the reservation, and the Papagos seem capable of many further developments.

The Anasazi made many kinds of baskets, but except for the Hopis and a few basketmakers in the Rio Grande villages, their Pueblo descendants have practically abandoned the craft. Besides the few coiled baskets made by the Gachupin brothers at Jemez, yucca ring baskets are made occasionally at Jemez, and a distinctive style of plaited wicker basket is still produced in several villages, notably by Tomás García at Santo Domingo, Arnold Herrera at Cochiti, and Evelyn Vigil at Jemez (fig. 128).

The Hopis are the most productive and proficient basketmakers among the Pueblos. They too make plaited yucca ring baskets, sometimes dyed with bright colors, and with weaving designs that are usually more complex than those of Rio Grande baskets. Isabel Coochyumptewa of Mishongnovi and other weavers still create patterns of crosses, scrolls, and labyrinths in natural colors. Like the traditional piki trays, these baskets are not in great demand by tourists, but they will probably survive because they are still used by the Hopis.

Figure 127. Norma Antone of Chuichu, Arizona, is known for her skill in making modern horsehair baskets. (Courtesy *American Indian Basketry*; photo by John M. Gogol, 1983.)

Figure 128. Evelyn Vigil of Jemez Pueblo makes willow plaited wicker baskets as well as yucca ring baskets. (Photo by Deborah Flynn, 1983.)

The brightly colored plaited wicker baskets made on Third Mesa are popular with tourists, and also with the Hopis, who use them on many occasions. Traditional designs prevail, but colors are softer now that the aniline dyes used at the beginning of the century have been abandoned. As in earlier days, plaited wicker baskets are made from rabbitbrush. On Second Mesa, traditional coiled baskets of galleta grass and yucca, still made in the old designs and shapes, are as finely crafted as at any time in known Hopi history. Hundreds of Hopi women make baskets, and the demand for them seems insatiable. Many are sold through the large salesroom at the crafts center, but well-known artisans such as Joyce Ann Saufkie, Edith Longhoma, Bertha Wadsworth, and Evangeline Talaheftewa usually deal directly with the urban traders and collectors who commision work from them. Hopi traditionalism, the most important factor in the continuity of their basketry, will sustain it well into the future.

It is evident that the native peoples of the Southwest are still making many baskets, some for their own use, but mostly for sale to visitors. Some tribes that once made fine baskets have nearly or completely lost the craft; others have modified their ancient products into baskets that are easier to make and sell. The resourceful Papagos followed the latter approach, but the Hopis continued their ancient ways with little modification except improved quality and increased production. Incipient revivals among the Navajos, San Juan Paiutes, and Hualapais suggest that other tribes may also be able to stimulate interest in basketmaking and begin training young weavers. The large number of recent basket exhibitions and publications about baskets indicate a growing appreciation of native American basketry by both whites and Indians. It is apparent that a ready market exists for almost any baskets of high quality, and as long as this continues to be the case, southwestern Indian basketmaking will survive and flourish.

The increasing shortage of native plant materials seriously affects most of the basketmakers in the Southwest. Even plants like yucca, which seems to grow everywhere, are no longer available on all parts of the Papago and Hopi reservations. The San Juan Paiutes and the Hualapais are often forced to travel many miles from their homes to obtain suitable stems of squawberry sumac, and they frequently trade for it or purchase it from other people. The Papagos and Paiutes grow devil's claw in their gardens if water is available, but the Cibecue Apaches gather it wherever they can. Because it is generally not in prime condition, they usually reinforce its color with black dye. As more land comes under cultivation or is turned into pasture for cattle, native plants become more difficult to find. There is a limit to how far basketmakers can travel for collection — even with pickups. Shortages may force them to give up the craft, adopt new materials, or participate in some kind of trading system with people who specialize in gathering and distributing raw materials.

SOUTHWESTERN INDIAN BASKETRY AND FINE ART

In recent years, many Indian artists have achieved recognition, not only in painting and sculpture, but also in the traditional crafts. Various publications (e.g., Windsor 1986) have featured the distinctive and original gold jewelry of James Little (Navajo) and Charles Pratt (Hopi); the unusual lapidary work of Ted Charveze (Isleta Pueblo); the sculptured silver vases of White Buffalo (Comanche); the unconventional pottery created by Jacque Stevens, Tom Polacca, Grace Medicine Flower, and Jody Folwell; the extraordinary wood carving of Dennis Tewa; and the work of many other artist/artisans of the Southwest. Their creations are regarded as so original in conception and so refined in execution that they transcend the boundaries of craft objects and become works of art.

The distinction between fine art and fine crafts has been discussed many times without producing a clear and acceptable definition. The matter is largely academic (semantic), and of no significance in classifying or evaluating particular creations. In any case, the concept of "fine art" came from Europe and had no meaning in traditional Indian life, where everyone's creative talents were employed in the embellishment of mundane objects and the design of ceremonial/religious paraphernalia. But Indian life has changed, and today, most Indians are to some extent part of a culture in which a distinction is made between things that are produced by techniques and designs that are repetitive and conventional, therefore "common," and things that are clearly unusual, innovative, and beyond tradition. Only the latter are considered to be "art," and these qualities, which distinguish the work of the outstanding southwestern potters, jewelers, painters, and sculptors, have been regarded as missing from the native textiles and baskets of the area (Monthan and Monthan 1975).

What does this judgement say about southwestern basketry? In its wealth and brilliance, are there no baskets that possess the qualities of art, none that are innovative and untraditional? How unusual or original would Indian baskets have to be to achieve recognition as art?

These questions might be answered by looking at the creations in basketry that are accepted as works of art in non-Indian society. Although wildly diverse, they seem to possess certain qualities that are esteemed by their creators. One example, by Douglas Fuchs, is a coiled cone 8 1/2 feet high with an 8-foot reed projecting from its tip. The cone is made of "reed, seagrass, [and] telephone wire" decorated with glitter and colored bands of acrylic paint (Malarcher 1984:35). Another, "Untitled Basket" by John McQueen, is a cushion 2 feet square and 7 inches thick made of openwork plaited ash splints stuffed with Spanish moss (Malarcher 1984:40). Others, as different from each other as these two examples, are made of materials that range from ash splints and cherry bark to plastic ribbons and hog casings. Regardless of their materials or shapes, they are all regarded as basketry products because they are "built up by the accumulation of stitchings, interlacings, or crossings" (Malarcher 1984:41; fig. 129) and because the artists define them as such.

If the objects themselves do not define clearly the reasons for their identification as objects of art, their creators are more loquacious, if not always more incisive: "The aim of my art is to make forms with universal emotional impact and spiritual presence, forms which talk about the mysterious process of creation. My circular shapes are a symbol of wholeness and 'innerness' which holds but cannot be seen. The sexual images of a cone and the opening, or split, of a vessel are archetypal" (Jane Sauer, quoted in Malarcher 1984:39). The personal relationship of the artist to her work, as expressed here by Joanne Segal Brandford, is a recurring theme: "My baskets function as objects of contemplation and pleasure, as gifts, as markers of significant events in my life. They do not hold water or food or unanswered mail, what they contain is less tangible but not less real or important (Malarcher 1984:39).

These statements reveal how the artists feel about their work, but they do not explain why their work is art. In "What Makes a Basket a Basket?"

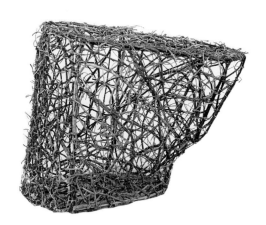

Patricia Malarcher (1984:34) defines this modern basketry-art as "free of function as a determinant of form, not dependent on indigenous plants, and not inhibited by inherited techniques." These negative traits appear to be the distinctive features held in common by the diverse creations of the art form, distinguishing the work of Indian basketmakers from modern basketry-art. Indian basketry embraces precisely what this definition abjures: its forms relate directly to functions, indigenous plants are used exclusively, and the techniques employed are inherited directly from the basketmakers' cultural traditions. It follows that in adhering to traditional ways, the practitioners of southwestern Indian basketry have not explored the esoteric prospect of making baskets for art's sake alone.

Why have basketmakers been so timid, when their relatives who are potters and jewelers are so bold? It may be that most potters and jewelers, as well as painters and sculptors, have had more intimate contact with the non-Indian world than basketweavers have. Metalworking, jewelrymaking, and pottery techniques are taught in off-reservation schools such as the Institute of American Indian Arts in Santa Fe. Some basketmaking is taught in reservation schools, but most basketmakers learn their craft from members of their families, and neither source is likely to expose apprentice weavers to concepts of weaving as a fine art form.

Figure 129. Two pieces by John McQueen, a modern basketry artist who was originally inspired by southwestern Indian baskets. *Left,* the lower edge of the bark collar is split into long fringes that are woven into the apparently random plaiting of the body. 15" high. (Private collection; photo by Roderick Hook.) *Right,* an asymmetrical basket of slender osiers tied in an eccentric open-work pattern. 17" high. (Courtesy Bellas Artes Gallery, Santa Fe.)

At the beginning of the twentieth century, the basketmakers of many southwestern tribes demonstrated that they were capable of extending their craft beyond the boundaries of tradition. When the first tourists arrived in the area and began buying baskets, the Jicarilla Apaches, Hualapais, and others eagerly courted customers with nontraditional baskets they believed would appeal to easterners: compotes with conical bases, sewing boxes with fitted lids, large laundry hampers, basket cups, brimmed hats, fishing creels, and other unusual forms. Bright aniline colors were employed, and baskets were "enhanced" with fancy rims, handles, lids, and other innovations. For a brief period, these creations were successful, and many were purchased by uncritical visitors, but their popularity and production were soon terminated by vociferous criticism from the growing ranks of "Indian basket collectors" and devotees. Influenced by dedicated, opinionated, and energetic people such as George Wharton James, buyers turned away from any baskets that appeared to be derived from Euro-American styles and began to search avidly for old baskets, which they believed reflected the unadulterated native traditions. This led them to the lasting conviction that the only good baskets were old baskets. Even today, most collectors are antiquarians at heart.

This addiction to old baskets and old styles inhibited change in southwestern basketmaking. If baskets were to be acceptable to collectors, museums, and knowledgable traders, they had to be old, or at least look old. Weavers soon learned to imitate, restricting their basket production to traditional forms, techniques, and designs. The tradition-breaking yucca baskets of the Papagos succeeded only because they bypassed the connoisseurs and appealed directly to the mass market. They were cheap, available in quantity, and genuinely Indian. Instead of following tradition, the Papagos established their own, and in recent years the finest examples, elegantly crafted and distinctly original in style, have achieved general acceptance and appreciation.

Even the bold and innovative Papagos were constrained by the economic considerations that affect all Indian basemakers. Most Indian families are poor, and the sale of baskets provides an important source of income. Because sales are so important to them, these Indian artisans are acutely aware of the kinds of baskets that are in demand. Navajo and Paiute women know the exact specifications of construction and design that must be observed to make their wedding baskets acceptable for ceremonial use. Even the best and most independent Hopi weavers understand what designs and shapes will earn them commissions from collectors and bring eager dealers to their door.

Financial returns are important, and some young weavers are determined to support themselves with their baskets. Sally Black (Navajo) is forthright about it when she says, "We're going for the money" (Herold 1984:63). Linda and Mike Guzmán make baskets all day and every day because the work provides a relatively stable income on the Cibecue Apache reservation, where

job opportunities are scarce and wages are low. Although some of these successful basketmakers occasionally experiment with new designs and may be seized at times with a desire to create a completely new and different kind of basket, they are restrained by the knowledge that they would be risking the welfare of their family for their own personal satisfaction (fig. 130). This has occurred, but few basketmakers can afford the luxury of the experience.

The devotion to tradition does not depend solely upon the interests of white antiquarians. Generally, tradition is revered by the basketmakers themselves, linking them to their tribal history, their long-enduring relationships with the gods, and their country. Most of them share a basic sense of contentment in who they are and what they are doing. They welcome changes that

Figure 130. Lydia Pesata, Jicarilla Apache, comes from an eminent family of basket makers. Her baskets are deeply rooted in tradition, although she is willing to experiment with dyes and techniques. (Photo by A. H. Whiteford, 1987.)

will improve life for their families, but not anything that might disturb the feeling of integration that comes from performing ancient rituals, dancing in the ceremonies, and working with kinfolk and neighbors. These sentiments are so deep and rewarding that even university-trained Indians return to their tribal settlements to participate in ceremonies, and most of them cherish the beliefs they acquired in their childhood. To most Indians of the Southwest, tradition is much more than a word.

Many basketmakers speak of the pleasure they find in their work. From the initial gathering and processing of raw materials to the final decoration of the basket rim, it is all done in the company of sisters, cousins, mothers, and neighbors. The women chat, gossip, exchange recipes, talk about their families, plan ceremonial activities, and often comment on each other's work. Basketmaking companions are the first and often the most important group of judges that a weaver tries to please. As good artisans, they praise excellent work and withhold praise when baskets do not meet their standards. For the younger workers, encouragement is usually mixed with advice. In many cases, the work group includes the mother, aunt, or mother-in-law who first taught the weaver to make baskets, and their praise and acceptance is especially treasured. Older women, the teachers who themselves learned from the preceding generation, exert a powerful influence for the maintenance of tradition and against strange or different designs and techniques. Among the Hopis, for example, refinement of stitching, enrichment of colors, and slight modification and enhancement of designs have been accepted without disturbing the continuity of tradition. Any innovations beyond these would arouse criticism, severely limiting the pleasure the women derive from their basketry.

The old ways are retained principally because Indians like them, and not just for the trade. This is evident in the many baskets that the Hopis and other people make for their own use in ceremonies and to give to their friends on special occasions. If anything, these baskets tend to be even more traditional than those made for sale. In some tribes, adherence to tradition provides a sense of continuity, reducing the weavers' fears that their beloved craft might be waning and may soon disappear — a pervading concern, and one that is not conducive to energetic experimentation and innovation.

Basketmakers take deep interest in each other's work and in the work of weavers in other tribes. Participation in crafts fairs and demonstrations, museum visits, reading, and travel have made many of them keenly aware of other types of Indian baskets and designs. Sometimes, as with the San Juan Paiutes and some Navajos, they admire the designs of other tribes and incorporate them into their own work. Such opportunities are open to almost all Indian basketmakers in the Southwest. Those who continue to work only within the bounds of their own tribal aesthetic do so not out of ignorance of other ways but because it is the most satisfying and productive thing for them to do.

Very few Indian basketmakers have seen or even heard about basketry art forms such as those created by Joanne Segal Brandford, Ed Rossbach, John McQueen, or Douglas Fuchs. If they have seen the creations of such modern artists, they probably did not recognize them as related in any way to the baskets they are making themselves. When or if native Americans start making basketry sculpture, they will be participating in a culture different from their own. In the meantime, traditional patterns of basketmaking will persist, and perhaps flourish, among the Indians of the Southwest.

Appendix:
The School of American Research Collection of Southwestern Indian Baskets

The School of American Research collection contains nearly six hundred southwestern baskets. Of these, more than half were donated to the School by the Indian Arts Fund (IAF), founded in 1922 as the Indian Pottery Fund by Harry P. Mera, Wesley Bradfield, Kenneth M. Chapman, and Elizabeth Shepley Sargeant. A few of the early members of the IAF were professional anthropologists, but participants from many backgrounds helped to build the collection, largely because they feared that the activities of eastern museums and collectors would soon leave the Southwest barren of its native arts.

The fund was incorporated in 1925. By 1972, when it disbanded, the IAF had acquired nearly six thousand artifacts. Some people contributed money to buy Indian art, while others gave pieces from their own collections. Pottery and textiles were acquired directly from Indian artists. Old specimens were sought out, and museum personnel and professional traders contributed their guidance and expertise. The IAF began deeding the collection to the School of American Research (SAR) in 1966, and in 1978 it was gathered together from various depositories and stored in the new Indian Arts Research Center, which had been built to house it.

There is some evidence that the IAF kept records of its acquisitions, but if they have survived, they unfortunately have not been found. As a result, most of the collection is undocumented. Baskets were not a major interest of the IAF: only a few of them can be attributed to a particular donor, and even fewer are accompanied by any collection data. The tribal identifications assigned to many of the baskets are those attributed to them by the IAF. I carefully reviewed these identifications during this study and changed a number of them on the basis of typological evaluations.

Part of the SAR collection was acquired through the donation of three private collections that included many baskets. Harry P. Mera, a Laboratory of Anthropology archaeologist who, from 1930 on, conducted extensive excavations in the Rio Grande Valley and other parts of New Mexico, gave a large collection to the School in 1941. There is no information to indicate which baskets in his collection were purchased from secondary sources and which he might have collected in the field.

Two other substantial collections were contributed by the families of trader/collectors who operated shops on the plaza in Santa Fe and were active participants in the early activities of the IAF. When the collection of one of these traders, J. F. Collins, was given to SAR in 1962, his wife, Elsie H. Collins, noted that it had been "collected in the 1920s." Aside from this important scrap of information, there is nothing further to indicate where or from whom the materials might have been acquired. It seems unlikely that Collins actually collected his baskets on the reservations, but it is not impossible. The fine collection from the other trader, Harold J. Gans, probably came from his inventory when his shop was closed. Although he probably maintained some records of his acquisitions, none has been preserved.

Other baskets, again without documentation, came from the estates of Amelia E. White, Margretta Dietrich, and Margaret Moses. Among the few baskets with acceptable documentation are a number of modern specimens collected and donated by Sallie R. Wagner, and a few that were purchased at the time of this study. The William Beaver collection of more than one hundred modern San Juan Paiute baskets, purchased in 1986, is completely documented and will be a valuable resource in the future.

As a whole, the SAR collection is strongest in baskets dating from the early decades of the twentieth century. It includes a good selection of classic Western Apache and Jicarilla Apache baskets, and a fine group of early Navajo baskets. One of its best segments consists of Pima coiled baskets, mostly from the Harold J. Gans collection. The Mera collection included some early Havasupai trays. The School has some typical Hualapai trade baskets, but no documented Yavapai baskets. The Hopi and Rio Grande Pueblo segment of the collection is rather meager, and except for baskets of the San Juan Paiutes, baskets made since 1935 are sparsely represented. In spite of its uneven distribution, the collection contains some excellent and some very fine representative baskets from most of the tribes in the Southwest.

The identifications presented here should be regarded as my best judgement, based upon the original identification, close comparison with documented baskets in other collections, examination of ethnological and historic documents, photographs, and illustrations, and many discussions with basketmakers and basket enthusiasts. I believe the majority of the identifications are correct and can be accepted with confidence, but the basis for the identifications should be taken into consideration. In some cases I have noted my own doubts and suggested an alternative identification. With this information at hand, those who peruse this list may gain some insights and possibly some assistance in identifying undocumented baskets in their own collections.

This appendix lists the southwestern Indian baskets housed in the Indian Arts Research Center at the School of American Research in Santa Fe and catalogued before 1987. An exception is the William Beaver collection of San Juan Paiute baskets, which the School purchased after its exhibition at the Wheelwright Museum of the American Indian. These baskets are described and illustrated in the catalogue for the exhibition (McGreevy and Whiteford 1985).

For each of the other baskets in the SAR collection, the following information is provided: tribal affiliation (documented or ascribed); type of basket (tray, olla, bottle, etc.); SAR catalogue number (illustrated baskets are marked with an asterisk); page number of photograph; dimensions in inches (diameter, diameter x height, or length x width x height, depending on the number of measurements given); type of construction; number of coils per inch (c/in); number of stitches per inch (st/in); shape; details of construction (rim, start, etc.); shape; weaving materials; decorative design and technique; collection data where available; name of donor; and date of acquisition.

PAIUTE BASKETS

Coiled Bowls

Unless noted otherwise, these bowls are coiled with three bunched rods, sewn with sumac stitching, and made for the Navajos with the traditional wedding basket design in dyed splints and a herringbone rim.

B.95 11" x 3.5", 5 c/in, 14–15 st/in. Gift of Flora W. Conrad. 1932.

B.143 15.5" x 3", 3.5 c/in, 14 st/in. Stacked open diamonds, one group faded red, the other blue-black. Identified as Ute by donor. Gift of H. P. Mera for Julia M. Ives collection. 1941.

B.229 5.75" x 1.5", 4 c/in, 9 st/in. Probably wedding basket design, badly faded. Identified as Ute by donor. H. P. Mera collection. 1941.

B.233 14" x 3.25", 4 c/in, 12 st/in. Identified as Ute by donor. H. P. Mera collection. 1941.

B.234 16.25" x 3.25", 2 c/in, 14 st/in. Identified as Ute by donor. H. P. Mera collection. 1941.

B.343 13.5" x 3.75", 3.5 c/in, 12 st/in. Gift of Mrs. Gerald Cassidy. 1962.

*B.368 (p. 35) 17.5" x 3.25", 3 c/in, 11–12 st/in. Wedding basket design with narrow band. J. F. Collins collection. 1962.

*B.369 (p. 22) 7" x 3.5", 3 c/in, 12 st/in. J. F. Collins collection. 1962.

B.370 16.25" x 4.5", 2.5 c/in, 13–14 st/in. J. F. Collins collection. 1962.

B.371 15.5" x 3", 3 c/in, 12 st/in. J. F. Collins collection. 1962.

B.372 15.5" x 3", 4.5 c/in, 12 st/in. J. F. Collins collection. 1962.

B.374 14.5" x 3", 4 c/in, 10–11 st/in. J. F. Collins collection. 1962.

1978-4-34 13.25" x 3.75", 4 c/in, 12 st/in. Harold J. Gans collection. 1978.

1978-4-35 12.75" x 2.75", 3 rods, 4.5 c/in, 11–12 st/in. Harold J. Gans collection. 1978.

1978-4-36 12.75" x 3.25", 4–5 c/in, 12–13 st/in. Harold J. Gans collection. 1978.

1978-4-38 13.75" x 3.5", 3 c/in, 10–11 st/in. Variation of wedding basket design. Harold J. Gans collection. 1978.

*1981-25-5 (p. 35) 15" x 3.5", 2.5 c/in, 9 st/in. Central cloth plug. Gift of Sallie Wagner. 1981.

*1984-21-1 (p. 27) 19" x 3.5", 2.5 c/in, 11 st/in. Sumac stitches. White lines separating red-brown quadrants, each with large white cross; ticked rim with black, red, white. Made by Rose Ann Whiskers in 1983, Hidden Springs, Arizona. Purchased from Sacred Mountain Trading Post. 1984.

1984-21-2 10.5" x 5", 2 c/in, 4 st/in. Globular bowl, three-rod stacked, spaced sumac stitches, spaced triangles and spots of devil's claw, crisscross rim stitching. Made by Mable Lehi, Hidden Springs, Arizona. Purchased from Sacred Mountain Trading Post. 1984.

1984-21-3 9" x 10", 2 c/in, 5 st/in. Deep jar, straight sides, wide mouth, three stacked rods, spaced sumac stitches, plain with yellow mottled areas. Made by Marie Lehi, Hidden Springs, Arizona. Purchased from Sacred Mountain Trading Post. 1984.

1984-21-4 12.5" x 2.5", 2.5 c/in, 4 st/in. Flat-based shallow bowl, spaced stitches, added two-strand black and brown crisscross on rim. Made by Mabel Lehi in 1983, Hidden Springs, Arizona. Purchased from Sacred Mountain Trading Post. 1984.

Water Jars and Bottles

These baskets are coiled with two stacked rods unless noted otherwise.

B.16 10" x 10", 3 c/in, 4 st/in. Globular body, spaced stitching, two carrying loops of twisted wood splints wrapped with splints. Formerly pitched on both surfaces. IAF. 1930.

*1984-4-23 (p. 21) 11.25" x 14.25", 3 c/in, 5 st/in. Globular body, vertical neck, spaced stitching, diagonal lashed rim. Two loops of braided horsehair strands. Originally pitched inside and out. Margaret Moses estate. 1984.

1984-4-24 10.5" x 11.75", 3.5–4 c/in, 7–8 st/in. Globular body, vertical neck, rim crisscrossed, canvas patch on base. Two loops of three or four horsehair braids. Originally pitched inside and out. Margaret Moses estate. 1984.

Twined Burden Basket

B.391 18" x 15.5". Subconical burden basket, twill twined with three bands of plain twine, one below the double rim (a willow rod and lower bundle of bark fibers). Two buckskin loops. J. F. Collins collection. 1962.

NAVAJO BASKETS

Coiled Tray/Bowls

Unless noted otherwise, these baskets are coiled with two rods and a fiber bundle, stitched with sumac, and decorated with natural dyes. The rims are flat and finished with herringbone false-braid. Designs have a "spirit opening" at the end of the final coil.

B.198 10.5" x 3", 4 c/in, 10 st/in. Deep red band edged with black. H. P. Mera collection. 1941.

B.199   12" x 4", 3 c/in, 7 st/in. Four-armed Maltese cross outlined in red and black. Cloth plug in start. H. P. Mera collection. 1941.

B.200   12.5" x 3.75", 3.5 c/in, 10–11 st/in. Broad russet zigzag band with central eight-pointed star. H. P. Mera collection. 1941.

B.230   11.75" x 3", 4 c/in, 12 st/in. Terraced red band outlined in black, cloth plug in start. H. P. Mera collection. 1941.

B.231   12.75" x 3.25", 4 c/in, 12 st/in. Red band edged with black line and spaced crosses. H. P. Mera collection. 1941.

*B.232   (p. 36) 13.75" x 4.25", 4 c/in, 18–19 st/in. Four large red block crosses outlined with black. Identified as Ute by donor. H. P. Mera collection. 1941.

B.237   5" x 1.5", 5 c/in, 13 st/in. Three radiating triangular red vanes outlined in black. H. P. Mera collection. 1941.

*B.238   (p. 36) 12.25" x 3.25", 6 c/in, 12 st/in. Six-armed black and red whirlwind design. H. P. Mera collection. 1941.

B.239   12.75" x 2.75", 5–6 c/in, 11 st/in. Four stepped diamonds with alternate quarters in red and black. H. P. Mera collection. 1941.

B.240   9.5" x 2.75", 5.5 c/in, 10–11 st/in. Red band edged with black triangles. H. P. Mera collection. 1941.

B.241   10.75" x 3", 4.5–5 c/in, 12 st/in. Red band outlined with black and divided into four quadrants. Cloth plug in start. H. P. Mera collection. 1941.

B.242   11.25" x 5", 5 c/in, 9 st/in. Dark red band outlined with black line and spaced right-angle hooks. H. P. Mera collection. 1941.

B.243   10.25" x 3.25", 4 c/in, 11 st/in. Three diagonal lines of red rectangles outlined in black. H. P. Mera collection. 1941.

B.244   10.25" x 3.25", 5 c/in, 11 st/in. Design very faded, resembles wedding-basket pattern. H. P. Mera collection. 1941.

B.245   11" x 3", 4.5 c/in, 10–11 st/in. Whirlwind of six red and black lines curving counterclockwise. Carved wood plug in start hole. H. P. Mera collection. 1941.

B.246   11.25" x 3", 4 c/in, 13–14 st/in. Zigzag band of rectangles, red outlined with black. H. P. Mera collection. 1941.

B.247   11.75" x 3.75", 4.5 c/in, 11 st/in. Band of red diamonds outlined with black blocks. H. P. Mera collection. 1941.

B.248   12.5" x 3", 5 c/in, 11–12 st/in. Three red block crosses outlined with black. H. P. Mera collection. 1941.

B.249   12.75" x 4", 5 c/in, 10 st/in. Four black and red double-stepped triangles. H. P. Mera collection. 1941.

*B.250   (p. 36) 11.75" x 4", 6 c/in, 14 st/in. Red band outlined with black line and hourglass figures. H. P. Mera collection. 1941.

*B.251   (p. 36) 12.5" x 4.5", 5.5 c/in, 14 st/in. Broad zigzag red band outlined with black. H. P. Mera collection. 1941.

B.252   12.75" x 4.5", 3 c/in, 13 st/in. Three block crosses, each arm divided diagonally into red and black halves. H. P. Mera collection. 1941.

B.253   15.5" x 4.5", 6 c/in, 12 st/in. Four red and black terraces producing a four-point star. H. P. Mera collection. 1941.

*B.266   (p. 37) 18" x 6", 6.5 c/in, 12 st/in. Two bands of interlocking terraced triangles, red edged with black. "Found in cave in the mountains west of Cochiti Pueblo." Possibly early Pueblo. IAF purchase from T. Harmon Parkhurst for Mary Austin collection. 1943.

*B.267   (p. 37) 20" x 6.5", 4 c/in, 14 st/in. Asymmetric bands of red terraced forms outlined with black. Color affected by fire. IAF purchase from Joseph Grubbs, White Mound Trading Post, Houck, Arizona, for Mary Austin collection. 1943.

B.276   13.5" x 4", 4 c/in, 12 st/in. Broad rust-red zigzag band outlined in black, central nine-pointed star. IAF purchase from War Bond Exchange for Mary Austin collection. 1945.

B.278   12.75" x 3.5", 5 c/in, 11 st/in. Broad red band with black outline and four terraced notches on each edge, broad "spirit path." Gift of H. P. Mera. 1946.

B.352   14.5" x 3.5", 5 c/in, 12 st/in. Four red rhomboidal vanes outlined in black forming whirlwind design. Gift of Mrs. Joseph M. Sundt. 1962.

B.373   14.5" x 3", 4 c/in, 10 st/in. Red band bordered with black terraces and red and black crosses on outer edge. J. F. Collins collection. 1962.

B.375   13" x 3.5", 5 c/in, 11 st/in. Zigzag red band with black outine forming five-pointed star. Yucca fiber plug in center hole. J. F. Collins collection. 1962.

B.376   11" x 2.75", 4 c/in, 12 st/in. Two open, rounded four-pointed stars, one inside the other, outlined with purple-black and russet rectangles. J. F. Collins collection. 1962.

B.377   11" x 3.25", 8 c/in, 16 st/in. Faded red zigzag band outlined in black. J. F. Collins collection. 1962.

B.378   9.5" x 2.25", 5 c/in, 11–12 st/in. Faded red band edged with black line and terraced triangles. J. F. Collins collection. 1962.

B.379 9.75" x 3.25", 4 c/in, 10 st/in. Narrow red band with black terraced triangles on both edges. J. F. Collins collection. 1962.

1978-4-27 12" x 3", 4 c/in, 10 st/in. Faded wedding-basket design. Harold J. Gans collection. 1978.

1978-4-28 12.25" x 2.5", 4 c/in, 9 st/in. Faded red band edged with black. Harold J. Gans collection. 1978.

1978-4-29 14" x 5", 3 c/in, 8 st/in. Open Maltese cross outlined in red and black. Harold J. Gans collection. 1978.

1978-4-30 12" x 3.5", 4 c/in, 12 st/in. Wedding-basket design, cotton fabric plug in center hole. Harold J. Gans collection. 1978.

1978-4-33 11.5" x 4.25", 4.5 c/in, 10–11 st/in. Broad red zigzag band edged with black. Twisted bundle. Harold J. Gans collection. 1978.

1978-4-36 12.75" x 3.25", 4 c/in, 9 st/in. Wedding-basket design, cotton cloth plug in center hole. Harold J. Gans collection. 1978.

1978-4-37 12.5" x 3.25", 3 c/in, 10 st/in. Four faded red crosses outlined in black, white wool plug in center hole. Harold J. Gans collection. 1978.

1981-25-6 13.5" x 4", 5 c/in, 12 st/in. Three red Spider Woman crosses with black outline and rectangles at corners. Gift of Sallie Wagner. 1981.

1981-25-7 8" x 1.5", 2.5 c/in, 9–11 st/in. Crude plate with black terraced triangles. Gift of Sallie Wagner. 1981.

*1982-5-4 (p. 67) 24" x 5", 2 c/in, 8 st/in. Five rods, white sumac with ten radiating *yei* figures in red, black, blue-green. Made by Sally Black of Medicine Hat, Utah. Purchased from Packard's Trading Post. 1982.

1984-4-30 13" x 3", 4 c/in, 7 st/in. Four red and black diamonds. Margaret Moses estate. 1984.

*1984-13-1 (p. 43) 18" x 9", 2 c/in, 10 st/in. Five rods, three black, spread-wing birds, and four black crosses with red centers. Purchased at Shonto Trading Post, maker unrecorded. 1984.

Coiled Jars

B.324 13.25" x 16.25", 4 c/in, 6 st/in. Three stacked rods. Globular body, tall cylindrical neck, diagonal lashed rim, coated with red ochre, pitched inside and out, thick horsehair carrying strap. Gift of Cornelia Thompson. 1956.

*1984-8-1 (p. 44) 5.75" x 7", 2 c/in, 4–5 st/in. Three stacked, unscraped sumac rods, spaced splint stitching, zigzag band of red-brown dyed splints. Lightly pitched inside and out. Two thin braided horsehair loops. Gift of Garrick and Roberta Bailey, purchased at Carson Trading Post, which acquired it from Shonto Trading Post. 1984.

*1984-21-5 (p. 44) 6.25" x 8.25", 2.5 c/in, 3 st/in. Pear shaped, coiled with bundle of flat willow splints, narrow spaced stitches. Lightly pitched inside and out. Made by Mei Bedone. Purchased at Shonto Trading Post. 1984.

JICARILLA APACHE BASKETS

These baskets have thick, smooth coils with three- or five-rod bunched foundations; noninterlocking stitching, generally with sumac splints; and mostly, herringbone rims. They are decorated with aniline and/or vegetal colors. Fag ends are often layed diagonally under the following stitches.

Bowl/Trays

Circular, shallow, round or flat bottoms, often large with flaring sides.

*B.69 (p. 51) 21" x 6.5", 3 thick rods, 3 c/in, 7 st/in. Vegetal brown "sunburst" and zigzag band. IAF. 1930.

B.70 21" x 7", 3 thick rods, 2.5 c/in, 6 st/in. Flat base, band of vegetal red-brown hexagonal figures. IAF. 1930.

B.71 18" x 5.5", 3 rods, 3 c/in, 7 st/in. Two brown bands with yellow rectangles, vegetal colors. IAF. 1930.

B.78 17.5" x 4.5", 5 rods, 2 c/in, 6 st/in. Terraced diamonds and triangles in aniline orange, red, blue. IAF, from D. M. Bacalski. 1930.

B.119 16.5" x 7", 3 rods, 3 c/in, 8 st/in. Coiled ring-base on bottom, bands of aniline red, green, brown. Gift of Dorothea K. Conrad. 1933.

B.132 18" x 4.5", 3 rods, 3 c/in, 8 st/in. Decoration entirely faded. Gift of Mary Cabot Wheelwright, said to have been used at Taos in "Maiden Ceremony" to hold corn meal. 1938.

B.156 18" x 6.75", 3 rods, 3 c/in, 7 st/in. Four vertical rows of faded vegetal brown crosses. From Old Santa Fe Trading Post for Mary Austin collection. 1941.

B.164 11.25" x 3.75", 3 rods, 3.5 c/in, 5 st/in. Stacked bars and triangles of vegetal brown. H. P. Mera collection. 1941.

B.165 13.75" x 3", 3 rods, 3.5 c/in, 6.5 st/in. Large terraced vegetal brown diamonds. H. P. Mera collection. 1941.

B.166 21.5" x 5.5", 3 rods, 3 c/in, 7 st/in. Figures of deer in vegetal brown with aniline purple triangles. H. P. Mera collection. 1941.

B.167 20" x 7", 3 rods, 3 c/in, 8 st/in. Four large rectangles in vegetal brown. H. P. Mera collection. 1941.

B.168 18.75" x 7.75", 5 rods, 2 c/in, 6 st/in. Four large vegetal brown crosses with one blue triangle. H. P. Mera collection. 1941.

*B.169 (p. 51) 20" x 9.5", 3 rods, 3 c/in, 7 st/in. Four deer between three rectangular vanes in vegetal brown. H. P. Mera collection. 1941.

B.280 18" x 5.75", 3 rods, 2.5 c/in, 6 st/in. Complex open design on vegetal brown central Maltese cross. IAF purchase for Mary Austin collection, from Old Santa Fe Trading Post. 1949.

B.287 17.75" x 4.75", 3 rods, 2 c/in, 7 st/in. Four terraced diamonds and triangles in red and green aniline colors. IAF purchase from the Arthur Seligman estate. 1954.

*B.288 (p. 69) 19.5" x 6.5", 3 rods, 2.5 c/in, 7 st/in. Three red and green (aniline) trianguloid vanes with red diamonds and crosses. IAF purchase from Arthur Seligman estate. 1954.

B.289 21.5" x 7.5", 3 rods, 2.5 c/in, 7 st/in. Five vegetal russet deer or horses. IAF purchase from Arthur Seligman estate. 1954.

B.320 8.25" x 2", 3 rods, 2.5 c/in, 8 st/in. Brown bands and central yellow (willow) disk. Gift of Dorothea K. Conrad. 1957.

B.361 17.5" x 6.5", 5 rods, 2.5 c/in, 8 st/in. Zigzag bands of aniline red, yellow, green rectangles, two handles made by pulling out rim coil. J. F. Collins collection. 1962.

B.362 16.25" x 6", 3 rods, 3 c/in, 6–7 st/in. Four swirling lines of aniline black and red rectangles. J. F. Collins collection. 1962.

B.363 15.75" x 4.75", 3 rods. Four sets of terraced blue diamonds with red borders, J. F. Collins collection. 1962.

B.364 20.5" x 17.75" x 6.25", 5 rods, 2 c/in, 6–7 st/in. Oval shape, red aniline red rim and eight vertical diamonds outlined with blue, remains of two loop handles. J. F. Collins collection. 1962.

1978-1-155 18" x 5.25", 5 rods, 2.25 c/in, 7 st/in. Five large faded terraced diamonds: yellow, red, blue-green. Green center. Amelia White collection. 1978.

1978-1-256 17" x .5", 5 rods, 2 c/in, 6–7 st/in. Flat plaque with four aniline red, green, purple, orange, rectanguloid figures radiating from center. Amelia White collection. 1978.

1978-1-257 16.5" x 5", 5 rods, 2 c/in, 6–8 st/in. Faded aniline red, green, purple crosses and triangles. Amelia White collection. 1978.

1978-4-31 9" x 2.5", 3 rods, 4 c/in, 8 st/in. Aniline yellow, blue, red bands, red cross painted at center. Remnants of mush. Harold J. Gans collection. 1978.

1978-4-32 9.5" x 3.25", 3 rods, 3–4 c/in, 7 st/in.

Four groups of small red and blue-black crosses (faded). Harold J. Gans collection. 1978.

1978-4-39 16.5" x 4.5", 3 rods, 3 c/in, 7 st/in. Four tan and purple aniline square crosses. Harold J. Gans collection. 1978.

1978-4-40 18.75" x 7", 3 rods, 2.5 c/in, 7 st/in. Aniline red and blue rectangles. Harold J. Gans collection. 1978.

1982-11-3 15" x 5", 3 rods, 3 c/in, 6 st/in. Three vegetal brown crosses with corner "ears." Gift of Mary Worman. 1982.

1983-7-1 16.5" x 5", 5 rods, 2 c/in, 6 st/in. Alternating aniline red and blue rectangles. Gift of Beatrice Chauvenet. 1983.

1984-2-1 4.25" x .25", 3 rods, 5 c/in, 8–9 st/in. Miniature, stitched with "boiled" willow, four stepped diamonds in black, white, red. Made by Lydia Pesata for A. H. Whiteford. 1984.

*1984-3-1 (p. 69) 13.5" x 2", 3 rods, 3 c/in, 10 st/in. Nine-point star at center outlined in red, with yellow, blue, and red heart-shaped figures in yellow. Made by Bertha Velarde. 1983.

*1984-6-1 (p. 54) 11.5" x 4", 3 rods, 4.5 c/in, 7–8 st/in. Open triangles and Vs in black and russet-brown. Made by Melissa Pesata on commission. 1984.

Deep Bowls with Straight Sides and Flat Bases

B.54 9" x 5.5", 3 rods, 3.5 c/in, 6–7 st/in. Slightly flaring sides, vertical diamonds and crosses in red and blue-green. IAF. 1930.

B.365 12" x 8.75" x 7.5", 5 rods, 2.5 c/in, 7 st/in. Oval with vertical sides, bands of open rectangles and terraced diamonds, faded green and red. Gift of Elsie H. Collins. 1962.

Jars and Bottles

These coiled water jars are pitched only on the inside and coated with white clay (kaolin) on the outside. The bodies are globular, and the necks are wide and quite vertical. Carrying loops are of horsehair.

B.140 10" x 9.25", 3 rods, 3 c/in, 6 st/in. Two pairs of long buckskin thongs, braided horsehair carrying loops, base covered with pitch-covered denim patch. Purchased by K. M. Chapman from Ralph Atencio, Jr., for the Mary Austin collection. 1940.

*B.163 (p. 53) 12" x 12.5", 3 rods, 3 c/in, 6 st/in. Two horsehair and sinew carrying loops on shoulder, four vertical lines of overstitching. H. P. Mera collection. 1941.

B.441 13.75" x 11.75", 3 rods, 2.5 c/in, 6 st/in. Two horsehair loops wrapped with cloth, base patch of denim, four vertical lines of overstitching, five pairs of buckskin thongs. Gift of John Gaw Meem. 1964.

Unusual Jars and Bottles

These jars and bottles, which were made for sale, are decorated with colored designs and have added handles and ring bases. They are not pitched.

B.290 12.5" x 14", 3 rods, 3 c/in, 7 st/in. Globose body and flaring neck, decorated with aniline red, yellow, and green wavy bands and six-pointed blue star on base. Two horsehair carrying loops wrapped with splints. IAF purchase from Arthur Seligman estate. 1954.

B.295 4.5" x 4.75", 3 rods, 6 c/in, 7 st/in. Small, undecorated, unpitched olla, herringbone rim, diagonal fag ends, subconical base. Purchased from Seligman estate. 1954.

*B.366 (p. 50) 12" x 15", 5 rods, 2.5 c/in, 7 st/in. Pitcher shape with globose body, straight neck with single loop handle, flaring ring base, concentric rectangles in red, orange, and green. J. F. Collins collection. 1962.

B.367 11" body diameter, 4.5" rim diameter x 15", 3 rods, 2.5 c, 7 st/in. Pitcher shape similar to B.366, band of large terraced diamonds in aniline orange, red, brown. J. F. Collins collection. 1962.

Large Cylindrical "Laundry Hampers"

All of these baskets have flat bases, most have two opposing handles, and some have flat, fitted covers or lids.

B.118 18" x 21.5", 5 rods, 2 c/in, 7 st/in. No lid, loop handles made with rim coil, zigzag band of red and blue aniline colors. Gift of Dorothea K. Conrad. 1933.

B.341 14.5" x 20", 5 rods, 2 c/in, 6–7 st/in. Fitted lid with overlapping edge, two rectangular openings for handles, broad zigzag bands of red, green, brown. Gift of Mrs. Gerald Cassidy. 1962.

1978-1-128 15.75" x 19.75", 5 rods, 2.25 c/in, 7.5 st/in. All-over pattern of interlocking terraced diamonds in blue, red, orange; two hole handles, no lid. From Amelia White estate. 1978.

*1978-1-129 (p. 68) 18.5" x 26.5", 5 rods, 2 c/in, 7 st/in. Lid with overlapping rim, two rectangular hole handles, five vertical rows of stepped diamonds in aniline red and blue with enclosed red crosses. Amelia White estate. 1978.

1979-6-53 9" x 12", 5 rods, 2.25 c/in, 8 st/in. Two loop handles, design of large diamonds or "butterflies" in faded aniline brown, red, green, orange. Gift of Mable Morrow estate. 1979.

MESCALERO APACHE BASKETS

Unless noted otherwise, these baskets are coiled with two sumac rods stacked above each other and topped with a bundle of yucca or grass fibers. Each stitch of yucca splits the stitch below and interlocks with half of it. They are decorated with yucca of various shades and deep red yucca root.

Bowl/Trays

Circular and shallow, with round bottoms and lashed rims.

B.159 16" x 4", sides of slat and bundle coils, base of one rod and bundle, 2.5 c/in, 8 st/in. Four yellow terraced diamonds outlined with red. H. P. Mera collection. 1941.

B.160 14" x 2", 2.5 c/in, 9–10 st/in. Five-pointed white star outlined with red. H. P. Mera collection. 1941.

B.161 16.25" x 2.25", 2–2.5 c/in, 7–8 st/in. Large five-pointed star outlined in red and ochre-yellow. H. P. Mera collection. 1941.

*B.162 (p. 58) 17.5" x 3", 2.5 c/in, 10–11 st/in. Large five-pointed star of ochre yucca outlined with red. H. P. Mera collection. 1941.

B.286 14" x 2", 2.5 c/in, 10–11 st/in. Four sets of ochre-yellow terraced triangles outlined in red and four small red crosses. Purchased from T. Harmon Parkhurst. 1951.

B.291 21" x 5.5", 1 rod with bundle, 2.5 c/in, 9 st/in. Large four-armed terraced cross outlined in red with four small red crosses inset. Purchased from the Arthur Seligman estate. 1954.

*B.323 (p. 58) 19.75" x 4", 2.25 c/in, 9 st/in. Open four-pointed star and red terraced diamonds. Gift of Amelia E. White. 1958.

B.380 16.25" x 2.5", 2–2.5 c/in, 9–11 st/in. Large five-pointed star and pendant triangles in yellow ochre outlined with red. Gift of Elsie H. Collins. 1962.

B.381 17.5" x 4.5", 2 c/in, 5–7 st/in. Green rectangles around rim and outlining large four-pointed star. J. F. Collins collection. 1962.

1978-1-53 16.25" x 2.25", 2 c/in, 7 st/in. Yellow four-pointed star outlined with red, intervening triangles. Amelia White estate. 1978.

1979-6-71 9" x 1", two rods and bundle bunched, 3 c/in, 7 st/in. Whirlwind design of tan blocks on yellow. Mable Morrow estate. 1979.

Deep Baskets with Vertical Sides and Flat Bases

Unless noted otherwise, these baskets are coiled with wood slats or heavy sumac rods topped with a bundle of yucca fibers and sewn with yucca splints.

*B.127 (p. 58) 14" x 8" x 8.25", 1.75 c/in, 7–8 st/in. Oval shape with a flat lid. The sides are vertical and made of slats about .75" wide. The lid and bottom are coiled with thick rods (.5" diameter). Broad zigzag band of ochre yellow with red spots. Gift of Amelia White. 1937.

B.158 7" x 9", 2.75 c/in, 8 st/in. One split rod and bundle, cylindrical with slightly flaring sides, no lid. Large red terraced diamonds and small crosses. H. P. Mera collection. 1941.

Deep Twined Baskets

*B.326 (p. 60) 14.5" x 14.5". Twill twined with sumac splints, no reinforcing rods, single rim rod (now missing), three bands of painted red diagonal lines encircled with conical metal dangles below rim and near the base. Identified as Chiricahua. Bequest of Margretta Dietrich. 1961.

WESTERN APACHE BASKETS

Coiled Trays and/or Bowls

These baskets are mostly circular and shallow with round bases. Some are deeper, and a few have flat bases. Their construction is three rods bunched sewn with fine willow splints, and they are decorated with splints of devil's claw and occasionally with red yucca root. Tondo and rim coils are usually of black devil's claw.

*B.18 (p. 80) 19.25" x 3.75", 5 c/in, 16–17 st/in. Interlocking triangles enclosing negative and positive crosses. IAF. 1930.

B.19 16" x 4.5", 5 c/in, 13–14 st/in. Radiating curved lines of black triangles. IAF. 1930.

B.39 13.25" x 4", 5 c/in, 9–10 st/in. Broad three-petaled open figures outlined with black rectangles, also triangular "fox heads," touches of red. IAF. 1930.

B.142 14" x 3.75", 6 c/in, 17 st/in. Central four-petal figure, interlocking triangles of black and white with negative crosses and human and animal figures in the black triangles. The style suggests that it may be Yavapai. H. P. Mera gift to Julia M. Ives collection. 1941.

B.157 15" x 4.75", 5 c/in, 13 st/in. Four pairs of checked diamonds, black and white rim. Purchase from Fred Wilson of Phoenix for Mary Austin collection, identified as San Carlos. 1941.

B.170 12" x 4.75", 6 c/in, 14 st/in. Interlocked open five-petaled figures. H. P. Mera collection. 1941.

B.171 17.5" x 4.75", 5–6 c/in, 11 st/in. Pattern of broad-line radiating rectangular zigzags. H. P. Mera collection. 1941.

B.172 15.5" x 3", 5 c/in, 9–10 st/in. Open four-petaled figure outlined with black triangles. H. P. Mera collection. 1941.

*B.173 (p. 81) 17.5" x 4.5", 6 c/in, 14 st/in. Band of open diamonds with circling zigzag lines below rim. H. P. Mera collection. 1941.

B.174 15.5" x 3.5", 3 c/in, 15 st/in. Composite pattern with meander below rim and five-petaled star at center. H. P. Mera collection. 1941.

*B.175 (p. 80) 21" x 5.5", 6.5 c/in, 8–9 st/in. Five-petaled open design. H. P. Mera collection. 1941.

*B.176 (p. 81) 23.5" x 6.75", 5 c/in, 9 st/in. Overlapping open five-petaled figures with black triangles pendant from rim. H. P. Mera collection. 1941.

B.275 8.5" x 3", 6.5 c/in, 7–9 st/in. Deeply indented angular meander of five parallel lines. Purchased for Mary Austin collection. 1945.

B.299 22.5" x 5.75", 6 c/in, 10 st/in. Rim band of diagonal rows of triangles with central band of three lines in angular meander. Rawhide patch on base. IAF purchase from Arthur Seligman estate. 1954.

*B.304 (p. 11) 17.12" x 10.12", 4 c/in, 10–11 st/in. Deep bowl with flat base and straight flaring sides, lines of checked diamonds, and red and black figures of animals, birds, and humans, some with horns. Gift of Amelia E. White. 1955.

B.331 15.5" x 3.5", 5 c/in, 11–12 st/in. Overlapping open four-petaled figures inset with checked diamonds, crosses, birds (?). Bequest of Margretta S. Dietrich. 1961.

*B.382 (p. 98) 22.5" x 4.75", 4 c/in, 15 st/in. Central figure of radiating lines ending in triangles, outer band of large black diamonds inset with figures of animals and humans. J. F. Collins collection. 1952.

*B.383 (p. 71) 22.75" x 5", 4 c/in, 13 st/in. Nine radiating lines of triangles and/or diamonds with animal and human figues in open rectangles. J. F. Collins collection. 1962.

B.384 20" x 4.5", 4 c/in, 13–14 st/in. Inner and outer five-pointed stars outlined with checks, inset crosses, and diamonds in black border. J. F. Collins collection. 1962.

B.385 20" x 5", 4.5 c/in, 14 st/in. White five-pointed star with unusual, complex U-shaped figures inset with animals. Possibly Yavapai. J. F. Collins collection. 1962.

B.387 16.25" x 4.5", 5 c/in, 13–15 st/in. Radiating triangular vanes and lines of checked diamonds with inset crosses. J. F. Collins collection. 1962.

1978-1-323 12" x 3.75", 4 c/in, 10 st/in. Two interlocked four-pointed stars with black crosses. Amelia White estate. 1978.

1978-4-44 19" x 5.5", 6 c/in, 11–12 st/in. Radiating lines of triangles, bottom patch of skin. Harold J. Gans collection. 1978.

1981-25-1 14.75" x 3.75", 6 c/in, 12–13 st/in. Central open seven-pointed star within a larger star, black animal figures inset. Gift of Sallie Wagner. 1981.

*1982-5-1 (p. 91) 13" x 2.5", 5 c/in, 8 st/in. Ticked rim, open bird and geometric figures. Made by Charlene Tuffley, purchased at Peridot Trading Post, San Carlos. 1982.

*1982-5-6 (p. 91) 11" x 2", 3.5 c/in, 11–12 st/in. Central black five-pointed star, small animals and checked diamonds. Made by Mary Porter, purchased at Peridot Trading Post, San Carlos. 1982.

1982-5-7 10" x 1.5", 3.5–4.5 c/in, 10 st/in. Five-pointed open star with another within it, small crosses. Made by Mary Porter, purchased at Peridot Trading Post, San Carlos. 1982.

Coiled Jar/Olla-Shaped Baskets

Unless noted otherwise, these baskets have straight, flaring sides, marked shoulders, short flaring necks, and flat bases. Proportions vary. Some are tall and slender; in others, the diameter equals the height.

B.285 15.75" x 14.5", 4 c/in, 8 st/in. Unpitched globular jar with straight neck, three rods with one rod and splint in neck, rim bound with commercial harness leather. May be protohistoric, with leather rim added later. Purchased from T. Harmon Parkhurst, who identified it as Jicarilla. 1951.

B.300 16.25" x 17.5", 4 c/in, 10 st/in. All-over net design enclosing crosses, triangles, and other geometric figures. IAF purchase from Arthur Seligman estate. 1954.

*B.301 (p. 83) 25.25" x 28.5", 4 c/in, 10 st/in. Large, broad olla with seven vertical lines of black triangles, open diamonds, deer, and asymmetrically scattered human figures. IAF purchase from Arthur Seligman estate. 1954.

*1978-4-25 (p. 70) 10" at shoulder x 12.5", 4 c/in, 13–14 st/in. Straight, flaring sides and slightly flaring neck; black, red, yellow, zigzag encircling bands. Harold J. Gans collection. 1978.

*1978-4-26 (p. 70) 10" x 14.5", 4 c/in, 8–9 st/in. Straight, slightly flaring sides and nearly vertical neck, all-over pattern of red and black lines forming open diamonds. Harold J. Gans collection. 1978.

1978-4-43 13" x 16.75", 3.5 c/in, 14–15 st/in. Slightly curved sides, wide flaring neck; zigzag band on

shoulder with angular meander below, six-pointed star on base. Harold J. Gans collection. 1978.

Twined Burden Baskets

Bucket shaped, these baskets are twined with willow, mulberry, or cottonwood. Many are decorated with fringed vertical bands of buckskin and painted or dyed with encircling geometric bands. They have two rim rods, the lower usually a bundle of bark and other fibers wrapped with splints, the upper of heavy galvanized wire bound between two splints with skin thongs. Some have U-shaped reinforcing rods.

B.327 9.5" x 12". Worked completely in three-strand twine, no reinforcing rods, double rim, six fringed strips, four bands of diagonal lines of devil's claw, base covered with buckskin. Margretta S. Dietrich bequest. 1961.

B.392 14" x 15". Completely three-strand twine of split sumac with bark on interior, no reinforcing rods, four buckskin fringed strips, encircling bands of painted orange and black diagonal lines, fringed and scalloped buckskin over red cotton fabric on base. J. F. Collins collection. 1962.

*1978-1-55 (p. 86) 17" x 17". Plain twining over double warps, two U-shaped reinforcing rods, double rim, four fringed bands, scalloped and fringed base patch over red cloth, black bands of devil's claw with pendant triangles and painted red band. Mable Morrow estate. 1979.

1978-1-127 13" x 14.5". Twill twined with bands of plain twine, half-twist with willow (?) bark on interior, three bands of devil's claw and rust-red paint, no reinforcing rods, double rim, four fringed buckskin bands, fringed skin base patch. Amelia White estate. 1978.

1978-1-154 11.75" x 10.5". Plain twined, half twist with bark covering interior, two U-shaped reinforcing rods, double rim, four fringed buckskin bands, fringed skin base patch. Three checked bands of black devil's claw. Amelia White estate. 1978.

1979-6-4 12.5" x 12.5". Plain twined, four reinforcing corner rods (not U-shaped), double rim, buckskin base patch with long fringe over red cloth, fringed skin bands, three bands of black devil's claw — one of triangles, and two checked. Mable Morrow estate. 1979.

1982-4-1 10.5" x 9.5". Cylindrical, alternating bands of twill twine with sumac splints and plain twine with yucca, no reinforcing rods, single flattened rod rim, base and lower part of sides covered with skin, four fringed bands, remnants of conical metal dangles. Probably Mescalero. Margretta Dietrick, gift to Mrs. T. Apsund. 1982.

*1983-8-2 (p. 72) 16" at rim x 13". Semiconical, plain twine with willow and cottonwood splints over two warps, half-twist twine to reverse colors for dark bands and figures of deer. Rim: two splints wrapped with leather around warp ends. Four fringed bands and fringed base patch of commercial russet leather. Made by Evelyn Henry, purchased at Peridot Trading Post, San Carlos. 1983.

Twined Pitched Jars and Bottles

These twill-twined water containers were coated with crushed juniper leaves or a similar concoction, and some with red ochre, before being coated inside and out with piñon pitch.

B.1 6.5" x 11.5". Double-bodied bottle with narrow neck. IAF. 1930.

*B.2 (p. 84) 6" x 11.5". Double-bodied bottle with narrow neck, several courses of three-strand twine around shoulder of upper body. IAF. 1930.

*B.79 (p. 84) 11" x 12". Globular body, narrow neck, twill twined, heavily pitched, three bent twig handles. IAF. 1930.

B.317 11.5" x 12.5". Coated with red ochre and heavy pitch. Flat base, nearly vertical sides, sharp shoulder, narrow neck. Three twig handles on shoulder. Said to be Chiricahua. Gift of Cornelia Thompson. 1956.

B.348 6" x 7". Flat base, wide flaring neck, two twig handles on shoulder, black line around shoulder shows under the pitch. Gift of Kenneth M. Chapman. 1961.

*B.447 (p. 84) 9.5" x 14.5". Twill twined with some three-strand. Flat base, nearly vertical sides, flared neck, bundle rim lashed with devil's claw. Coated with red ochre and pitched inside and out, two twig handles. IAF, purchased from James Ahmie Joe. 1968.

*1983-8-4 (p. 90) 8" x 13". Plain twined neck. Flat base, round body, flaring neck. Coated with amber pitch over red ochre, two thin bent wood handles. Purchased from Dicey Lupe, Cibecue reservation. 1983.

Miscellaneous Twined Baskets

1982-5-2 20" x 18". Large round-bodied olla with vertical neck. Plain and twill twined with willow splints of cottonwood, broad meander around body and encircling bands around neck worked with half-twist twining. Made by Cecilia Henry, purchased at Peridot Trading Post, San Carlos. 1982.

1982-5-3 9" x 14.5". Willow-twined, double-bodied jar with wide flaring neck. Decorated with light bands of half-twist twining. Made by Cecilia Henry, purchased at San Carlos Tribal Enterprises. 1982.

YAVAPAI BASKETS

Coiled Trays

These trays have three-rod bunched foundations and are sewn with willow and devil's claw. Two baskets in the SAR collection (B.142 and B.385) that have been ascribed to the Western Apaches may actually be Yavapai.

*B.386 (p. 100) 17.75" x 3.25", 4.25 c/in, 14 st/in. Four broad white radiating Y figures with negative animals and small crosses in black areas between them. J. F. Collins collection. 1962.

*1983-8-1 (p. 100) 17.25" x 1.75", 2.5 c/in, 10 st/in. A heavy tray with a unique devil's claw design of a three-lobed leaf with a small antelope and a spread-winged eagle within it. Made by Bessie Mike, Fort McDowell Reservation, Arizona. 1983.

HUALAPAI BASKETS

Twined Bowls

Twill twined with sumac splints on stiff, whole-rod sumac warps. Decorated with dyed bands and finished with flat rims made with two splints bound inside and outside the warp ends.

*B.347 (p. 105) 6.75" x 3.75". Two bands of aniline purple and red stripes. Purchased in California in 1912. Gift of Mrs. Gerald Cassidy. 1962.

B.356 4" x 3.75". Two bands of red yucca root, unbound rim finished with three-strand twine. Possibly Havasupai. Gift of Mrs. Joseph M. Sundt. 1962.

B.388 4.5 x 6". Rim bound on fiber bundle, bands of orange, russet, cerise, and yucca root. Also some three-strand twine. Possibly early Havasupai. J. F. Collins collection. 1962.

*1983-17-2 (p. 106) 7.5" x 4.25". Twill twined with half-twist sumac splints, band of orange and ochre yellow. Made by Elnora Mapatis, Peach Springs, Arizona. Purchased at Indian Market. 1983.

*1983-17-4 (p. 106) 9.25 x 6.25". Twill twined, bark on inside with half twist, three bands of dyed red, blue, maroon splints. Made by Elnora Mapatis, Peach Springs, Arizona. Purchased at Indian Market. 1983.

Twined Burden Baskets

*B.390 (p. 103) 17" at rim x 15.5". Conical, twill twined, double rim of wire and splint bundle, buckskin base cap. Narrow line and hachured band of devil's claw. J. F. Collins collection. 1962.

B.393 20" at rim x 13". Large, subconical, plain twine with bands of three-strand, double rim of wire and wood rod, two devil's claw bands of hachures and two of terraced triangles. J. F. Collins collection. 1962.

HAVASUPAI BASKETS

Coiled Bowls

Three-rod bunched foundations; sumac, cottonwood, and willow stitching; devil's claw for decoration.

B.211 14" x 2.75", 4.5 c/in, 10–11 st/in. Eleven-pointed star with large black center, zigzag band below herringbone rim. H. P. Mera collection. 1941.

*B.212 (p. 111) 15.25" x 4.5", 5 c/in, 8–9 st/in. Thirteen-pointed open star edged with black diamonds, herringbone rim. "An old basket." H. P. Mera collection. 1941.

*B.213 (p. 111) 10.5" x 1", 4.5 c/in, 11 st/in. Six radiating curved bands with one serrated edge, lashed rim, knot start. H. P. Mera collection. 1941.

B.214 10.5" x 2", 5 c/in, 10–12 st/in. Spiral pattern of zigzag lines. H. P. Mera collection. 1941.

B.215 12.75" x 1.75", 4.5 c/in, 9 st/in. Black ring with triangles and four broken double zigzags. H. P. Mera collection. 1941.

*B.216 (p. 112) 16.25" x 2.5", 5 c/in, 12 st/in. Open nine-pointed star bordered with double-line zigzag band, lashed rim, knot start. H. P. Mera collection. 1941.

B.297 18.25" x 4", 6 c/in, 9–10 st/in. Open star with ten spire-shaped points and zigzag border, lashed rim. An old basket. Purchased from Arthur Seligman estate. 1954.

B.298 12" x 2.5", 4 c/in, 10 st/in. Five curved radiating bands edged with triangles, rim missing. Purchased from Arthur Seligman estate. 1954.

1978-4-45 16" x 3.5", 5 c/in, 12 st/in. Black four-pointed star within an open eight-petaled figure outlined in black and faded red. Harold J. Gans collection. 1978.

Twined Jars and Bowls

Twill twined with catclaw and/or squawberry sumac, some willow and devil's claw.

*B.128 (p. 115) 9" x 8". Jar with round body and flaring neck, bands of three-strand, half-twist plain twine, some crossing two warps and others one warp. Two bands of devil's claw. Bundle rim with herringbone finish. Gift of Frank Patania. 1937.

*B.273 (p. 115) 8" x 8". Flat base jar with flared neck, bundle rim diagonally lashed with devil's claw. Compact plain twine over one warp, bands of three-strand twine. Half twist with bark on interior. Gift of Mrs. Frank Applegate. 1944.

B.274 11" x 13.5". Biconical bottle, lashed bundle rim, canvas base, heavy coat of black pitch inside and out, two braided horsehair loops. Found at Ash Fork, Arizona, by donor, Mrs. Frank Applegate. 1944.

B.355 6" x 6". Small jar, plain and twill twined with courses of three-strand, fiber-bundle rim lashed with splints. Gift of Mrs. Joseph M. Sundt. 1962.

*B.389 (p. 6) 8.75" x 7.25". Jar with bands of three-strand twine, devil's claw bands of pendant triangles and diagonal hachures. Lashed bundle rim. J. F. Collins collection. 1962.

Twined Burden Basket

1984-4-41 28" at rim x 21". Conical, double rim (bundle of wood splints and a solid rod). Half-twist twill twined with band of three-strand below rim, sumac (?) splints with bark on interior. Devil's claw band with pendant triangles. Harold J. Gans collection. 1978.

PIMA BASKETS

Coiled Bowl/Trays

These baskets are coiled with a bundle of cattail fibers and stitched with willow splints. Designs are in black devil's claw with occasional color. Most are shallow and rounded, with thin walls of flattened coils.

B.20 18" x 5", 4 c/in, 10 st/in. Five segments with interlocking frets, lashed rim. IAF. 1930.

*B.22 (p. 73) 18.5" x 6.25", 4 c/in, 9 st/in. Five large H figures with small crosses, herringbone rim. IAF. 1930.

*B.23 (p. 128) 19.75" x 7", 5 c/in, 9 st/in. Four large radiating petals with interlocking hachures, diagonal rim. IAF. 1930.

B.24 19" x 6", 5 c/in, 9 st/in. Black vortex with swastikas at each point, herringbone rim, twill-plaited start. IAF. 1930.

*B.25 (p. 126) 21" x 2.5", 4 c/in, 9–10 st/in. Three radiating arms joined to horizontal lines, diagonal rim. IAF. 1930.

B.26 16" x 5", 5 c/in, 10 st/in. Concentric six-pointed stars of small black rectangles, diagonal rim. IAF. 1930.

B.27 16" x 5", 5–6 c/in, 11 st/in. Radiating curved serrated lines ending with swastikas and/or rectangles, diagonal rim. IAF. 1930.

B.28 17.5" x 3.75", 4–5 c/in, 9–10 st/in. Large swastika figure with border of interlocking angular frets, diagonal lashed rim. IAF. 1930.

B.29 17" x 5.5", 5 c/in, 10 st/in. Central light cross in a black diamond with black and white framing zigzags, herringbone rim. IAF. 1930.

B.30 17" x 5", 4–5 c/in, 8–10 st/in. Six vertical panels of interlocking angular frets, four-square knot start, diagonal lashed rim. IAF. 1930.

*B.31 (p. 127) 18" x 6.5", 5 c/in, 13 st/in. Angular, five-petaled squashblossom pattern, herringbone rim. IAF. 1930.

B.32 15.5" x 5.5", 5 c/in, 12 st/in. Band of five frets terminating in swastikas, herringbone rim. IAF. 1930.

*B.33 (p. 126) 15" x 3.75", 7 c/in, 11 st/in. Four-pointed vortex and band of interlocking frets. IAF. 1930.

B.34 11" x 3.5", 5–6 c/in, 11–12 st/in. Four diagonal panels of black squares connected by horizontal lines, diagonal rim. IAF. 1930.

*B.35 (p. 127) 15.5" x 5", 5 c/in, 9–12 st/in. Four panels with black hourglass figures known as "butterfly wings" topped with crosses and figure-fours, lashed rim. IAF. 1930.

B.36 15" x 3.75", 5–6 c/in, 10–11 st/in. Four diagonal vanes outlined with concentric lines, diagonal rim, four-square knot start. IAF. 1930.

B.37 14" x 4.75", 5 c/in, 9 st/in. Inner and outer bands of swastikas, herringbone rim. IAF. 1930.

B.38 14" x .5", 3–4 c/in, 9 st/in. Flat plaque with three broad radiating arms ending in swastikas, diagonal rim. IAF 1930.

*B.40 (p. 73) 12" x 3.5", 6 c/in, 13 st/in. Four radiating black bands with hachured trapezoids bordered with hooks, diagonal rim. IAF. 1930.

B.41 10.5" x 1.75", 5 c/in, 9 st/in. Four-pointed vortex joined to parallel horizontal lines, diagonally lashed rim. IAF. 1930.

B.42 11" x 3", 5 c/in, 11–12 st/in. Four radiating black bands with parallel horizontal lines between them, simple lashed rim. IAF. 1930.

B.43 10.75" x 2", 5 c/in, 13–24 st/in. Three radiating complex figures of frets, plumes, swastikas; herringbone rim. IAF. 1930.

B.44 11" x 1", 7 c/in, 12–14 st/in. Five-petaled figure with band of black terraced diamonds inside, herringbone rim. IAF. 1930.

B.67 19" x 6", 3–4 c/in, 9 st/in. Four radiating curved lines with spiral hooks, diagonally lashed rim. IAF. 1930.

*B.68 (p. 73) 15" x 5", 6 c/in, 10 st/in. Mounted on a ring base to form a compote. Two bands of interlocking angular scroll-frets, design filled in with green and magenta (faded) color, herringbone rim. Gift of Frank Applegate. 1930.

B.81 12", 5 c/in, 10–11 st/in. Plaque with four whirling lines of triangles, final coil bent to form open scallop. Gift of H. P. Mera. 1930.

B.82 9" x 1.75", 6 c/in, 8–9 st/in. Two bands of spaced black triangles, diagonal rim. Gift of H. P. Mera. 1930.

B.83 8" x 2.5", 6 c/in, 10–12 st/in. Two overlapping open five-pointed stars. H. P. Mera collection. 1930.

B.84 9" x 2.5", 4–5 c/in, 9–10 st/in. Eight radiating curved zigzag lines forming spiral, diagonal rim. H. P. Mera collection. 1930.

B.141 14.5" x 5.25", 5 c/in, 11 st/in. Four angular spirals with center of banded rectangles. Purchased in Santa Fe about 1906. Gift of H. P. Mera for Julia Ives collection. 1941.

B.219 4.75" x .75", 8 c/in, 14 st/in. Circle with four radiating curved serrated bands with angular spirals between them. H. P. Mera collection. 1941.

B.220 8" x 1.25", 9–10 c/in, 15 st/in. Maltese cross with triangles between arms, diagonal rim, four-square knot start. H. P. Mera collection. 1941.

B.221 12.75" x 3", 5 c/in, 8–9 st/in. Complex pattern of interlocking open frets, herringbone rim, four-square knot start. H. P. Mera collection. 1941.

B.222 17.5" x 6", 4 c/in, 9 st/in. Three bands of open angular hooked meanders, herringbone rim, four-square knot start. H. P. Mera collection. 1941.

B.223 15.75" x 3.5", 6 c/in, 11 st/in. Four rhomboidal panels filled with horizontal lines, diagonal rim. H. P. Mera collection. 1941.

B.224 15" x 2.5", 4–5 c/in, 11 st/in. Vortex with four points terminating in swastikas, diagonal rim, four-square knot start. H. P. Mera collection. 1941.

B.225 14" x 2.75", 5 c/in, 7–9 st/in. Diagonally radiating zigzag lines with triangles, herringbone rim, four-square knot start. H. P. Mera collection. 1941.

*B.226 (p. 128) 18.75" x 6.5", 5 c/in, 12 st/in. Bands of angular meanders enclosing swastikas, herringbone rim, vestiges of red paint. H. P. Mera collection. 1941.

B.227 19.5" x 7.5", 5 c/in, 9 st/in. Four panels of triangles and interlocking frets, lashed rim, four-square knot start. H. P. Mera collection. 1941.

B.228 22.5" x 8.75", 4 c/in, 9–10 st/in. Vortex with points ending in horizontal lines, outer band of angular S shapes, lashed rim. H. P. Mera collection. 1941.

B.293 14.5" x 3.5", 5 c/in, 9 st/in. Outer band of open T shapes interlocking with inner band of brackets, large twill-plaited start. IAF purchase from Arthur Seligman estate. 1954.

B.342 14.75" x 2.5", 6 c/in, 10 st/in. Black vortex with four points ending in swastikas, herringbone rim, four-square knot start. Gift of Mrs. Gerald Cassidy. 1962.

B.353 10.75" x 3", 5 c/in, 9 st/in. Radiating panels of rectangular black checks, lashed rim. Gift of Mrs. Joseph M. Sundt. 1962.

B.354 10.5" x 3.5", 3 c/in, 10 st/in. Six cross-hachured petals with crosses between them. Gift of Mrs. Joseph M. Sundt. 1962.

B.394 18" x 4.75", 4 c/in, 12 st/in. Two bands of open diamonds forming central four-pointed star, diagonal lashed rim. J. F. Collins collection. 1962.

B.397 20.5" x 6.75". Vortex with five points ending in triangles that interlock with border of lines and pendant hourglass figures. J. F. Collins collection. 1962.

B.398 21.25" x 7", 4–5 c/in, 10–11 st/in. Two bands of large interlocking angular hooks, herringbone rim, four-square knot start. J. F. Collins collection. 1962.

B.399 21.5" x 6", 4 c/in, 10 st/in. Large black swastika, border of interlocking black and white frets, diagonal rim, four-square knot start. J. F. Collins collection. 1962.

B.400 19" x 5.5", 4 c/in, 11 st/in. Open vortex with five arms terminating in swastikas, herringbone rim. J. F. Collins collection. 1962.

B.401 21" x 8", 5 c/in, 10–11 st/in. Black vortex with parallel horizontal lines from its four points, herringbone rim, four-square knot start. J. F. Collins collection. 1962.

B.402 19" x 6.25", 4 c/in, 9 st/in. Black vortex with four points ending in fret border, diagonal lashed rim. J. F. Collins collection. 1962.

B.403 17" x 6.75", 5 c/in, 9 st/in. Three central triangles joined to lines forming border with swastikas, herringbone rim, twill-plaited start. J. F. Collins collection. 1962.

B.405 16.5" x 2.5", 5 c/in, 10 st/in. Central cross with concentric terraces that form type of rectangular squashblossom, diagonal rim. J. F. Collins collection. 1962.

B.406 18" x 4.5", 4 c/in, 11 st/in. Five diagonal bands of crosses formed with black rectangles, lashed rim. J. F. Collins collection. 1962.

B.407 18.25" x 4.25". Large black tondo, outer band of four swastikas, twill-plaited start. J. F. Collins collection. 1962.

*B.408 (p. 126) 17.25" x 4", 5 c/in, 11 st/in. Radiating parallel diagonal zigzag lines with black squares, four-square knot start, diagonal rim. J. F. Collins collection. 1962.

B.409 16.5" x 4.5", 5 c/in, 10 st/in. Rectangular squashblossom design with scattered spots of red yucca root, four-square knot start, diagonal rim. J. F. Collins collection. 1962.

B.410 16" x 5.25", 6 c/in, 12 st/in. Black vortex with parallel zigzag lines, herringbone rim. J. F. Collins collection. 1962.

B.411 16.25" x 6", 6 c/in, 11 st/in. Diagonal rectangular meander with crosses, four-square knot start, herringbone rim. J. F. Collins collection. 1962.

B.412 15.5" x 4", 5.5–6 c/in, 11 st/in. Black vortex with band of crosses with three offset arms, lashed rim. J. F. Collins collection. 1962.

B.413 19.75" x 5.5", 4 c/in, 9–10 st/in. Five curved radiating lines edged with triangles and angular hooks, silver button at center, diagonal rim. J. F. Collins collection. 1962.

B.414 16.5" x 5.25", 5 c/in, 10 st/in. Broad band of open interlocking frets, herringbone rim. J. F. Collins collection. 1962.

*B.415 (p. 73) 12.75" x 4", 5 c/in, 12 st/in. Eight radiating open petals, each containing a cross; plaited start; diagonal rim. J. F. Collins collection. 1962.

B.416 11.25" x 3", 5 c/in, 12 st/in. Five encircling angular zigzag lines with black squares at corners, herringbone rim. J. F. Collins collection. 1962.

B.417 10.75" x 3", 4 c/in, 10 st/in. Four small three-armed crosses, vestige of green dyed hourglass figures on exterior, four-square knot start, diagonal lashed rim. J. F. Collins collection. 1962.

*B.418 (p. 126) 9.5" x 2", 6 c/in, 12 st/in. Black vortex with band of parallel black lines, four-square knot start, herringbone rim. J. F. Collins collection. 1962.

B.419 9.5" x 1.25", 6 c/in, 7–8 st/in. Four open radiating zigzags, diagonal lashed ticked rim. J. F. Collins collection. 1962.

B.420 7.25" x 1.5", 8–10 c/in, 12 st/in. Small bowl with three black radiating zizags, intervening lines and crosses, diagonal lashed ticked rim. J. F. Collins collection. 1962.

B.422 12.5" x .25", 3–4 c/in, 11–12 st/in. Plaque with three curved radiating black vanes with swastikas, diagonal rim. J. F. Collins collection. 1962.

B.423 12.5" x .25", 4–5 c/in, 10 st/in. Plaque with three radiating black vanes with outlining, diagonal rim. J. F. Collins collection. 1962.

B.424 10.75" x .25", 6 c/in, 13–14 st/in. Plaque with three black radiating petals with outlining. J. F. Collins collection. 1962.

1978-1-52 21.25" x 6.5", 3.5–4 c/in, 9–10 st/in. Six black triangles radiating from tondo which become swastika panels, twill-plaited start, herringbone rim. Amelia White collection. 1978.

1978-4-42 17.5" x 6", 4–4.5 c/in, 10 st/in. Band of large checked rectangles, herringbone rim. Harold J. Gans collection. 1978.

*1983-17-3 (p. 133) 6.25" x 1.5", 6 c/in, 13 st/in. Small bowl with Man in the Maze or Elder Brother design. Made by Hilda Manuel at Indian Market. 1983.

1984-22-1 15.5" x 4.5", 3 c/in, 10 st/in. Large mottled five-pointed star, herringbone rim. Gift of Peggy Pond Church. 1984.

Small and/or Deep Bowls and Olla-Shaped Baskets

*B.52 (p. 124) 12" at shoulder x 8.5", 4 c/in, 10 st/in. Olla with flat base, angular shoulder, short flaring neck, four black vertical bands with border lines, four bands of checks, lashed rim, four-square knot start. IAF. 1930.

B.53 6.5" x 4.5", 5 c/in, 10 st/in. Small cylindrical bowl with four panels of concentric rectangles. IAF. 1930.

B.217 4" x 2.75", 8 c/in, 11 st/in. Cup-shaped, flat base, fret design. H. P. Mera collection. 1941.

B.218 6.5" x 3", 9 c/in., 13–14 st/in. Flat-base, slightly curved sides, fret designs. H. P. Mera collection. 1941.

*B.292 (p. 125) 7.5" x 5", 5 c/in, 9 st/in. Bowl with flat base, nearly vertical sides, five pairs of men and women, herringbone rim. IAF purchase from Arthur Seligman estate. 1954.

B.318 6.75 x 3.25". Small bowl with flat base and straight flaring sides, irregular interlocking frets, diagonal lashed rim. Gift of Dorothea K. Conrad. 1957.

*B.319 (p. 125) 11.25" x 4", 4.5 c/in, 9 st/in. Bowl with flat base and curved flaring sides, angular squashblossom design, diagonal lashed rim. Gift of Dorothea K. Conrad. 1957.

B.358 2.5" x 1.25", 11 c/in, 16 st/in. Miniature bowl, interlocking black and tan triangles, herringbone rim. Gift of Mrs. H. P. Mera. 1962.

*B.359 (p. 125) 7.75" x 4.75", 5–6 c/in, 11 st/in. Small bowl, flat base, straight flaring sides, four human figures, four crosses. Gift of Clare Jones. 1962.

B.421 15.5" x 7.5", 2.5–3 c/in, 9–10 st/in. Flat base, straight vertical sides, heavy meander design with swastikas, herringbone rim. J. F. Collins collection. 1962.

B.425 9" x 9.5", 3.5 c/in, 10–11 st/in. Olla with low shoulder and short flaring neck, two bands of frets. J. F. Collins collection. 1962.

B.426 6.25" x 2.25", 8 c/in, 15 st/in. Small bowl, flat base, straight flaring sides, net of negative hexagonal figures, diagonal lashed rim. J. F. Collins collection. 1962.

B.427 4.5" x 2.25", 7 c/in, 1 st/in. Small bowl, flat base, straight vertical sides, six panels checked with rectangles. J. F. Collins collection. 1962.

B.428 3.75" x 2.5", 5–6 c/in, 15–16 st/in. Miniature bowl, flat base, straight sides, bands of stacked rectangles, diagonal rim. J. F. Collins collection. 1962.

B.429 3.75" x 2.5", 5–6 c/in, 15–16 st/in. Miniature bowl, flat base, slightly flaring straight sides, vertical black diamonds, some with border lines, small white porcelain beads sewn around rim. J. F. Collins collection. 1962.

B.430 3.75" x 1.75", 8 c/in, 21 st/in. Miniature bowl, flat base, straight sides, four large swastikas, diagonal rim. J. F. Collins collection. 1962.

B.431 3.25" x 1.75", 9 c/in, 16 st/in. Miniature bowl, flat base, continuous rectilinear meander, lashed rim. J. F. Collins collection. 1962.

B.432 9.5" x 11.5", 4 c/in, 5 st/in. Olla with short flaring neck, spaced willow stitches, lashed rim. J. F. Collins collection. 1962.

*B.444 (p. 125) 3.5" x .5", 14 c/in, 24 st/in. Miniature low bowl, compact spiral design of parallel zigzags, lashed rim. Gift of Kenneth Chapman. 1965.

1978-4-46 17.25" x 16.25", 3 c/in, 9–10 st/in. Large olla, flat base, slightly angular shoulder, short vertical neck, ticked diagonal rim, all-over net of diamonds and crosses. Harold J. Gans collection. 1978.

1982-7-30 10" x 6" x 2", 4–5 c/in, 12 st/in. Rectangular bowl, flat base, straight sides, diagonal rows of black rectangles, herringbone rim. Gift of Sallie Wagner. 1982.

1984-14-1 5" x 4", 3–4 c/in, 12 st/in. Small cup-shaped bowl, straight sides, angular meander design, diagonal lashed rim, four-square knot start. Gift of Jack Campbell. 1984.

PAPAGO BASKETS

These baskets are coiled on a bundle of beargrass splints. The old baskets are sewn with willow and devil's claw splints, and the recent commercial baskets are sewn with yucca splints of various colors and black devil's claw. In most of these baskets, the coils have been flattened between stones. The rims are finished with lashed devil's claw splints.

Bowl/Trays

Sewn with willow splints, decorated with devil's claw.

*B.21 (p. 134) 18.5" x 7", 4–5 c/in, 9–10 st/in. Round base, negative design of interlocking angular hooks, four-square knot start, herringbone rim. IAF. 1930.

B.129 5.25" x 2.75", 6–7 c/in, 8–9 st/in. Small hemispherical winebowl. Four sets of angular black scrolls, plain rim, four-square knot start, much used. Gift of Frank Patania. 1937.

B.277 15.5" x 8.5", 4.5 c/in, 9 st/in. Hemispherical wine bowl, vortex with four short points becoming angular scrolls with central swastikas, lashed rim. IAF purchase from War Bond Exchange for Mary Austin collection. 1945.

B.321 19" x 6.5", 3 c/in, 9 st/in. Four-petaled squashblossom design, four-square knot start, lashed rim. Gift of Amelia E. White. 1958.

B.322 16" x 6.5", 3 c/in, 8 st/in. Black vortex with three-lined fret band, lashed rim, four-square knot start. Gift of Amelia E. White. 1958.

B.330 17.5" x 4", 4 c/in, 8 st/in. Whirlwind design of multiple rectangular zigzags radiating diagonally from center, four-square knot start, lashed rim. Bequest of Margretta S. Dietrich. 1961.

*B.404 (p. 134) 20.25" x 4", 2.5 c/in, 10 st/in. Five-point vortex with band of four broad-line (two coils wide) frets, diagonal lashed rim. J. F. Collins collection. 1962.

1986-9-1 10.5" x 3", 3.5 c/in, 15 st/in. Three-petal rectangular squashblossom design, diagonal overstitching on rim. Made by Josephine Thomas, Chuichu, Arizona. 1986.

*1986-9-4 (p. 135) 18.5" x 8", 3.5 c/in, 8 st/in. Hemispherical saguaro wine bowl, rectangular squashblossom design, rim coil missing, four-square knot start. Purchased from Case Trading Post. 1986.

Commercial Baskets

Sewn with yucca and devil's claw splints.

B.45 12.5" x 8.25", 3 c/in, 6 st/in. Bowl with flat base, vertical sides, black devil's claw birds. IAF. 1930.

B.46 11" x 5", 3 c/in, 7 st/in. Bowl with flat base, vertical sides, four double zigzag diagonal lines in black, diagonal ticked rim. IAF. 1930.

B.47 9" x 2", 3–4 c/in, 7 st/in. Shallow bowl, three diagonal stacks of black rectangles. IAF. 1930.

B.48 4.5" x 6", 4 c/in, 6–7 st/in. Deep bowl with flat base, vertical sides, four double-lined large black zigzags, ticked rim. IAF. 1930.

B.49 5.5" x 2.75", 3–3.5 c/in, 6–8 st/in. Small bowl, flat base, slightly curved sides, black diagonal lines of rectangles. IAF. 1930.

*B.303 (p. 74) 7" x 10.75", 3 c/in, 9 st/in. Deep bowl with flat base and straight sides, five yellow-green saguaro cacti with red yucca root tops, four-square knot start. Gift of Amelia E. White. 1955.

B.442 .5" x 2.25", 10 c/in, 10–14 st/in. Miniature bowl, three black angular whirling lines, black diagonal overstitching on rim, four-square knot start. Gift of Laura Gilpin. 1964.

B.448 7.75" x 1.25", 3–4 c/in, 6–8 st/in. Shallow bowl, four groups of black rectangles, black diagonal overstitched rim, four-square knot start. IAF purchase at Indian Market. 1969.

*B.449 (p. 139) 10.75" x 2", 4 c/in, 1 st/in. Shallow bowl of heavy beargrass with spaced yucca wheat stitches, four-square knot start. IAF purchase at Indian Market. 1969.

1969-34 15" x 15.5", 2 c/in, 4–5 st/in. Globular olla with flaring rim, parallel black zigzag vertical bands, diagonal black overstitch on rim, four-square knot start. Gift of Mr. and Mrs. Marshall McCune. 1969.

*1978-4-47 (p. 137) 18" x 16", 2 c/in, 6–7 st/in. Large olla, flat base, straight flaring sides, short wide flaring neck, seven vertical black bands edged with triangles, four-square knot start, rim crisscrossed with devil's claw. Harold J. Gans collection. 1978.

1979-6-2 15" x 9", 4 c/in, 10 st/in. Deep bowl, flat base, straight flaring sides, vertical zigzag lines of black rectangles, diagonal ticked rim. Gift of Mrs. Leo Woolman. 1978.

1979-6-65 6.5" x 1", 5 c/in, 7–9 st/in. Small shallow bowl, black five-pointed star and five crosses, four-square knot start, crisscross rim. Mable Morrow estate. 1979.

1980-16-1 13.75" x .5", 3–4 c/in, 7–8 st/in. Plaque with yellow-ochre maze and black devil's claw man figure, four-square start. Gift of Sallie Wagner, purchased from trader Clay Lockett, 1950, in Tucson. 1980.

*1981-2-18 (p. 138) 13" x 7.5", 4 c/in, 3–4 st/in. Globular jar with fitted lid, spaced and split yucca stitching in curved diagonal lines, small loop handle on lid, flat bottom. Gift of Sallie Wagner. 1981.

1981-2-19 7.75" x .5", 4–5 c/in, 7–8 st/in. Plaque with ochre-yellow five-pointed star outlined in black. Gift of Sallie Wagner. 1981.

*1981-2-20 (p. 74) 5.5" x .5", 6 c/in, 11 st/in. Flat plaque with turtle design in black and yellow-ochre. Gift of Sallie Wagner. 1981.

1981-2-21 7.5" x .5", 4 c/in, 7 st/in. Small plaque, large open four-armed cross outlined with black and yellow. Gift of Sallie Wagner. 1981.

*1981-2-22 (p. 74) 13.5" x 11.75" x 2.5", 2.5 c/in, 7 st/in. Shallow oval bowl with yellow-ochre and black deer figure. Gift of Sallie Wagner. 1982.

1981-25-10   5" x 3.5", 2.5 c/in, 2.5 st/in. Small globular jar with lid, diagonal lines of spaced stitches, small loop handle. Gift of Sallie Wagner. 1981.

1983-2-1   9" x 3", 4 c/in, 7–8 st/in. Bowl with flat base and flaring sides, black fret design, four-square knot start. Gift of Sallie Wagner. 1983.

1984-4-28   17" long x 12.5" wide, 2 c/in, 8–9 st/in. Oval tray with arched handle, four yellow block crosses outlined with black. Margaret Moses estate. 1984.

1985-8-1   5.5" x 2.75", 3.5 c/in, 7–8 st/in. Bowl with flat base, straight sides, angular meander in black, black diagonal plain rim. Gift of Rick Dillingham. 1985.

1985-8-2   5.5" x 1", 3 c/in, 6–7 st/in. Shallow bowl, four crosses and rim overstitching with maroon yucca root, four-square start. Gift of Rick Dillingham. 1985.

1985-8-3   4.5" x 2", 4 c/in, 2 st/in. Globular jar with lid, diagonal lines of spaced and split yucca stitches, four-square knot start. Fitted lid with loop handle. Gift of Rick Dillingham. 1985.

*1985-8-4   (p. 140) 7" x 11", 2 c/in, 6–7 st/in. Bird effigy with fitted head, added oval wings, ochre stitching for feathers, devil's claw for eyes, feet, other details. Gift of Rick Dillingham. 1985.

1986-9-2   8.5" x 1.75", 3 c/in, 2.5 st/in. Crude shallow bowl, sewn with plain stitches at center, four coils of large wheat stitches, and final coil with spaced plain stitches, rim finished with added diagonal splint, four-square knot start. Purchased from maker, Josephine Thomas of Chuichu, Arizona. 1986.

*1986-9-3   (p. 139) 11.5" x 2.5", 4 c/in, 2.5 st/in. Shallow bowl with flat base, straight flaring sides, complex pattern of small yucca wheat stitches and plain stitches to form lacy pattern, black crisscross overstitching on rim. Purchased at Heard Museum Shop. 1985.

HOPI BASKETS

Coiled Baskets

Made in the villages of Second Mesa. Thick to medium coils with galleta grass bundle foundations, closely sewn with fine splints of yucca. Spiral starts and lashed rims. Geometric designs in vegetal and commercial colors.

B.179   11.5", 1.5 c/in, 18 st/in. Old plaque with unfinished terminus, four yellow petals with areas between them checkered in black and yellow, vegetal colors. H. P. Mera collection. 1941.

B.180   12", 2.5 c/in, 16 st/in. Plaque with Navajo wedding-basket design in blue-black and rust natural colors. H. P. Mera collection. 1941.

B.181   13", 2 c/in, 14 st/in. Crow Mother kachina in black and yellow-tan, wrapped fillet at brow. H. P. Mera collection. 1941.

*B.182   (p. 75) 16.5", 1.5 c/in, 15 st/in. Plaque with bilateral design: two central petals, radiating black lines, ochre-yellow rectangles in natural colors. H. P. Mera collection. 1941.

B.283   14", 2.5 c/in, 14 st/in. Kachina mask, zigzag overstitching for mouth and teeth, black, brown, green, yellow. Gift of H. P. Mera. 1949.

*B.305   (pp. 75 and 146) 12.25" x 2.5", 2.5 c/in, 13 st/in. Shallow bowl, full figure of kachina in black, yellow, red, tan natural colors. Overstitching on headdress, etc. Gift of Amelia E. White. 1955.

B.306   13.5" x 0.75", 2 c/in, 12 st/in. Plaque with orange four-pointed star and four radiating vanes. Amelia White estate. 1955.

B.395   12.5", 1.5 c/in, 14 st/in. Plaque with four-petaled ochre-yellow star outlined in black, natural colors. J. F. Collins collection. 1962.

1978-1-194   10.75", 2 c/in, 11 st/in. Plaque with four-pointed star bordered with orange, black, yellow checks in natural colors. Amelia White estate. 1978.

1978-1-195   12.5", 2 c/in, 14 st/in. Plaque with whirling vanes checked with bright red, black, yellow, green commercial colors. Amelia White estate. 1978.

1978-4-48   15.25", 1.5 c/in, 11 st/in. Plaque with four-pointed star made with checked terraced diamonds in black, yellow, deep red. Harold J. Gans collection. 1978.

*1979-6-57   (p. 76) 8.5" x 6", 2.5 c/in, 15–17 st/in. Deep bowl with vertical sides, zigzag band of red, yellow rectangles bordered with black, seven antelope heads in black, white, red. Mable Morrow estate. 1979.

*1981-6-1   (p. 76) 9.5" x 5.25", 2 c/in, 15–16 st/in. Deep bowl, flat base, straight sides, design of four red, yellow checked rectangles and four antelopes: two red, two black. Collected at Oraibi by donor, Barbara Cook. 1981.

*1981-25-3   (p. 146) 13", 2 c/in, 15 st/in. Plaque with two symmetrical trianguloid vanes and "feathers": black, yellow, red natural colors. Gift of Sallie Wagner. 1981.

1981-25-4   7" x 1", 4 c/in, 18 st/in. Small tray with Navajo wedding-basket design: black, red, lemon yellow. Collected at Hopi by donor, Sallie Wagner. 1981.

*1984-4-27   (p. 75) 17.5" x 2", 2.5 c/in, 14 st/in. Large tray with symmetrical terraced hourglass figure outlined with yellow and black natural colors. Margaret Moses estate. 1984.

1984-4-32 12", 2 c/in, 16 st/in. Plaque with two four-pointed stars, one imposed on the other, outlined with orange-red and yellow checks edged with black. Margaret Moses estate. 1984.

1984-4-33 9.5", 3 c/in, 14 st/in. Plaque with four black checked diamonds. Margaret Moses estate. 1984.

1984-4-34 8" x 1", 3.5 c/in, 17 st/in. Shallow bowl with full kachina figure with tablita; deep red, black, yellow with some overstitching. Margaret Moses estate. 1984.

1984-4-35 11.5", 2.5 c/in, 12 st/in. Plaque with symmetrical design of black zigzag lines. Margaret Moses estate. 1984.

*1984-4-38 (p. 147) 18" at rim x 16", 2.5 c/in, 12 st/in. Deep bowl with flat base, straight flaring sides, five full kachina figures: Crow Mother, terraced rain clouds, etc. Black, red, yellow. Much overstitching. Margaret Moses estate. 1984.

1984-4-39 14" at rim x 16.5", 2.5 c/in, 16 st/in. Deep bowl, flat base, slightly curved flaring sides. Four large kachina masks and terraced bands in yellow, black, orange-red. Margaret Moses estate. 1984.

Plaited Wicker Baskets

Typical of Third Mesa villages. Plaited with whole (unsplit) stems of rabbitbrush wefts on unscraped sumac warps, brightly colored with natural and commercial dyes. Trays and bowls. Rims are wrapped with yucca splints.

*B.92 (p. 150) 10.5". Tray with Hopi wedding-basket design: band of blue rectangles linked with black and orange. Gift of Bryce Sewell. 1931.

*B.151 (p. 151) 8.5" x 7.5". Small bowl, diagonal bands of green, black, brown. Gift of H. P. Mera to Julia M. Ives collection. 1941.

B.178 13". Plaque with three trianguloid vanes radiating from disk, orange and yellow natural colors. H. P. Mera collection. 1941.

*B.282 (p. 150) 14" x 1.25". Tray with full-figure Crow Mother kachina, blue-black, purple, ochre, deep green. Gift of H. P. Mera. 1949.

*B.335 (p. 151) 12.25" x 9.5". Bowl with four antelope figures and two bands of yellow-brown and blue-gray. Collected by donor, Mrs. Gerald Cassidy, at Hopi between 1912 and 1915. 1962.

B.336 10.5 x 12.5". Bowl with two yellow and green checked bands. Collected before 1915 by donor, Mrs. Gerald Cassidy. 1962.

B.337 10" x 13". Deep bowl with spiraling whirlwind design in faded yellow, blue-green, blue. Gift of Mrs. Gerald Cassidy. 1962.

B.338 13.25". Plaque with central kachina mask with radiating lines to border band: blue-black, ochre, pale green, orange. Collected at Hopi between 1912 and 1915 by donor, Mrs. Gerald Cassidy. 1962.

B.339 14". Tray with raised center and raised rim finished with double twist of sumac; black and blue-green butterfly or bird design. Gift of Mrs. Gerald Cassidy. 1962.

*B.340 (p. 152) 11". Tray with raised center and rim, loop handle at center, rim finished with double course of twisted sumac. Design of concentric bands: yellow, blue, black. Gift of Mrs. Gerald Cassidy. 1962.

B.438 12.5" x 11.75". Deep bowl with flat base and straight flaring sides, checked and terraced meander around center. Purchased by donor, Ina Sizer Cassidy, in 1916 at Oraibi. 1964.

*1978-1-51 (p. 153) 17.5" x 3.75". Shallow bowl, plaited wicker, sumac warps, rabbitbrush wefts, yucca rim. Amelia White estate. 1978.

1978-1-140 11.5" x 6.25". Bowl with checked bands of yellow, black, green, white. Amelia White estate. 1978.

1978-1-141 11" x 10.25". Deep bowl with two bands of black, green, yellow rectangles. Amelia White estate 1978.

1979-6-58 13" x 11.5" x 3.5". Oval tray with edges covered with checkered band of white, yellow, black. Mable Morrow estate. 1979.

*1983-6-2 (p. 77) 13.5" x 1". Tray with spread-wing bird in black and white on rust, terraced outer band of green. Purchased at Oraibi in 1983 by Barbara Stanislawski. 1983.

1984-4-29 17". Plaque with wide rectangular start, kachina mask of white, rust, black. Some colors possibly painted on. Margaret Moses estate. 1984.

Carrying Baskets (Peach Baskets)

Plaited with whole and split sumac withes, over cottonwood in some.

B.7 7" x 10". Small carrying basket, semiconical and square in section. Multiple sumac warps, rabbitbrush wefts, four reinforcing rods in corners (bottom broken), rim unbound. IAF. 1930.

B.8 7" x 9". Small peach basket, semiconical with two U-shaped reinforcing rods rim bound with sumac splints. Two light bands of scraped wefts. IAF. 1930.

B.80 15.5" x 8.5" x 7". Burden basket or pannier plaited with whole and split sumac, crude U-shaped rods that project above the untreated rim. A carrying sash of green, red, and black is still attached. Gift of Frank Applegate to IAF. 1930.

B.272   16.5" x 5" x 9.5". Coarse-plaited oblong pannier made with two parallel U-shaped rods that cross bottom and project above the unbound rim. Gift of Mrs. Frank Applegate. 1944.

Plaited Piki Tray

*1984-5-1   (p. 155) 24" long x 20" wide. Rectangular tray, twill plaited in diamond design at center with multiple withes of dunebroom, bordered with plain-plaited sumac, edges bound with yucca splints. Made by Dora Tawahonqua. Purchased at Hopi Culture Center, Honani Crafts, by Deborah Flynn. 1984.

Yucca Plaited Ring Baskets

The designs of these baskets are complex labyrinths, crosses, diamonds, and squares, some worked with white, yellow, and green yucca splints. Some are dyed red, green, or blue to produce brightly colored patterns. The yucca splints are tied over a hoop of sumac. The baskets are plaited with spaces between the yucca splints.

B.271   5" x 6.75". Not a ring basket, but a jar. Open diagonal plain plaiting, over two under two, of yucca splints, rim finished with splints bent over a stiff rod. Gift of Mrs. Frank Applegate. 1944.

1983-17-1   10.25". Twill plaited with concentric rectangles in green yucca. Made by Isabel Coochyumptewa of Mishongnovi, Second Mesa. 1983.

BASKETS OF THE RIO GRANDE PUEBLOS

Coiled Baskets

Rio Grande baskets of two-rod-and-bundle construction such as these have not been made in the twentieth century.

*B.3   (p. 159) 9.5" x 8", 4 c/in, 13–14 st/in. Squat jar with flat base, flaring neck, all-over pattern of interlocking diamonds of black dyed rectangles, flat herringbone rim. IAF. 1930.

B.235   7.25" x 6", 4 c/in, 14–15 st/in. Jar with flat base, straight contracted neck, herringbone rim, red zigzag band edged with black below shoulder. H. P. Mera collection. 1941.

*B.236   (p. 159) 7.75" x 6.5", 4.5 c/in, 14–15 st/in. Two-rod-and-bundle jar with flat base, short flaring neck, herringbone rim. Band of large open diamonds edged with black and red dyed rectangles (possibly some devil's claw). H. P. Mera collection. 1941.

Plaited Wicker Baskets with Lacy Scalloped Rims

Bowl shapes. The whole withes of red-barked young willow give these baskets a deep red or maroon color. The designs were produced by scraping off the bark.

The withes in the scalloped rims are bent down and plaited into a thick, reinforcing band.

*B.123   (p. 165) 32" x 12". Large shallow bowl, flat base, straight flaring sides of split willow splints, 1/2 inch wide. Two loop handles on opposite sides of rim. Made by Pasqual Martínez of San Ildefonso about 1912. Gift of Kenneth M. Chapman. 1934.

B.351   14" x 4". Shallow bowl, flat base of unpeeled withes, sides completely peeled. Hole in center for use as lamp shade. Gift of Mrs. Joseph M. Sundt. 1962.

B.360   9.75" x 3.25". Small bowl, mostly scraped withes. Gift of Elizabeth Derr. 1962.

B.445   16.5" x 4". Shallow bowl, flat base made with thick warps, bands of white peeled wefts in sides. Made by Tomás García at Santo Domingo. Gift of Mrs. C. J. Cahusac. 1966.

1978-1-126   21.5" x 7". Bowl with flat base; withes in scalloped edge are half peeled for red and white contrast. Amelia White estate. 1978.

1978-1-201   12.5" x 3.5". Bowl with flat base, scalloped border is scraped, sides and base are twined with slender whole withes. Amelia White estate. 1978.

1978-4-49   31.5" x 6.75". Large bowl with flat base, peeled splints form rectangular blocks on sides and base. San Juan Pueblo (?), Harold J. Gans collection. 1978.

1979-6-61   10.5" x 4.25". Bowl with flat base of unscraped withes, white scalloped border. Santo Domingo Pueblo. Mable Morrow estate. 1979.

*1982-16-11   (p. 165) 18.5" x 6.5". Bowl with flat base, peeled and unpeeled wefts. Made by Tomás García, Santo Domingo. Purchased by Barbara Stanislawski. 1981.

Plaited Yucca Ring Baskets

The designs of these baskets are twilled in concentric squares with tan or yellow splints.

B.177   20" x 7.5". Large, old basket. The rim rod is unusually heavy. From Jemez Pueblo, according to donor, H. P. Mera. 1941.

B.446   14.5" x 5.75". Purchased for IAF from Leonora Toledo of Jemez Pueblo at Indian Market. 1968.

1979-6-67   10" x 4.5". Mable Morrow estate. 1979.

1979-6-68   11" x 4". Added bale handle of five-strand, flat-braided yucca splints. Mable Morrow estate. 1979.

1982-16-10   15.5" x 5". Made by Sefora Tosa, Jemez Pueblo. 1982.

*1984-4-36   (p. 10) 15" x 4.75". Margaret Moses estate. 1984.

1984-4-37   20" x 5.25". Thick rim rod. Margaret Moses estate. 1984.

Burden Baskets

B.9   13.5" x 13.5". Bucket shape with two U-shaped reinforcing rods. The sides are plain twined over two warps, bands of three-strand twine at base and below rim. Single rim rod lashed with buckskin to warps as they are bent and plaited through each other. IAF. 1930.

B.10   14" x 17.5". Bucket shape, four corner reinforcing rods unconnected at base. Plaited with sumac (?) withes, some scraped to create two or three light bands. The rim is lashed to the wefts with sumac splints. IAF. 1930.

B.12   11.75" x 13". Bucket shape with two U-shaped reinforcing rods, plain twined with sumac splints with bark on interior, two dark bands of bark in half-twist twine. Rim finished as in B.9. IAF. 1930.

B.13   14" x 17". Bucket shape with two U-shaped reinforcing rods exposed on base, twined with willow or sumac splints in bands of plain and twill twine. Decorated with bands of red and black, possibly painted. Interior heavily coated. Rim finished as in B.9. IAF. 1930.

B.14   15" x 18". Bucket shape, identical to B.13 with addition of four vertical buckskin fringed bands and remnants of clumps of fringe below the rim (as in Apache baskets). Rim finished as in B.9. IAF. 1930.

*B.15   (p. 161) 12" x 12". Bucket shape with corner reinforcing rods that do not cross the base. Plain twined with sumac (?) splints with band of three-strand twine near base and single course below rim. Decorated with three and one-half stacked diamonds on each side, half-twist twine to bring bark surfaces to exterior. Rim finished as in B.9. IAF. 1930.

1978-1-10   13" x 6". Carrying basket, bowl shape with two loop handles (one missing), plain and twill twined with bark of sumac splints on interior. Light bands and rectangles with half-twist twining. Rim finished like B.9 but with yucca lashing. Amelia White estate. 1978.

Southwestern tribes not treated in text:
CHEMEHUEVI BASKETS

These baskets are coiled with three-rod bunched foundations and tightly sewn with willow and devil's claw splints. The designs, in black, are crisp and precise.

B.64   6" x 5", 7–8 c/in, 19 st/in. Small bowl olla with flat base and short, slightly flaring neck. Black rim and scattered small X figures made with rectangles. IAF. 1930.

B.65   10.75" x 2.75", 6 c/in, 12–23 st/in. Shallow bowl with flat base and flaring sides. Black diagonal zigzag bands between rim and central ring. IAF. 1930.

B.66   15" x 3.5", 6 c/in, 10 st/in. Shallow curved bowl, black ring with six radiating paired lines edged with triangles. IAF. 1930.

B.186   5.75" x 5.25", 7 c/in, 14 st/in. Olla with four vertical bands bordered on each side with black triangles. H. P. Mera collection. 1941.

B.187   8" x 2.75", 7 c/in, 14 st/in. Small bowl with black rim and zigzag band. H. P. Mera collection. 1941.

B.284   8" x 4". Bowl with double zigzag black band. Gift of Mrs. Cornelia Thompson (specimen missing). 1954.

MARICOPA BASKETS

A few baskets in the collection are attributed to the Maricopas, who acquired most of their baskets from the Pimas.

B.201   6.75" x 3", 5 c/in, 6 st/in. Small bowl with flat base and straight flaring sides. Black design of stacked crosses, large blue glass beads around the rim. H. P. Mera collection. 1941.

B.202   10.25" x 7" x 4.75", 4.5 c/in, 6–7 st/in. Oval bowl with flat base and straight sides, six black stylized lizards on sides. H. P. Mera collection. 1941.

B.203   12.75" x 1.75", 4 c/in, 9 st/in. Shallow bowl, three radiating triangles hooked into angular meander. Probably Pima. H. P. Mera collection. 1941.

B.204   12.5" x 9" x 4", 5 c/in, 4 st/in. Oval bowl with flat base and straight, slightly flaring sides, spaced stitches. Entirely coated with fugitive red color (now pink). H. P. Mera collection. 1941.

UTE BASKETS

The three baskets in the collection identified by Mera as Ute are indistinguishable from the baskets of the Southern Paiutes. They are coiled with three bunched rods, sewn with sumac splints, and dyed to produce the Navajo wedding-basket design.

B.143   15.5" x 3", 3.5 c/in, 14 st/in. Shallow bowl, unusual design of two and one-half vertical open diamonds; one group was originally red, the other blue-black. Gift to Julia M. Ives collection by H. P. Mera. 1941.

B.229   5.75" x 1.5". Small bowl with faded suggestion of wedding-basket design. H. P. Mera collection. 1941.

B.234   16.25 x 3.25", 2 c/in, 14 st/in. Wedding basket, red and purple. H. P. Mera collection. 1941.

References

Abel, Annie H., ed.
1915 *The Official Correspondence of James S. Calhoun While Indian Agent at Santa Fe and Superintendent of Indian Affairs in New Mexico.* Washington: U.S. Government Printing Office.

Adams, William Y.
1963 *Shonto: A Study of the Role of the Trader in a Modern Navajo Community.* Bureau of American Ethnology Bulletin, no. 188. Washington: Smithsonian Institution.

Adavasio, J. M.
1974 *Prehistoric North American Basketry.* Nevada State Museum Anthropological Papers, no. 16. Carson City, Utah: Nevada State Museum.

1977 *Basketry Technology: A Guide to Identification and Analysis.* Aldine Manuals on Archaeology. Chicago: Aldine Publishing.

Bahr, Donald M.
1983 "Pima and Papago Social Organization." *In Handbook of North American Indians*, vol. 10, edited by Alfonso Ortiz. Washington: Smithsonian Institution.

Barnett, Franklin
1968 *Viola Jimulla: The Indian Chieftess.* Prescott, Arizona: Prescott Yavapai Indians.

Barrows, D. P.
1900 *Ethno-Botany of the Coahuilla Indians of Southern California.* Chicago: University of Chicago Press.

Bartlett, Katherine
1949 "Hopi Yucca Baskets." *Plateau* 21 (3).

Basso, Keith
1970 *The Cibecue Apache.* New York: Holt, Rinehart & Winston.

1983 "Western Apache." In *Handbook of North American Indians*, vol. 10, edited by Alfonso Ortiz. Washington: Smithsonian Institution.

Bateman, Paul
1972 "Cultural Change and Revival in Pai Basketry." Master's thesis, Northern Arizona University, Flagstaff.

Bennett, Noel
1974 *The Weaver's Pathway: A Clarification of the "Spirit Trail" in Navajo Weaving.* Flagstaff: Northland Press.

Bohrer, Vorsila L.
1983 "New Life from Ashes: The Tale of the Burnt Bush *(Rhus trilobata)*." *Desert Plants* 5 (3): 122–24 (Superior, Arizona: Boyce Thompson Southwest Arboretum).

Breazeale, J. F.
1923 *The Pima and His Basket.* Tucson: Arizona Archaeological and Historical Society.

Breunig, Robert
1982 "Cultural Fiber: Function and Symbolism in Hopi Basketry." In *The Basket Weavers of the Southwest,* Plateau 53 (4). Flagstaff: Museum of Northern Arizona.

Brew, J. O.
1979 "Hopi Prehistory and History to 1850." In *Handbook of North American Indians,* vol. 9, edited by Alfonso Ortiz. Washington: Smithsonian Institution.

Brugge, David M.
1983 "Navajo Prehistory and History to 1850." *In Handbook of North American Indians,* vol. 10, edited by Alfonso Ortiz. Washington: Smithsonian Institution.

Bunte, Pamela A.
1985 "Ethnohistory of the San Juan Paiute Tribe." In *Translating Tradition: Basketry Arts of the San Juan Paiute,* edited by Susan Brown McGreevy and Andrew Hunter Whiteford. Santa Fe: Wheelwright Museum of the American Indian.

Cain, H. Thomas
1962 *Pima Indian Basketry.* Heard Museum Research Project no. 2. Phoenix: Heard Museum of Anthropology and Primitive Art.

Castetter, Edward F., and Ruth M. Underhill
1935 *The Ethnobiology of the Papago Indians.* Ethnobiological Studies in the American Southwest II, University of New Mexico Bulletin, no. 275. Albuquerque: University of New Mexico.

Chapman, Kenneth M., and Bruce T. Ellis
1951 "The Line-break, Problem Child of Pueblo Pottery." *El Palacio* 58 (9).

Codallos y Rabal, Joachín
1744 "Original Depositions Sent to the Superior Government of the Most Excellent Count of Fuenclara, Viceroy, Governor, and Captain General of this New Spain." Manuscript in the Pinart Collection of the Bancroft Library, University of California, Berkeley (also in Hill 1940).

Collings, Jerold L.
1976 "Basketry." In *Indian Arts and Crafts,* edited by Clara Lee Tanner. Phoenix: Arizona Highways.

Colton, Mary-Russell Ferrell
1965 *Hopi Dyes.* Museum of Northern Arizona Bulletin, no. 14. Flagstaff: Museum of Northern Arizona.

Cushing, Frank Hamilton
1882 "The Nation of Willows." *Atlantic Monthly* 50:362–74. Reprinted 1965, Northland Press, Flagstaff.

1886 "A Study of Pueblo Pottery as Illustrative of Zuni Culture Growth." Bureau of American Ethnology Annual Report, no. 4. Washington: Smithsonian Institution.

Cutter, Donald C.
1974 "An Inquiry into Indian Land Rights in the Jicarilla Apache Area in the American Southwest under Spain, Mexico, and the United States, with Particular Reference to the Jicarilla Apache Area of Northeastern New Mexico." *In American Indian Ethnohistory: Indians of the Southwest*, vol. 6, *Apache Indians*. New York: Garland Press.

DeWald, Terry
1979 *The Papago Indians and Their Basketry*. Tucson: Terry DeWald.

Di Peso, Charles C.
1953 *The Sobaipuri Indians of the Upper San Pedro River Valley, Southeastern Arizona*. Amerind Foundation Publication no. 6. Dragoon, Arizona: Amerind Foundation.

Dockstader, Frederick J.
1979 "Hopi History, 1850–1940." In *Handbook of North American Indians*, vol. 9, edited by Alfonso Ortiz. Washington: Smithsonian Institution.

Douglas, Frederic H.
1930 *Pima Indian Close Coiled Basketry*. Denver Art Museum Leaflet no. 5. Denver: Denver Art Museum.

Dunnington, Jean
1985 "Emily Quanimptewa — Hopi Basket Maker." *American Indian Basketry* 5 (3): 22–25.

Eggan, Fred
1979 "Pueblos: Introduction." In *Handbook of North American Indians*, vol. 9, edited by Alfonso Ortiz. Washington: Smithsonian Institution.

Ellis, Florence Hawley
1959 "An Outline of Laguna Pueblo History and Social Organization." *Southwestern Journal of Anthropology* 15:4.

Ellis, Florence Hawley, and Mary Walpole
1959 "Possible Pueblo, Navajo, and Jicarilla Basketry Relationships." *El Palacio* 66 (6).

Elmore, Francis H.
1944 *Ethnobotany of the Navajo*. University of New Mexico and the School of American Research, Monograph 8. Albuquerque: University of New Mexico.

1976 *Shrubs and Trees of the Southwest Uplands*. Southwest Parks and Monuments Association, Popular Series, no. 19. Globe, Arizona: Southwest Parks and Monuments Association.

Euler, Robert C.
1966 *Southern Paiute Ethnohistory*. Glen Canyon Series, Anthropological Papers, no. 78. Salt Lake City: University of Utah.

1981 "Havasupai-Cohonina Relationships in the Grand Canyon." In *Collected Papers in Honor of Erik Kellerman Reed*. Papers of the Archaeological Society of New Mexico, no. 6. Albuquerque: Archaeological Society Press.

Euler, Robert C., and Henry Dobyns
1984 "The Ethnoarchaeology of Upland Arizona Ceramics." In *Collected Papers in Honor of Albert H. Schroeder*, edited by Charles Lange, Papers of the Archaeological Society of New Mexico. Albuquerque: Albuquerque Archaeological Society.

Evans, Glen L., and T. N. Campbell
1952 *Indian Baskets*. Austin: Texas Memorial Museum.

Farrer, Claire R.
1982 "Signs of Self and Other in Mescalero Apache Basketry." Unpublished paper prepared for third annual conference of the Native American Art Studies Association, Ames, Iowa.

Ferg, Alan, and William B. Kessel
1987 "Subsistence." In *Western Apache Material Culture,* edited by Alan Ferg. Tucson: University of Arizona Press.

Fontana, Bernard L.
1983 "Pima and Papago: Introduction." In *Handbook of North American Indians,* vol. 10, edited by Alfonso Ortiz. Washington: Smithsonian Institution.

Fowler, Catherine S., and Don D. Fowler
1971 "Notes on the History of the Southern Paiutes and Eastern Shoshonis." *Utah Historical Quarterly* 39:95–113.

Fowler, Don D., and Catherine S. Fowler, eds.
1971 *Anthropology of the Numa: John Wesley Powell's Manuscripts on the Numic Peoples of Western North America, 1868–1880.* Smithsonian Contributions to Anthropology, no. 14. Washington: Smithsonian Institution.

Fowler, Don D., Robert E. Euler, and Catherine S. Fowler
1969 *John Wesley Powell and the Anthropology of the Canyon Country.* United States Geological Survey, Professional Papers, no. 670. Washington: U.S. Geological Survey.

Fowler, Don D., and John F. Matley
1979 *Material Culture of the Numa: The John Wesley Powell Collection, 1867–1880.* Smithsonian Contributions to Anthropology, no. 6. Washington: Smithsonian Institution.

Franciscan Fathers
1910 *An Ethnologic Dictionary of the Navajo Language.* St. Michaels, Arizona: The Franciscan Fathers.

Gifford, Edward W.
1932 *The Southeastern Yavapai.* University of California Publications in American Archaeology and Ethnology, vol. 29, no. 3. Berkeley: University of California.

1936 *The Northeastern and Western Yavapai.* University of California Publications in American Archaeology and Ethnology, vol. 34, no. 4. Berkeley: University of California.

Gilpin, Laura
1968 *The Enduring Navaho.* Austin: University of Texas Press.

Gogol, John M.
1982 "Pima Indian Basketry." *American Indian Basketry* 2 (3).

1983 "Papago Horsehair Basketry." *American Indian Basketry* 3 (3).

Gunnerson, James H.
1969 "Apache Archaeology in Northeastern New Mexico." *American Antiquity* 34 (1).

1979 "Southern Athapaskan Archaeology." In *Handbook of North American Indians,* vol. 9, edited by Alfonso Ortiz. Washington: Smithsonian Institution.

Guy, Hubert
1977 "Baskets, Beads and Buckskin." *Arizona Highways* 53 (7).

Hackenberg, Robert A.
1983 "Pima and Papago Ecological Adaptations." In *Handbook of North American Indians,* vol. 10, edited by Alfonso Ortiz. Washington: Smithsonian Institution.

Hart, Elizabeth
1935 "Arts and Crafts of the Pima Jurisdiction." *Indians at Work* 2 (19).

Harvey, Byron, III
1976 "The Fred Harvey Fine Arts Collections." In *The Fred Harvey Fine Arts Collection.* Phoenix: The Heard Museum.

Heatwole, Thelma
1967 "Artistry of Mesquite Baskets May Die With Pima Weaver." *Arizona Republic* (January 2).

Heizer, Robert, and Alex Krieger
1956 *The Archaeology of Humboldt Cave, Churchill County, Nevada.* University of California Publications in American Archaeology and Ethnology, vol. 47, no. 1. Berkeley: University of California.

Herold, Joyce
1978 "The Basketry of Tanzanita Pesata." *American Indian Art* 3 (2).

1979 "Havasupai Basketry: Theme and Variation." *American Indian Art* 4 (4).

1982 "One Hundred Years of Havasupai Basketry." In *The Basket Weavers of the Southwest,* Plateau 53 (4). Flagstaff: Museum of Northern Arizona.

1984 "Basket Weaver Individualists in the Southwest Today." *American Indian Art* 9 (2).

Hill, W. W.
1940 "Some Navajo Culture Changes During Two Centuries." In *Essays in Historical Anthropology in Honor of John R. Swanton,* Smithsonian Miscellaneous Collections, no. 100. Washington: Smithsonian Institution.

1982 *An Ethnography of Santa Clara Pueblo New Mexico.* Edited and annotated by Charles H. Lange. Albuquerque: University of New Mexico Press.

Irwin-Williams, Cynthia
1979 "Post-Pleistocene Archaeology, 7000–2000 B.C." In *Handbook of North American Indians,* vol. 9, edited by Alfonso Ortiz. Washington: Smithsonian Institution.

James, George Wharton
1902 *Indian Basketry.* Privately printed, Pasadena, California; reprinted 1972, New York: Dover.

1903 "Palomas Apaches and Their Baskets." *Sunset* 2:146–53.

Kelly, Isabel T.
1964 *Southern Paiute Ethnography.* University of Utah Anthropology Papers, no. 69. Salt Lake City: University of Utah.

Kent, Kate Peck
1985 *Navajo Weaving: Three Centuries of Change.* Santa Fe: School of American Research.

Khera, Sigrid, and Patricia S. Mariella
1983 "Yavapai." In *Handbook of North American Indians,* vol. 9, edited by Alfonso Ortiz. Washington: Smithsonian Institution.

Kidder, Alfred V., and Samuel J. Guernsey
1919 *Archaeological Explorations in Northeastern Arizona.* Bureau of American Ethnology Bulletin, no. 65. Washington: Smithsonian Institution.

Kissell, Mary Lois
1916 *Basketry of the Papago and Pima.* Anthropological Papers of the American Museum of Natural History, vol. 17, no. 4. New York: American Museum of Natural History.

Kluckhohn, Clyde, W. W. Hill, and Lucy Wales Kluckhohn
1971 *Navajo Material Culture.* Cambridge, Massachusetts: Belknap Press.

Lange, Charles H.
1959 *Cochiti: A New Mexico Pueblo, Past and Present.* Austin: University of Texas Press; reissued 1968, Carbondale, Illinois: Southern Illinois University.

Loud, L. L., and M. R. Harrington
1929 *Lovelock Cave.* University of California Publications in American Archaeology and Ethnology, vol. 25, no. 1. Berkeley: University of California.

Malarcher, Patricia
1984 "What Makes a Basket a Basket?" *Fiberarts* 11 (1).

Mason, Otis Tufton
1904 *Aboriginal American Basketry: Studies in a Textile Art Without Machinery.* Annual Report of the Smithsonian Institution for 1902. Washington: Smithsonian Institution.

Matthews, Washington
1894 "The Basketry Drum." *American Anthropologist* 7 (2).

Mauldin, Barbara
1983 "Curator's Choice: Baskets." *El Palacio* 89 (1).

1984 *Traditions in Transition: Contemporary Basket Weaving of the Southwestern Indians.* Santa Fe: Museum of New Mexico Press.

McGreevy, Susan Brown
1985a "The Other Weavers: Navajo Basket Makers." *Phoebus* 4.

1985b "Translating Tradition: Contemporary Basketry Arts." In *Translating Tradition: Basketry Arts of the San Juan Paiute,* edited by Susan Brown McGreevy and Andrew Hunter Whiteford. Santa Fe: Wheelwright Museum of the American Indian.

McGreevy, Susan Brown, and Andrew Hunter Whiteford, eds.
1985 *Translating Tradition: Basketry Arts of the San Juan Paiute.* Santa Fe: Wheelwright Museum of the American Indian.

McKee, Barbara, Edwin McKee, and Joyce Herold
1975 *Havasupai Baskets and Their Makers: 1930–1940.* Flagstaff: Northland Press.

Monthan, Guy, and Doris Monthan
1975 *Art and Indian Individualists: The Art of Seventeen Contemporary Southwestern Artists and Craftsmen.* Flagstaff: Northland Press.

Morris, Earl H., and Robert F. Burgh
1941 *Anasazi Basketry: Basket Maker II Through Pueblo III.* Carnegie Institution of Washington Publication no. 533. Washington: Carnegie Institution.

Newman, Sandra Corrie
1974 *Indian Basket Weaving: How to Weave Pomo, Yurok, Pima and Navajo Baskets.* Flagstaff: Northland Press.

Opler, Morris E.
1941 *An Apache Life-way: The Economic, Social, and Religious Institutions of the Chiricahua Indians.* Chicago: University of Chicago.

1969 *Apache Odyssey: A Journey Between Two Worlds.* New York: Holt, Rinehart & Winston.

1983a "The Apachean Culture Pattern and Its Origins." In *Handbook of North American Indians,* vol. 10, edited by Alfonso Ortiz. Washington: Smithsonian Institution.

1983b "Chiricahua Apache." In *Handbook of North American Indians,* vol. 10, edited by Alfonso Ortiz. Washington: Smithsonian Institution.

Parent, Annette R.
1984 "A Clean Sweep: Bear Grass Harvesting in Grant County." *New Mexico* 62 (4): 69–74.

Powell, John Wesley
1874 *Report of Explorations in 1873 of the Colorado of the West and its Tributaries under the Direction of the Smithsonian Institution.* Washington: U.S. Government Printing Office.

1875 *Explorations of the Colorado River of the West and its Tributaries; Explored in 1869, 1870, 1871, and 1872 under the Direction of the Secretary of the Smithsonian Institution.* Washington: U.S. Government Printing Office.

Quintero, Nita
1980 "Coming of Age the Apache Way." *National Geographic* 157 (2): 262–71.

Roberts, Helen H.
1916 "San Carlos Apache Double Coiled Basket." *American Anthropologist* 18 (4): 601–2.

1929 *Basketry of the San Carlos Apache.* Anthropological Papers of the American Museum of Natural History, vol. 21, no. 2. New York: American Museum of Natural History.

Robinson, Bert
1954 *The Basket Weavers of Arizona.* Albuquerque: University of New Mexico Press.

Roessel, Ruth
1983 "Navajo Arts and Crafts." In *Handbook of North American Indians,* vol. 10, edited by Alfonso Ortiz. Washington: Smithsonian Institution.

Russell, Frank
1908 *The Pima Indians.* Annual Report of the Bureau of American Ethnology, no. 26. Washington: Smithsonian Institution.

Sandlin, Scott
1983 "Navajo Basketry." *The Indian Trader* (October): 9–10.

Schroeder, Albert H.
1979 "Prehistory: Hakataya." In *Handbook of North American Indians,* vol. 9, edited by Alfonso Ortiz. Washington: Smithsonian Institution.

Schwartz, Douglas W.
1956a "The Havasupai 600 A.D.–1955 A.D.: A Short Culture History." *Plateau* 28 (4): 77–85.

1956b "Demographic Changes in the Early Periods of Cohonina Prehistory." In *Prehistoric Settlement Patterns in the New World,* edited by G. R. Willey, Viking Fund Publications in Anthropology, no. 23. New York: Wenner-Gren Foundation for Anthropological Research.

1959 "Culture Area and Time Depth: The Four Worlds of the Havasupai." *American Anthropologist* 61 (6): 1060–70.

1983 "Havasupai." In *Handbook of North American Indians,* vol. 10, edited by Alfonso Ortiz. Washington: Smithsonian Institution.

Shepardson, Mary, and Blodwen Hammond
1970 *The Navajo Mountain Community, Social Organization and Kinship Terminology.* Berkeley: University of California Press.

Shreve, Margaret
1943 "Modern Papago Basketry." *The Kiva* 8 (2): 10–16.

Smithson, Carma Lee
1959 *The Havasupai Woman.* Anthropological Papers, no. 38. Salt Lake City: University of Utah.

Smithsonian Institution
1979 *The Year of the Hopi: Paintings and Photographs by Joseph Mora, 1904–06.* Washington: Smithsonian Institution Traveling Exhibition Service.

Spicer, Edmund H.
1962 *Cycles of Conquest: The Impact of Spain, Mexico, and the United States on the Indians of the Southwest, 1533–1960.* Tucson: University of Arizona Press.

Spier, Leslie
1928 *Havasupai Ethnography.* Anthroplogical Papers of the American Museum of Natural History, vol. 29, no. 3. New York: American Museum of Natural History.

1933 *Yuman Tribes of the Gila River.* Chicago: University of Chicago Press.

Stevenson, James
1883 *Illustrated Catalogue of the Collections Obtained from the Indians of New Mexico and Arizona in 1879.* Bureau of American Ethnology Annual Report, no. 2. Washington: U.S. Government Printing Office.

1884 *Illustrated Catalogue of the Collections Obtained from the Pueblos of Zuni, New Mexico, and Wolpi, Arizona.* Bureau of American Ethnology Annual Report, no. 3. Washington: U.S. Government Printing Office.

Stewart, Kenneth M.
1983a "Yumans: Introduction." In *Handbook of North American Indians,* vol. 10, edited by Alfonso Ortiz. Washington: Smithsonian Institution.

1983b "Mohave." In *Handbook of North American Indians,* vol. 10, edited by Alfonso Ortiz. Washington: Smithsonian Institution.

Stewart, Omer C.
1938 *The Navajo Wedding Basket.* Museum Notes, vol. 10, no. 9. Flagstaff: Museum of Northern Arizona.

1942 *Ute-Southern Paiute.* Culture Element Distributions 18, University of California Anthropological Records, vol. 6, no. 4. Berkeley: University of California.

Tanner, Clara Lee
1968 *Southwest Indian Craft Arts.* Tucson: University of Arizona Press.

1982 *Apache Indian Baskets.* Tucson: University of Arizona Press.

1983 *Indian Baskets of the Southwest.* Tucson: University of Arizona Press.

Teleki, Gloria Roth
1975 *The Baskets of Rural America.* New York: E. P. Dutton.

Thomas, Alfred B., ed. and trans.
1935 *After Coronado: Spanish Exploration Northeast of New Mexico, 1696–1727; Documents from the Archives of Spain, Mexico and New Mexico.* Norman: University of Oklahoma Press.

Tiller, Veronica V.
1983 "Jicarilla Apache." In *Handbook of North American Indians,* vol. 10, edited by Alfonso Ortiz. Washington: Smithsonian Institution.

Trimble, Marshall
1983 "The Gadsden Purchase Survey, from Los Nogales to Fort Yuma, along El Camino del Diablo." *Arizona Highways* 59 (4).

Tschopik, Harry, Jr.
1938 "Taboo as a Possible Factor Involved in the Obsolescence of Navaho Pottery and Basketry." *American Anthroplogist* 40 (2).

1939 "Coiled Basketry in the Southwest: Distributions and Continuities." In *Preliminary Report on the 1937 Excavations, Bc50–5l, Chaco Canyon, New Mexico.* University of New Mexico Bulletin, Anthropological Series, vol. 3, no. 2. Albuquerque: University of New Mexico.

1940   "Navajo Basketry: A Study of Culture Change." Pt. 1. *American Anthropologist* 42 (2).

Vivian, Gordon
1957   "Two Navajo Baskets." *El Palacio* (May–June): 145–55.

Watahomigie, Lucille J., Malinda Powskey, and Jorigine Bender, with Elnora Malpatis and Eva Schrum.
1982a *Hualapai Gwadi, Hualapai Spudi.* Peach Springs, Arizona: Hualapai Bilingual Program, School District 8.
1982b *Ethnobotany of the Hualapai.* Peach Springs, Arizona: Hualapai Bilingual Program, School District 8.

Waters, Frank
1963   *The Book of the Hopi.* New York: Viking Press.

Webb, William, and Robert A. Weinstein
1973   *Dwellers at the Source: Southwestern Indian Photographs of A. C. Vroman, 1895–1904.* New York: Grossman.

Weltfish, Gene
1930   "Prehistoric North American Basketry Techniques and Modern Distributions." *American Anthropologist* 32:454–95.
1932   "Problems in the Study of Ancient and Modern Basket Makers." *American Anthropologist* 34 (2): 108–17.

Whiteford, Andrew Hunter
1985   "Traditional Baskets of the San Juan Paiutes." In *Translating Tradition: Basketry Arts of the San Juan Paiute,* edited by Susan Brown McGreevy and Andrew Hunter Whiteford. Santa Fe: Wheelwright Museum of the American Indian.

Wilson, Maggie
1972   "Precious Petal Baskets Sold for Precious Little Years Ago." *Arizona Republic* (May 13).

Windsor, Merrill, ed.
1986   "The New Individualists: A Spectacular Visual Journey Through the Realm of Native American Fine Art." *Arizona Highways* 62 (5).

Witherspoon, Gary
1983   "Navajo Social Organization." In *Handbook of North American Indians,* vol. 10, edited by Alfonso Ortiz. Washington: Smithsonian Institution.

Worcester, Donald E.
1979   *The Apaches: Eagles of the Southwest.* Norman: University of Oklahoma Press.

Wright, Barton
1979   *Hopi Material Culture: Artifacts Gathered by H. R. Voth in the Fred Harvey Collection.* Flagstaff: Northland Press and The Heard Museum.

Wyllys, Rufus K.
1931   "Padre Luis Velarde's Relacion of Pimeria Alta, 1716." *New Mexico Historical Review* 7 (2): 111–57.

Wyman, Leland C.
1983a "Navajo Ceremonial System." In *Handbook of North American Indians,* vol. 10, edited by Alfonso Ortiz. Washington: Smithsonian Institution.
1983b *Southwest Indian Drypainting.* School of American Research Southwest Indian Art Series. Albuquerque: University of New Mexico.

Index